GUIDELINES

TEFILLAH

GUIDELINES

Questions & Answers
about the Laws of
TEFILLAH

Volume One

Rabbi Elozor Barclay
Rabbi Yitzchok Jaeger

TARGUM/FELDHEIM

First published 2004
Copyright © 2004 by E. Barclay & Y. Jaeger
ISBN 1-56871-344-4

Please address any questions or comments
regarding these notes to the authors:
E. Barclay (02) 583 0914
Y. Jaeger (02) 583 4889
email: yjaeger@013.net.il

By the same authors:
GUIDELINES TO PESACH
GUIDELINES TO THE THREE WEEKS
GUIDELINES TO THE YOMIM NORAIM
GUIDELINES TO SUCCOS
GUIDELINES TO CHANUKAH
GUIDELINES TO PURIM
GUIDELINES TO FAMILY PURITY

Published by:
Targum Press, Inc.
22700 W. Eleven Mile Rd.
Southfield, MI 48034
E-mail: targum@netvision.net.il
Fax toll free: (888) 298-9992
www.targum.com

Distributed by:
Feldheim Publishers
200 Airport Executive Park
Nanuet, NY 10954

Printed in Israel

Rabbi CHAIM P. SCHEINBERG

Rosh Hayeshiva "TORAH ORE"

and Morah Hora'ah of Kiryat Mattersdorf

הרב חיים פינחס שיינברג

ראש ישיבת "תורה אור"

ומורה הוראה דקרית מטרסדורף

בס"ד, חודש שבט, תשס"ג

מכתב ברכה

I was pleased to see "**Guidelines**", an impressive six volume work which encompasses the *halachos* of the *Moadim* and other relevant topics, written by Rabbi Elozor Barclay, *shlita* and Rabbi Yitzchok Jaeger, *shlita*. These books have been praised highly by numerous *Gedolei HaRabbonim* and have been received warmly by the English speaking Torah community.

As a matter of policy, I do not endorse *halachic* rulings in any published *sefer*. However, since so many *Gedolei Torah* have already agreed to what is written and offered their approbation to "**Guidelines**", I join them and offer my heartfelt blessing that *Hashem* should guide and assist the authors in producing more successful *halachic* works, which glorify and strengthen the Torah.

Signed in the honor of the Torah,

Rabbi Chaim Pinchas Scheinberg

רחוב פנים מאירות 2, ירושלים, ת.ד. 6979, טל. 537-1513 (02), ישראל

2 Panim Meirot St., Jerusalem, P.O.B. 6979, Tel. (02) 537-1513, Israel

Letter of Approbation received from
Rabbi Nachman Bulman zt"l for Guidelines to Succos

Rabbi Nachman Bulman
Yeshivat Ohr Somayach
Beit Knesset Nachliel

רב נחמן בולמן
מנהל רוחני ישיבת אור שמח
רב ק"ק נחליאל נוה יעקב מזרח

בע"ה

יום ו', י"ח תמוז, תשס"ב פה עיה"ק ת"ו

Friday, eighteenth of Tammuz, 5672, the holy city of Yerushalayim.

I was delighted to see the fifth volume of the **Guidelines** series. The questions and answers in **Guidelines** provide a clear and easily understood format and clarify relevant halachic issues.

It is clear from the quality of this work that Rabbi Elozor Barclay and Rabbi Yitzchok Jaeger have invested great amounts of time and effort in their thorough investigation of these dinim. Every answer has been written carefully and thoughtfully, considering both the classic and the most up-to-date halachic authorities. The accurate Hebrew references will certainly be an invaluable aid for any reader who wishes to investigate further.

I highly recommend this book to any person who is truly searching to know the correct conduct.

Signed with admiration,

נחמן בולמן

מנהל רוחני ישיבת אור שמח
רב ק"ק נחליאל נוה יעקב מזרח ביום הנ"ל
ועיני נשואות לשמים להסכמת שוכן במרומים

משה הלברשטאם

חבר הבד"צ העדה החרדית

ראש ישיבת "דברי חיים" טשאקאווע

מח"ס שו"ת "דברי משה"

פעיה"ק ירושלים תובב"א

רח' יואל 8 טל. 5370514

בס"ד

ערב ט"ו בשבט לסדר "והיה ביום הששי" תשס"ג לפ"ק

מאד שמחתי ונהנתי כשהובאו לפני ליקוטים נפלאים לעת עתה על הלכות פורים, פסח, ימים נוראים, סוכה וחנוכה ואי"ה עוד יד נטוי' להשלים המלאכה, שחיברו האברכים החשובים חו"ב מוהר"ר אלעזר ברקלי שליט"א ומוהר"ר יצחק ייגר שליט"א אוצר בלום מה שאספו וליקטו הלכות רבות ונחוצות מהשו"ע ונושאי כליו מספרי הפוסקים ראשונים ואחרונים מסודר בתבונה והשכל בטטו"ד לתועלת וזיכוי הרבים.

ונוכחתי לראות כי הלכו מישרים לאסוקי שמעתתא אליבא דהלכתא והיטב אשר עשו שציינו מקור לכל הלכה והלכה למען אשר כבר הזהירו גאוני קדמאי שלא לפסוק הלכה למעשה מספרי הקיצורים.

ואמינא לפעלא טבא יישר כוחם וחילם לאורייתא והנני נותן להם בזה ברכת מו"ר הגה"צ שליט"א שיזכו להמשיך לעלות במעלות התורה להו"ל עוד חיבורים יקרים ולזכות את הרבים מתוך נחת ושפע ברכות והצלחה, אכי"ר.

ובעה"ח בפקודת הקודש

יהונתן וינר

מו"ץ בבית הוראה

שע"י מרן הגה"צ שליט"א

נ.ב. בספר על הלכות חנוכה שאלה 15, בגדר איסור מלאכה לנשים בחנוכה עיין בן איש חי פרשת וישב סי' כז, וט"ז ס' תרע סק"ב דמשמע דומיא דר"ח, וכן שמעתי מכרכא דכולי ביה מרא דכולא תלמודא (לשון מוה"ר הגה"צ בשו"ת דברי משה ס' יד) ממוה"ר חיים קנייבסקי שליט"א.

Rabbi E. Falk

146 Whitehall Road
Gateshead NE8 1TP
England

פסח אליהו פאלק

דומ״ץ בק״ק גייטסהעד יצ״ו
מח״ס שו״ת מחזה אליהו
יזכור ושמורי על הלכות שבת
יעוז והדר לבושהי על הלי צניעות דלבוש
מו״ץ בק״ק גייטסהעד יצ״ו

בס״ד

20 Kislev 5765 - Gateshead UK

Once again a great service has been rendered to the Jewish English-speaking public by the great "partners in *zikuy horabim*" - Rabbi Elozor Barclay *shlita* and Rabbi Yitzchok Jaeger *shlita*. They have prepared a sefer on the laws of *tefillah* - thereby giving the person who is praying easy access to the numerous intricate laws that could apply to him at any point during his prayers. With this production they have earned themselves an enormous merit, for *tefillah* is a duty that stands towering above everything else (See *Gemara Brachos* 32b), and to ensure the correct execution of such a duty by a multitude of people, is an immeasurable merit.

As with their other works in the **"Guidelines"** series, this *sefer* is concise, accurate, and well structured. The authors have performed a great service, presenting these vital and complex laws in a clear and straightforward questions and answers format. This style arouses the interest and opens the mind, enabling the reader to fully integrate the information. As clarity of material assists the memory, the person who learns the relevant *halachos* in this manner is likely to remember them and know exactly how to react when a given situation arises.

Unfortunately, my busy schedule does not allow me to thoroughly review every *halacha*, and therefore I cannot accept personal responsibility for the rulings given. However, the authors have themselves invested vast amounts of time and effort researching the sources and clarifying the laws. Apart from this, they have had access to the excellent *seforim* that have been published on the laws of *tefillah* over the last two decades. I am therefore confident that the *halachos* have been correctly presented and I add my approval of its printing for the benefit of the public.

May *Hashem Yisborach* bless the authors with great success in the publication of this work, and other works that they will produce *b'ezer Hashem* in the future. I pray that this *sefer* will be warmly accepted and will lead to increased appreciation and greater dedication to the great gift *Hashem Yisborach* has given us - the means to approach Him thrice daily and present our needs to Him through the medium of *tefillah*.

With Torah blessings,

Rabbi Pesach Eliyahu Falk

הרב רפאל צבי ובר

רב דקהילת קמניץ
ונוה יעקב מזרח, ירושלים

ז׳ כסלו תשס״ד
בס״ד

מכתב ברכה

שמחתי לראות ששני תלמידי חכמים יקרים
הרב אלעזר ברקלי שליט״א והרב יצחק ייגר שליט״א
חיברו ספר פסקי הלכות בהלכות תפלה בשפה
האנגלית.

וכבר זכו לחבר פסקי הלכות על המועדים
שהתפרסמו הרבה, וזיכו את הרבים. ויש תועלת רבה
בצורת הכתיבה בלשון שאלות ותשובות ועי״ז
מתבררת ההלכה היטב.

ואע״פ שאיני מבין שפה האנגלית, אבל אני
מכירם ויודעם בהשתדלות לאסוקי שמעתתא אליבא
דהלכתא, ונשאו ונתנו אתי בהרבה נושאים שבספר,
והנני מברכם שיקבלו דבריהם בביהמ״ד.

בברכת התורה,

צבי ובר

RABBI ZEV LEFF
Rabbi of Moshav Matisyahu
Rosh Hayeshiva Yeshiva Gedola Matisyahu

בס"ד
ט"ז שבט תשס"ג

It is with great pleasure that I reviewed the manuscript of "**Guidelines**" to Pesach by Rabbi Elozor Barclay שליט"א and Rabbi Yitzchok Jaeger שליט"א.

A siyum - completion - is a very special and joyous occasion. This volume is a siyum and culminates the series of **Guidelines** to the various Yomim Tovim of the year. As in the previous volumes, the laws and customs are presented in a concise, lucid, and organized fashion. The fact that the vastness of the laws of Pesach could be condensed so masterfully into this volume of **Guidelines** is truly impressive. This volume, as well as the entire complete series of **Guidelines**, will serve as a guide for those who cannot learn these laws from their original sources, and as a valuable aid even to those who can.

May Hashem grant the authors the ability to continue to benefit Klal Yisrael with further works of Torah and mitzvos for many long happy and healthy years.

With Torah blessings,

Rabbi Zev Leff

Table of Contents

Foreword

With praise and thanks to Hashem, we present a basic guide to the laws of *tefillah*. Our books on the laws of the Yomim Tovim and Family Purity were warmly received by the public, which encouraged and motivated us to produce this new addition to the series.

There is probably no activity more deeply and naturally ingrained in the human soul than prayer. In the words of *Dovid Hamelech*, "And [as for me,] I am prayer" (*Tehillim* 109:4). Although man serves Hashem in many ways, the most fundamental form of service to Hashem is *tefillah*, in which a person can pour out his heart and express his complete dependence upon his Creator. Throughout the generations, the Jewish nation has relied upon prayer as the sole means of survival in times of distress and oppression. Today more than ever, as Jews the world over are living like sheep surrounded by seventy hungry wolves, the nation must turn to its only source of salvation, our Father in Heaven.

As precious as the gift of prayer is, it is surprising and tragic that so many people are ignorant or negligent about the observation of its laws. Like any other mitzvah, prayer is regulated by numerous restrictions, and a person cannot hope to experience fulfillment of his supplications unless he follows the rules, exactly as they have been formulated. In the words of Harav Chaim Kanievsky, *shlita*, "It is an absolute obligation to be proficient in the laws of prayer, since a person who approaches the King and does not know how to behave, will certainly be expelled by the King. All those who are careless about this will eventually be held accountable, and there is no doubt that the study of these laws takes precedence over all other studies, since they apply three times a day" (*Orchos Yosher*, page 100).

Rarely will a written work be a perfect substitute for a one-to-one discussion with a rav. The answer to a query often depends upon various factors that only further questioning can clarify. Even though much thought and effort has been invested in the phrasing and wording used, it is possible that *halachos* may be misunderstood or misconstrued. As in other topics of *halacha*, the laws of prayer include many varying customs that were accepted by different communities around the world. The rulings in this book are based upon the decisions of the Chofetz Chaim, *zt'l*, as found in his classic work *Mishna Brura*, and may occasionally differ from the local custom. In addition, we have presented the laws according to the Ashkenazic custom, and Sephardim should follow their own traditions. Any doubts that arise should be discussed with one's local rav.

Our primary intent is to guide the reader through the maze of laws and customs that abound in the area of prayer, hence the title GUIDELINES. Although the present volume contains much of the most basic information, it is far from complete, and it is our hope to continue the subject in a second volume, with the help of Hashem. This will deal with topics such as *krias hatorah*, prayer on Shabbos and Yom Tov, *kiddush levanah*, bedtime shema, prayer in the house of a mourner, visitors to and from *Eretz Yisroel*, and laws for a traveler.

We would like to thank a few individuals, whose contribution to this book was of major significance. First and foremost, the great *posek* and community leader, *HaGaon* Rav Nachman Bulman, *zt'l*. Rav Bulman was a source of great encouragement when the series of GUIDELINES was launched, and this book is imbued with his invaluable perspective, reliability, and practicality.

We would like to express our thanks to two exceptional *talmidei chachamim*, who graciously took time from their busy schedules to help turn this book into a reality. Rav Yirmiyahu Kaganoff, *shlita, posek* in *Neveh Ya'akov*, thoroughly checked the entire manuscript, providing many invaluable comments and insights. His observations have left their impression on much of the book. Rav Yehuda Berson, *shlita, maggid shiur in yeshivas Nachalas Shmuel*, with his keen perception and comprehensive mastery of the topic, provided many valuable changes and additions throughout the entire book.

Thanks are also due to Rabbi Moshe Dombey and all the staff at Targum Press, who have once again demonstrated their professional expertise with the production of this book.

Deepest feelings of appreciation are extended to our wives for their endless patience and untiring support during the preparation of the ongoing series of Guidelines books. May Hashem bless them with good health and strength, and may we merit together to see much *nachas* from our children.

It is our hope that in the merit of keeping the laws of *tefillah* punctiliously, Hashem will graciously accept our prayers, and we will be worthy to experience the final salvation and the building of the holy Temple, speedily in our days.

Elozor Barclay   Yitzchok Jaeger
                        Yerushalayim, Kisleiv 5765

Chapter One

Introduction

1.   What is the meaning of prayer?

The Hebrew word for prayer - *tefillah* - is derived from the word *pallel* - to think. The reflexive form of this root - *lehispallel* - to pray, therefore means **to make oneself think**. The purpose of prayer is to bring into one's mind and to declare the fundamental truths about Hashem, and man's relationship with Him. The classic work *Chovos Halevavos* (Duties of the Heart) lists five goals that can be achieved by prayer:

1. To express the yearning of the soul to make contact with Hashem.
2. To feel humility towards Hashem.
3. To recognize the greatness of Hashem.
4. To praise and thank Hashem for His many kindnesses.
5. To cast one's burden on Hashem by requesting all one's needs and realizing that all one's affairs are in His hands.

In addition, Rabbi Moshe Chaim Luzzato writes that although Hashem knows exactly what we require, he will not bestow His blessings upon us until we ask for them. Even if a person has a multitude of merits, the gates of the Heavenly storehouses remain closed, and the only way that one can open them is through prayer.

It is no wonder that our Sages state that prayer stands at the peak of the universe, yet people belittle it. Prayer is an immense challenge, and if used correctly can be one of the greatest opportunities for spiritual growth.

2.   Does prayer without thought have any value?

The problem of lip service is not a modern one. The prophet *Yeshayahu* berated the Jewish people in the name of Hashem, "Behold this nation approaches Me, they honor Me with their mouth and lips, but their heart is far from me" (29:13). Intelligent people will surely realize that prayer is not a mitzvah to be performed solely with one's mouth by reciting certain words found in the siddur, while one's thoughts wander to entirely different areas. Our Sages describe prayer as service of the heart, and this idea has become a well-known saying: "A prayer without thought is like a body without a soul". Although a person does not fulfill his obligation with a prayer recited without any thought, it is not regarded as a prayer in vain (see also questions 558 and 599).

3.   What if a person does not understand the Hebrew words?

The Avudraham writes, "Most of the masses raise their voices in prayer before Hashem, but are aimlessly going about like a blind man in darkness, not understanding the words they are praying". The first step towards *davening* with thought must surely be to study a translation of the prayers. Only after mastering the meaning of the words can one hope to proceed to deeper levels of concentration.

4.   May a person *daven* in English?

- If he cannot read Hebrew, he may temporarily *daven* using a reliable English translation, until he is able to read Hebrew.
- If he can read Hebrew, he should *daven* in Hebrew. In this day and age, when there is a proliferation of siddurim that provide a running translation, there is no excuse for *davening*

in English. With persistent use of such a siddur, a person will soon master the Hebrew language, making his *davening* more meaningful.

- In extenuating circumstances, a rav should be consulted.

5.   Is a person obligated to pray daily?

The Torah commands, "And you shall serve Hashem your G-d" (*Shemos* 23:25). By linking this to the verse in shema, "And serve Him with all your heart" (*Devarim* 11:13), our Sages derive that this refers to prayer, which is service of the heart. According to Rambam (Maimonides), every man and woman is obligated by the Torah to pray once a day. Although the Torah does not require any particular text, the prayer must comprise three basic elements in this order: praise, request, and thanksgiving. According to Ramban (Nachmanides), there is only a Torah commandment to pray in times of distress, but not on a daily basis.

6.   When was formal prayer instituted?

During the Babylonian exile, the Jewish people were dispersed among foreign nations and began to speak their languages. In the course of time, many people found it difficult to express themselves coherently in prayer in their original Hebrew language. This prompted Ezra and his court (later to become The Men of the Great Assembly) to formalize prayer, so that everyone would have access to a suitable text. Three fundamental ideas were introduced:

1. The *shemoneh esrei* (literally eighteen *brachos*) was compiled, using the structure required by the Torah. The first three *brachos* are praises, the last three are thanksgiving, and the central twelve contain requests for all the general needs of

the individual and the community. A nineteenth *b'racha* was added to the central requests at a later time.

2. Prayers are to be recited in the morning (*shacharis*) and the afternoon (*mincha*), corresponding to the communal sacrifices that were brought daily in the holy Temple. The evening prayer (*ma'ariv*) was originally voluntary, but in the course of time it was accepted by the nation as an obligation. An additional prayer (*mussaf*) is to be recited on Shabbos, Yom Tov, and *rosh chodesh*.

3. Prayers must be recited at certain times of the day.

According to Ramban, an additional major change occurred. Until the days of Ezra, prayer was completely voluntary, required by the Torah only in times of distress. With the advent of Ezra and his court, prayer became a rabbinic obligation.

7.   Are women obligated to pray?

• According to Rambam, prayer is a Torah mitzvah that is not bound by time. Women are therefore obligated to pray once a day, using a short prayer in any language that comprises a praise, request, and thanksgiving. They are exempt from all formal prayer, since that is a rabbinic mitzvah bound by time.

• According to Ramban, women are rabbinically obligated to *daven shacharis* and *mincha*. Although these are bound by time, the Sages made prayer an exception to the rule and obligated women in this mitzvah. The reason is that prayer is a request for mercy, and women need Hashem's mercy as much as men do.

8.   Which view should a woman follow?

Most opinions agree with the view of Ramban, which obligates women to *daven shacharis* and *mincha* on a daily basis. However, many women are heavily involved with raising a family and are not required to follow this ruling. In such circumstances, a woman may follow the view of Rambam, and can fulfill her obligation by reciting a short prayer comprising a praise, request, and thanksgiving. In addition, it is correct for her to recite the first two lines of shema.

Note: Women are advised to discuss this matter with a rav, who will be able to provide a ruling based upon individual circumstances.

Unfortunately, many women do not realize the tremendous benefit of *davening* at least *shemoneh esrei* twice a day. Even if a woman is unable to find time to *daven* anything else, she still fulfills the stricter view of Ramban by doing so. This will greatly enhance the spiritual content of her day and enrich the atmosphere of her home.

9.   Must a woman follow one view consistently?

No. Therefore:

• A woman who has been *davening shacharis* and *mincha* regularly may follow the lenient opinion if circumstances change and she is unable to maintain her custom.

• A woman who usually follows the lenient view must *daven shacharis* and *mincha* if circumstances permit it. For example, if her husband is home on vacation or when the children grow older and no longer require constant attention.

If she wishes to be strict on a temporary basis, she should have in mind that she is doing so *b'li neder*, in order not to become permanently bound by it.

10. What is a suitable short prayer?

One of the following:
- *Birchos hatorah* (when said with the intention to fulfill the mitzvah of *tefillah*).
- The *b'racha hama'avir sheina* including *yehi ratzon*.
- A personal prayer in any language that includes a praise, request, and thanksgiving.

11. According to the stricter opinion, must a woman *daven* the entire *shacharis*?

Women are often mistaken in this matter and are unaware that most of *shacharis* is voluntary for them, even according to the stricter view. According to most opinions, women should ideally *daven* the following sections of *shacharis*:
- The morning *brachos*.
- *Baruch she'amar, ashrei, yishtabach* (on Shabbos and Yom Tov, *nishmas* should also be said).
- The first paragraph of shema.
- *Emes veyatziv* until *ga'al yisroel*.
- *Shemoneh esrei*.
- *Aleinu*.

According to some opinions, women should also say the section of *korbanos* dealing with the daily sacrifices (*parshas hatamid*). However, the widespread custom is to omit it (see question 446).

12. Are women obligated to *daven mussaf*?

Opinions differ about this, and the custom is for women to make an effort to *daven mussaf*.

13. Are women obligated to *daven ma'ariv*?

No. Although men accepted upon themselves to *daven ma'ariv*, women did not do so. A woman who wishes to *daven ma'ariv* on a regular basis (e.g. on Friday night) should have in mind that she is doing so *b'li neder*, in order not to become permanently bound by it.

14. Are women obligated to recite hallel?

No, this is a time-bound mitzvah and women are exempt. If they wish to recite hallel on the appropriate days, they may do so. A woman who has limited time and wishes to *daven* either *mussaf* or hallel, should *daven mussaf* rather than hallel.

15. Are children obligated to *daven*?

• Boys should be trained to *daven shacharis* and *mincha* from the age of six or seven, but opinions differ whether one must train them to *daven ma'ariv*. See also question 94.

• According to most opinions, girls should be trained to *daven shacharis* and *mincha* from the age of six or seven, but do not need to be trained to *daven ma'ariv*.

16. Must a person *daven* with the same *nusach* as his parents?

Generally speaking, a person should adhere to the *nusach* of his parents. This is derived from the verse, "And do not forsake the Torah of your mother" (*Mishlei* 1:8).

17. What if one's parents deviated from the *nusach* of their ancestors?

According to some opinions, it is a mitzvah to return to the original *nusach* of one's ancestors.

18. What if one is already accustomed to a different *nusach*?

If it is difficult for him to change to the original family *nusach*, he may continue with his present *nusach*.

19. What if one's parents are not religious and do not *daven*?

He should attempt to clarify the *nusach* that was used by his ancestors. If this cannot be discovered, he may choose whichever *nusach* that he prefers.

20. May a married woman *daven* with a different *nusach* from her husband?

She should make every effort to *daven* with the same *nusach* as that of her husband. It is important for her to do this before her children begin to *daven*.

Chapter Two
Times of Prayers

Although most people are aware that prayers are restricted to certain hours of the day, many do not realize that the earliest and latest times for each prayer are calculated exactly. Just as Shabbos commences and terminates at a precise minute of the day, so too do each of the prayers - *shacharis, mincha, ma'ariv,* and *mussaf.* It is vital to understand that a prayer recited at the wrong time is at best second-rate, and at worst totally invalid. These times vary greatly throughout the year, and from one country to another. A person who wishes to perform the mitzvah of prayer correctly must regularly consult a local Jewish calendar in order to check the relevant times. All times mentioned in this book are *halachic* times; for example, *halachic* noon is not twelve o'clock, but halfway between sunrise and sunset. A *halachic* (seasonal) hour is a twelfth of the time between sunrise and sunset.

21. What is the best time for *shacharis*?

The best time to begin *shemoneh esrei* of *shacharis* is at the moment of sunrise (known as *zericha,* or *haneitz*). This necessitates beginning *shacharis* some time before sunrise, in order to reach *shemoneh esrei* at the right time. Care must be taken not to begin *shemoneh esrei* even a few moments before sunrise. In normal circumstances this is the earliest time for *shacharis,* and is known as *kevasikin.*

22. May one *daven* earlier?

In difficult situations, one may *daven shacharis* before sunrise. E.g., if he must set out early on a journey, or in order to arrive at work on time.

23. What is the earliest time for *shacharis*?

Halachic dawn. This is known as *alos hashachar*, and is approximately seventy-two minutes before sunrise. Nevertheless, the *brachos* for tallis and *tefillin*, and shema may not be recited until some time later. This time is known as *misheyakir*, and since opinions differ as to its calculation, a rav should be consulted. (See also question 399.)

24. Is it preferable to *daven shacharis* alone after sunrise or with a minyan before sunrise?

It is preferable to *daven* alone after sunrise. If possible, he should attend the minyan in order to hear *kaddish, kedusha, krias hatorah*, etc. See also questions 26, 45 and 51.

25. What is the latest time for *shacharis*?

Every effort must be made to **finish** *shemoneh esrei* before the end of one third of the day, and it is reprehensible to deliberately allow this deadline to pass. However, if one accidentally missed this time, he may still *daven shacharis* until *halachic* noon, although the value of such a prayer is much lower. See also questions 38 and 522.

26. Is it preferable to *daven shacharis* alone before a third of the day or with a minyan after this time?

It is preferable to *daven* alone before a third of the day.

27. Is it preferable to *daven shacharis* before sunrise or after a third of the day?

If a person is unable to *daven shacharis* at the correct time, it is better to *daven* before sunrise than after a third of the day.

28. What if a person willfully delayed *davening shacharis* until one third of the day?

Although it is questionable whether he may *daven shacharis* until noon, he should nevertheless do so. However, due to the doubt, he should stipulate beforehand that if he is exempt, his prayer is a voluntary one. If this occurs on Shabbos or Yom Tov, he should *daven* without making the stipulation.

29. Should a man omit parts of *shacharis* in order to *daven shemoneh esrei* before one third of the day?

In normal circumstances, such a situation should not arise. However, if this did occur, he should omit most of *shacharis* in order to *daven shemoneh esrei* before one third of the day. He should say at least the following before *shemoneh esrei*:

- *Al netilas yadayim, asher yatzar,* and *elohai neshamah.*
- *Birchos hatorah.*
- From *yotzeir ohr* until *shemoneh esrei.*

If by saying this he will not be able to finish *shemoneh esrei* before one third of the day, he should *daven shacharis* as usual without omissions.

30. If a man follows this procedure, should he say all the omitted sections after *shemoneh esrei*?

He should say everything except *baruch she'amar* and *yishtabach,* since these *brachos* may not be recited after *shemoneh esrei.*

31. Should a woman omit parts of *shacharis* in order to *daven shemoneh esrei* before one third of the day?

Yes. If necessary, she should recite the *b'racha al netilas yadayim*, the last verse of shema, omit everything else, and begin *shemoneh esrei* immediately.

32. What else should a woman say before *shemoneh esrei* if time allows?

If it is close to one third of the day, but there is time to *daven* a little before *shemoneh esrei* besides the *b'racha al netilas yadayim*, she should say from *emes veyatziv* until *shemoneh esrei*. If more time is available, she should also say *baruch she'amar, ashrei,* and *yishtabach*.

33. Why does *emes veyatziv* have such high priority?

The *b'racha emes veyatziv* through *ga'al yisroel* discusses the Exodus from Egypt. According to most opinions, women are obligated in the mitzvah of remembering the Exodus daily, and should preferably fulfill it by reciting this *b'racha*.

34. May a woman skip most of this section and begin from *tehillos l'eil elyon*?

This is totally forbidden and tantamount to reciting a *b'racha* in vain. The section beginning at *emes veyatziv* and ending at *ga'al yisroel* is one *b'racha* and should be either said in its entirety or omitted completely. See also question 521.

35. May she say all the omitted sections after *shemoneh esrei*?

• The *brachos baruch she'amar* and *yishtabach* may not be recited after *shemoneh esrei*, irrespective of the time.

• According to many opinions, women may not recite the three *birchos shema* after one third of the day (see next question).

In effect this means that she may say after *shemoneh esrei*:

• The morning *brachos* including *birchos hatorah*.

• *Korbanos*.

• *Pesukei dezimra* excluding *baruch she'amar* and *yishtabach*.

• Shema.

• Any sections following *shemoneh esrei*.

36. What if she begins to *daven* after one third of the day?

According to many opinions, she may say everything except the three *birchos shema*. Therefore, following *yishtabach* she should skip to shema, and following shema she should skip to *shemoneh esrei*. See also question 524.

37. What if she begins to *daven* close to *halachic* noon?

If there is very little time, she should say *al netilas yadayim*, the last verse of shema, and *shemoneh esrei*. If time allows, she should also say *baruch she'amar*, *ashrei*, and *yishtabach*.

38. May one begin *shemoneh esrei* just before noon?

If one will be unable to finish before noon, one should not begin *shemoneh esrei*, but rather *daven mincha* twice (see chapter three).

39. What is the earliest time for *mincha*?

The earliest time, known as *mincha gedola*, is half an hour after noon.

40. Is this half a *halachic* hour or thirty minutes?

According to the main opinion, it is half a *halachic* hour. However, some communities have the custom to wait thirty minutes after noon during the winter, when half a *halachic* hour is less than thirty minutes.

41. What if a person accidentally *davened mincha* during this half hour?

Although it is forbidden to *daven* during this half hour even in an emergency, if one accidentally did so, he should not *daven* again.

42. Is it preferable to *daven mincha* later in the afternoon?

According to some opinions, it is preferable to *daven mincha ketana*, which begins two and a half *halachic* hours before sunset. However, according to many opinions, *mincha gedola* is equally acceptable.

43. What is the latest time for *mincha*?

- According to many opinions, one must finish *shemoneh esrei* before sunset, and this is the prevalent custom in *Eretz Yisroel*.
- According to some opinions, one may *daven* until close to nightfall, and this is the custom in some communities in *chutz la'aretz*.

44. According to the main view, may one *daven* after sunset if one did not *daven* earlier?

- According to most opinions, this is permitted, but one must finish *shemoneh esrei* no later than fifteen minutes before nightfall.
- According to some opinions, it is forbidden to begin *mincha* if one cannot finish *shemoneh esrei* by sunset, and certainly forbidden to begin after sunset.

45. Is it preferable to *daven mincha* alone before sunset or with a minyan after sunset?

According to many opinions, it is preferable to *daven* alone before sunset.

46. What is the correct time for *ma'ariv*?

The ideal time is as soon as it is nightfall. A person should make an effort to *daven* at this time, since enthusiastic people perform mitzvos at the first opportunity.

47. May one *daven ma'ariv* before nightfall?

In normal circumstances, one should not *daven* before nightfall. However, on Friday afternoon or in extenuating circumstances on other days, one may *daven* after *plag hamincha* (one and a quarter *halachic* hours before sunset). A man who does so must recite shema again after nightfall. A man who has *yahrzeit* should make every effort to *daven* after nightfall.

48. May one *daven ma'ariv* immediately after *mincha*?

• It is forbidden for an individual to *daven mincha* and *ma'ariv* together, unless *plag hamincha* falls between them. Therefore, an individual who wishes to *daven ma'ariv* before nightfall, must *daven* the previous *mincha* before *plag hamincha*.

• A shul that cannot arrange *mincha* and *ma'ariv* at the ideal times may *daven ma'ariv* immediately after *mincha*. If possible, the prayers should be scheduled so that *plag hamincha* (or sunset) falls between *mincha* and *ma'ariv*. Shema must be recited again after nightfall.

49. Is it preferable to *daven ma'ariv* with a minyan before nightfall or alone after nightfall?

• If he *davened mincha* before *plag hamincha*, he should *daven ma'ariv* with the minyan, and repeat shema after nightfall.

• If he *davened mincha* after *plag hamincha*, he should *daven ma'ariv* alone after nightfall.

50. What is the latest time for *ma'ariv*?

Ideally, one should *daven* before *halachic* midnight. A man who misses this time is a transgressor, but must nevertheless still *daven ma'ariv* before dawn of the following day.

51. Is it preferable to *daven ma'ariv* alone before midnight or with a minyan after midnight?

It is preferable to *daven* alone before midnight.

52. What is the earliest time for *mussaf*?

Immediately following *shacharis*.

53. What if a person *davened mussaf* before *shacharis*?

Although this is forbidden, one who did so has fulfilled his obligation.

54. What is the latest time for *mussaf*?

- Ideally, one should start *davening* before *mincha gedola*.
- If this time passed, one should make every effort to finish *davening* before one *halachic* hour after noon.
- If this time passed, one has transgressed, but may nevertheless still *daven mussaf* until sunset.

55. May one *daven mussaf* after sunset?

- A man should follow the same rules as for *mincha* (see question 44).
- A woman should not *daven mussaf* after sunset.

56. If a person wishes to *daven mussaf* and *mincha* together, which one should he say first?

- If it is close to an hour after noon, he should *daven mussaf* first, in order to meet the ideal deadline.
- At other times he should *daven mincha* first, since *mincha* is a more important prayer.

57. May one *daven mussaf* and *mincha* at different times during the afternoon?

Yes.

• Before the time of *mincha ketana* one may *daven* these prayers in either order.

• After the time of *mincha ketana*, one should *daven mincha* first.

58. What if it is close to sunset and there is not enough time for both *mussaf* and *mincha*?

One should *daven mincha*.

The following summary chart may be useful to readers:

	Earliest Time		Latest time	
	Normally	In times of need	Normally	*Bedieved*
Shacharis	Sunrise	Dawn	One third of the day	Noon
Mincha	Half an hour after noon	-	Sunset	15 minutes before nightfall
Ma'ariv	Nightfall	*Plag hamincha*	Midnight	Dawn
Mussaf	After shacharis	-	½ hour/ one hour after noon	Sunset/ 15 minutes before nightfall

Chapter Three

Replacement Tefillos

59. Can one replace a missed *tefillah*?

If a person accidentally missed a *tefillah*, he can correct the situation by reciting *shemoneh esrei* twice at the next *tefillah*. If he deliberately missed a *tefillah*, the situation cannot be corrected.

60. What is considered accidental?

The following situations are included:
- He forgot to *daven*.
- He thought that he *davened* and realized too late that he did not.
- He was ill or intoxicated.
- He was engrossed in an activity and thought that he would be able to *daven* later, but the time passed.

61. What if he was involved in urgent communal needs?

A rav should be consulted.

62. Is there an obligation to replace the missed *tefillah*?

- A man is obligated to do so.
- A woman who missed *shacharis* is obligated to *daven* *mincha* twice.

- A woman who missed *mincha* is not obligated to *daven ma'ariv shemoneh esrei* twice, but it is praiseworthy for her to do so. It is not sufficient to *daven ma'ariv* once, since this would be considered as *ma'ariv* and not a replacement for *mincha*. This is true even if she does not usually *daven ma'ariv*.

63. Can a woman replace a missed *mincha* by *davening* the next *shacharis* twice?

No. Since the correction must be made at the subsequent *tefillah*, a missed *mincha* can only be replaced at *ma'ariv*.

64. If a woman *davens ma'ariv* regularly and missed it once, is she obligated to replace it at *shacharis*?

She is not obligated, but may do so if she wishes.

65. If a woman did not *daven shacharis* due to household obligations, should she *daven mincha* twice?

- If she *davens shacharis* regularly, she should *daven mincha* twice.
- If she does not *daven shacharis* regularly, she does not need to *daven mincha* twice.

66. How do these laws apply on a day when there is *mussaf*?

The *mussaf* prayer has no connection whatsoever to these laws. Therefore:

- A missed *mussaf* cannot be replaced by any *tefillah*.
- A missed *shacharis* is replaced by *mincha* and not by *mussaf*. If this occurs and *mussaf* has not yet been said, the

correct sequence of prayers is: *mincha, mussaf,* repetition of *mincha* to replace *shacharis.*

67. What if a person missed more than one *tefillah* (e.g. he was ill)?

- The last missed *tefillah* may certainly be replaced.
- Opinions differ whether he may also replace the other missed *tefillos.* A rav should be consulted for details.

68. Should the second *shemoneh esrei* be said immediately after the first?

If one is not *davening* with a minyan, he should do the following:

- When *davening shacharis* twice, he should say *tachanun* and *ashrei* after the first *shemoneh esrei,* and then repeat *shemoneh esrei.* This is followed by *ashrei, uva le'tziyon,* etc.
- When *davening mincha* twice, he should say *tachanun* and *ashrei* after the first *shemoneh esrei,* and then repeat *shemoneh esrei.* This is followed by *aleinu.*
- When *davening ma'ariv* twice, he should wait a few moments after concluding the first *shemoneh esrei,* and then repeat *shemoneh esrei.* This is followed by *aleinu.*

69. What if one is *davening* with a minyan?

- When *davening shacharis* twice, he should repeat *shemoneh esrei* after saying with the congregation the *ashrei* that follows *tachanun* [and *krias hatorah*].
- When *davening mincha* twice, he should wait until after saying *tachanun* with the congregation, and then repeat *ashrei* and *shemoneh esrei.*

- When *davening ma'ariv* twice, he should wait a few moments after concluding the first *shemoneh esrei*, and then repeat *shemoneh esrei*.

70. What if the chazan needs to say a replacement *shemoneh esrei*?

He should have in mind that the repetition *shemoneh esrei* that he says aloud should also count as his replacement. If he needs to *daven ma'ariv* twice, he should repeat *shemoneh esrei* after the conclusion of the entire *ma'ariv*.

71. May the second *shemoneh esrei* be said later in the day (or night)?

It is forbidden to postpone the second *shemoneh esrei*. In addition, one may not eat, do any work, or even study Torah before saying the second *shemoneh esrei*. If a person began any of these activities, he must stop and *daven* the replacement *shemoneh esrei* immediately.

72. Is the replacement *shemoneh esrei* valid if recited later?

Yes. However, since some opinions disagree, it is preferable to stipulate that the *shemoneh esrei* is a voluntary prayer if he is exempt. (On Shabbos or Yom Tov he should not stipulate this.)

73. What is the latest time for saying the replacement *shemoneh esrei*?

- At *shacharis* (replacing *ma'ariv*), the latest time is one third of the day. Although regular *shacharis* may be said after this time if necessary, a replacement *shemoneh esrei* may not.
- At *mincha* (replacing *shacharis*), the latest time is sunset.

- At *ma'ariv* (replacing *mincha*), the replacement *shemoneh esrei* should preferably be recited before *halachic* midnight. If this time passed, it may be said until dawn.

74. What should one have in mind when reciting each *shemoneh esrei*?

He should intend the first *shemoneh esrei* to be the current obligation, and the second *shemoneh esrei* to replace the previously missed *tefillah*.

75. What if he intended the reverse?

If he intended the first *shemoneh esrei* to be the replacement, he has not fulfilled his obligation, and is required to *daven* a third time, as a replacement *shemoneh esrei*. However, since some opinions disagree, it is preferable to stipulate that this third *shemoneh esrei* is a voluntary prayer if he is exempt.

76. What if he had no specific intention for either *shemoneh esrei*?

He has fulfilled his obligation.

77. What if the replacement *shemoneh esrei* is not the same as the missed one?

The replacement *shemoneh esrei* must be the appropriate one at the time he is *davening*. For example, if a person missed *mincha* on Friday afternoon, he must say the Friday night *shemoneh esrei* twice, although this does not match the missed weekday *shemoneh esrei*. Similarly, if he missed *mincha* on Shabbos afternoon, he must say the weekday *shemoneh esrei* twice on *motzai* Shabbos.

78. When *davening* twice on *motzai* Shabbos, when should he recite *ata chonantanu?*

In the first *shemoneh esrei* only.

79. What if he added it in *shemoneh esrei* both times?

The mistake does not need to be corrected.

80. What if he forgot to add it in the first *shemoneh esrei?*

He should **not** say it in the second *shemoneh esrei*.

81. What if he added it in the second *shemoneh esrei* only?

• If he intended the second *shemoneh esrei* to be the replacement, he has fulfilled his obligation.
• If he had no specific intention, he has not fulfilled his obligation and must *daven* a third time for the replacement *shemoneh esrei*.

82. May a woman *daven mincha* after lighting Shabbos candles?

No, since it is now Shabbos for her. It is praiseworthy for her to make amends by *davening shemoneh esrei* twice at *ma'ariv*. (See also question 62.) The same applies on Yom Tov.

83. What if a person must repeat *shemoneh esrei* due to an error, but did not realize the mistake until the next *tefillah?*

He must *daven shemoneh esrei* twice at the next *tefillah*. For example, if he forgot to add *ya'aleh veyavo* in *shacharis* of *rosh chodesh* and realized in the afternoon, he must *daven mincha* twice. Similarly, if he added *morid hageshem* or *tal u'matar* in the wrong season, he must *daven* a replacement *shemoneh esrei* if the error was not corrected.

84. What if a person forgot to add *ya'aleh veyavo* during *mincha* on *rosh chodesh* and did not realize until the evening?

- If the next day is also *rosh chodesh*, he should *daven ma'ariv* twice and add *ya'aleh veyavo* in each *shemoneh esrei*.
- If the next day is not *rosh chodesh*, opinions differ whether he is obligated to say a replacement *shemoneh esrei*. Therefore, he should *daven ma'ariv* twice (omitting *ya'aleh veyavo*) and stipulate that the second *shemoneh esrei* is a voluntary prayer if he is exempt. If the next day is Shabbos, he should *daven ma'ariv* only once.

85. What if a person wrongly added or omitted *tal u'matar* during *mincha* on Friday and did not realize until the evening?

The mistake cannot be corrected and he should *daven ma'ariv* only once.

Chapter Four
Place of Prayer

86. Where is the best place to *daven*?

The most ideal place is a *beis midrash* where the voice of Torah is constantly heard, and the next best place is a shul. This is based on the verse, "Hashem loves the gates of Zion more than all the dwellings of Ya'akov" (*Tehillim* 87:2). Our Sages explain that "the gates of Zion" are the gates that excel in *halacha*. These surpass "the dwellings of Ya'akov", which are the shuls.

87. Is there any other factor to consider?

The verse says, "In the multitude of the people is the King's glory" (*Mishlei* 14:28). Therefore, it is preferable to *daven* in a *beis midrash* or shul that has a larger congregation.

88. What if the *davening* is rushed in the larger minyan?

It is better for a person to *daven* with a smaller congregation if this will enable him to *daven* slowly and with more concentration.

89. Is it better to *daven* with a small minyan in a *beis midrash* or with a large minyan in a shul?

It is better to *daven* with a small minyan in a *beis midrash*.

90. What if a person *davens* with a different *nusach* from the shul?

He should *daven* with his own *nusach*. However, for the sections of *davening* that are said aloud by the congregation (e.g. *kaddish*, *kedusha*), he must use the *nusach* of the shul. See also questions 758, 773, 801, and 824.

91. Should one *daven* in shul even if he has missed the minyan?

Yes. Even if one must *daven* alone, it is better to do so in shul, since it is a place of holiness and more conducive to prayer. This is derived from the verse, "To listen to the cry and to the prayer" (*Melachim* I 8:28). Our Sages explain that this refers to a shul, where a person's prayers are always heard.

92. Is it better to *daven* alone in shul, or at home at the same time as the minyan in shul?

It is better to *daven* at home at the same time as the shul (see questions 226-229).

93. Should women make an effort to *daven* in shul?

Women are not obligated to *daven* in shul, but it is praiseworthy and a great merit for them to do so. Although the *Vilna Gaon* discouraged women from going to shul, the reasons that he gave no longer apply today. A woman should not go to shul if this entails neglect of her household duties, since these responsibilities take priority.

94. Should one bring children to shul?

Boys should be trained to *daven* in shul from the age of six or seven (see question 15). The father must instruct them to sit in their place with awe and respect, and encourage them to answer amen, *kedusha*, etc., and not allow them to wander around the shul. Very young children who are incapable of remaining still for more than a short time must certainly not be brought to shul. Such children make a great deal of noise as they run around and play, causing enormous disturbance to the congregation and desecrating the holiness of the shul. They will find it difficult to change their bad habits when they are older, and the father will be punished severely for all this. See also question 655.

95. Should one try to *daven* always in the same shul?

If this does not cause inconvenience, it is correct to *daven* always in the same shul. This is learned from *Avraham Avinu*, about whom it says, "And Avraham went early in the morning to [pray in] the place where he had stood before Hashem" (*Bereishis* 19:27). Our Sages comment that whoever has a fixed place for prayer will be assisted by the God of Avraham.

96. May three different shuls be used for the three daily prayers?

Yes. It is sufficient to have one fixed shul for each of *shacharis*, *mincha*, and *ma'ariv*. Similarly, a person may use one shul for weekday prayers and another for Shabbos prayers.

97. Should one try to *daven* in the same seat in shul?

Yes, this too is a mitzvah and enhances one's prayers.

98. What is the reason for this?

• Prayer is in place of offerings, and should have a fixed place, as did each animal that was brought in the holy Temple.

• Each successive prayer adds sanctity to that place and the accumulated holiness assists the prayers to rise.

99. What if another person is occupying one's regular place?

One should not embarrass the person by asking him to change his place. If possible, one should *daven* within four *amos* (approx. 2m) of one's regular seat.

100. Should one have a fixed place at home for *davening*?

Yes, women who usually *daven* at home should have a fixed place in the house for *davening*. The same applies to a man on the occasions when he is unable to *daven* in shul.

101. Must the entire *tefillah* be said in the fixed place?

No, the main requirement is to *daven shemoneh esrei* in a fixed place. The rest of *davening* may be said in a different place.

102. What if there is a disturbance in one's fixed place?

He should move to another place where he can *daven* with more concentration.

103. Where in the shul or home is the best place to *daven*?

The most ideal place is facing a wall without any intervening object between the person and the wall.

104. What is the reason for this?

- As a comparison to offerings in the holy Temple, for which interventions were forbidden.
- So that one will not be distracted.

105. Are all objects considered to be interventions?

No. The following are not interventions:
- Permanent furniture such as a closet or bookcase.
- An object that is less than ten *tefachim* high (80 cm) or less than four *tefachim* wide (32cm).
- An object that is being used during *davening*, e.g. a table or *shtender*, on which the siddur is placed.
- According to some opinions, an object that is more than four *amos* away (approx. 2m).

106. Is another person an intervention?

No, but it is still preferable to avoid this, if possible.

107. What if an intervention is unavoidable?

Avoiding an intervention is not an essential requirement, but an enhancement of one's prayers. If necessary, a person may *daven* where there is an intervening object, but he should either close his eyes or keep them focused on the siddur, in order not to be distracted.

108. May one *daven* facing a picture?

One should not *daven* any section of the *tefillah* facing a picture, in order not to be distracted. If this cannot be avoided, he should either close his eyes or hold the siddur in front of his face.

109. What if the picture is not directly in front of him?

He may *daven* there, if the picture is either to his side or above his head.

110. May one *daven* facing a mirror?

This is forbidden, since one would appear to be praying to oneself.

111. May one *daven* facing a window?

• During the day this is permitted, unless the window faces a busy street, etc., that may cause a distraction.
• At night this should preferably be avoided, since the window acts as a mirror, reflecting one's image.

112. May one *daven* outside?

• Ideally, this should be avoided. *Davening* indoors is more conducive to humility and fear of Hashem, and a person who willfully ignores this is considered insolent. This applies only to *shemoneh esrei*.
• If the area is surrounded by a wall or fence one may *daven* there.
• The area in front of the *Kosel Hama'aravi* is an exception, since it is designated for prayer.

113. What if one must *daven* outside, e.g. while traveling?

If possible, he should *daven* near a wall or between trees.

114. Which direction should one face?

See question 590.

Chapter Five

Forbidden Places of Prayer

115. In which places is it forbidden to pray?

The two main restrictions are:
- In the presence of an improperly dressed person.
- In the presence of waste substances, foul material, etc.

The details of these topics are complex, and only the basic guidelines are given here. Other types of restrictions are mentioned at the end of this chapter.

116. What is meant by an improperly dressed person?

There are three levels:

1. A male or female whose genitals are exposed.

2. A female whose genitals are covered, but other parts of the body are not sufficiently covered according to the *halacha*.

3. A male whose genitals are covered, but other parts of the body are exposed.

- It is forbidden for either a man or a woman to *daven*, recite a *b'racha*, or say anything of Torah content when facing an undressed person of level 1.

- It is forbidden for a man, but permitted for a woman, to *daven*, recite a *b'racha*, or say anything of Torah content when facing an undressed person of level 2.

- It is permitted for either a man or a woman to *daven*, recite a *b'racha*, or say anything of Torah content when facing an undressed person of level 3.

117. What if the undressed person is a child?

The laws apply to an undressed boy from the age of nine and an undressed girl from the age of three. There is no difference whether the undressed person is Jewish or non-Jewish. According to some opinions, the restrictions of level 2 begin only from the age of approximately six.

118. Do the same restrictions apply to members of one's family?

Basically, yes. Even a husband is restricted if his wife is not fully covered. The only exception is for a father, who is not restricted in the presence of his partially exposed daughter (level 2) until she reaches the age of eleven.

119. Is it sufficient to close one's eyes?

• When facing level 1 nakedness, it is not sufficient to close the eyes, nor even to turn one's face aside. It is permitted to *daven* only if one turns the entire body away from the undressed person.

• When facing level 2 nakedness, if the woman's body is covered with a thin see-through garment, it is sufficient for the man to turn his face aside or close his eyes. If the woman's body is exposed, he must try to turn his body away, but if this is extremely difficult, he may be lenient to turn his gaze away or close his eyes.

120. May a man *daven* while facing a woman's exposed hair?

This is forbidden only if she is Jewish and married (or was married). However, it is sufficient for him to turn his face away or close his eyes.

121. What if a person *davened* in one of the forbidden situations?

• If one *davened* facing level 1 nakedness, one must *daven* again.

• If a man *davened* facing level 2 nakedness, or facing a woman's hair, he should not *daven* again. However, the mitzvah of shema cannot be fulfilled in this situation, and must be repeated.

122. May a man *daven* if he can hear a woman singing?

Ideally, he must go somewhere else to *daven*, or ask the woman to stop singing. If this is impossible, he may *daven*, but he must make every effort to ignore the singing and focus his mind on the *davening*. This restriction applies even to the voices of non-Jewish women and single girls from the age of eleven, and even to close relatives such as one's wife or daughter.

123. What are the restrictions regarding waste substances?

It is forbidden to *daven*, recite a *b'racha*, or even think anything of Torah content if one can either see or smell waste substances, garbage, rotting objects, etc. In addition, one must distance oneself four *amos* (approx. 2m) from the point where the odor ends.

124. What if the substances are enclosed in a plastic bag?

If no foul odor is emitted from the bag one may *daven* nearby, even if the substances are visible through the bag.

125. May one *daven* near a child who is wearing a soiled diaper?

It is forbidden to *daven*, unless one is at least four *amos* away from the point where the odor ends (or from the child if there is no odor). This does not apply to a child who is less than three months old.

126. What if the child has been changed but there is still a bad odor in the room?

It is still forbidden to *daven* there. If one sprays the room with an air-freshener to create a pleasant smell, one may *daven* there.

127. What if a child is wearing a wet diaper?

One may *daven* nearby, unless there is a bad odor.

128. Is there an obligation to check a child's diaper before *davening*?

As long as one does not suspect that the child may be dirty, there is no requirement to check him.

129. What if a child soils himself while one is *davening*?

If one can smell the bad odor, he must stop *davening* immediately and attend to the problem. Either the child should be changed or moved, or one must move away four *amos* from the point where the odor ends. This applies even if one is in the middle of *shemoneh esrei*.

130. May one *daven* in the presence of a child's potty?

This is permitted if the potty is thoroughly clean and does not smell.

131. May one *daven* facing the open door of a bathroom or toilet?

- If one can smell a foul odor, this is forbidden.
- If there is no foul odor, opinions differ about this and it is preferable to close the door, if possible.

132. What if there is an offensive odor from tar, kerosene, paint, etc.?

One may *daven* in the presence of such odors, even if he is nauseated by them.

133. What if a person accidentally *davened* in the presence of waste matter?

This is a complex issue depending on several factors, and a rav should be consulted.

134. May a person *daven* if there is used *nagel vasser* in the room?

It is preferable to remove the water.

135. May one *daven* in a shul that lacks a proper *mechitza*?

It is forbidden to *daven* in such a shul when there are women present, even if the women dress modestly. If one is unsure whether the *mechitza* meets the *halachic* requirements, he should consult a rav.

136. May men *daven* in a hall or house when women are present?

- If all the men and women are members of the family, it is permitted.
- If they are not all relatives, the women should be asked to go to another room. If they do not agree to leave, it is permitted to *daven* there.

137. May one *daven* in a hall that is used for mixed dancing?

Such a place is an abomination and it is forbidden to *daven* there, even when the hall is not in use.

138. May one *daven* in a reform or conservative temple?

It is forbidden to *daven* in such a place.

139. May one *daven* in the house of a gentile?

Ideally, this should be avoided. If necessary one may *daven* there, provided that one does not face an item or picture of idol worship.

Chapter Six
Proper Attire for Tefillah

140. Are there any dress requirements for prayer?

The verse says, "Prepare to meet Hashem" (*Amos* 4:12). Our Sages derive from this verse that when a person *davens* he must dress in a dignified manner, as he would when appearing before a king.

141. What does this mean in practice?

A person must dress in clothing that he would wear when standing before an important dignitary.

142. Should a man wear a jacket?

It is praiseworthy to do so.

143. May the jacket be draped over the shoulders?

It is preferable to wear it correctly.

144. Should a man wear a hat?

It is praiseworthy to do so, or to drape a tallis over his head.

145. Is it better to *daven* with a minyan without a hat or jacket or alone with a hat and jacket?

If a man is unable to obtain a hat or jacket, it is better to *daven* without them in a minyan. However, if he can *daven* with a later minyan with a hat and jacket, he should preferably do so. Alternatively, he could cover his head and body with a tallis.

146. May a woman *daven* while wearing a robe?

Ideally, this should be avoided, since a robe is not sufficiently dignified. According to some opinions, it is permitted if she would wear it in the street.

147. May one *daven* while wearing a coat?

Yes.

148. May one wear a scarf or gloves?

If one is feeling cold, this is permitted.

149. May one wear a plastic cover over one's hat?

It is preferable to remove it.

150. Must footwear be worn?

Yes. Even if one is wearing socks, one must also wear shoes or sandals, since it would be improper to stand before a dignitary without them. Yom Kippur and Tisha b'Av are exceptions.

151. Must socks be worn?

Yes. Even when wearing shoes or sandals, one must also wear socks.

152. May one wear slippers?

No, this is not sufficiently dignified.

153. May one wear boots?

Only if one would wear them in front of a dignitary.

154. May one wear work clothes?

Ideally, a laborer should change into respectable clothes for *davening*. Similarly, a woman should not wear a work apron.

155. May one wear dignified clothes above one's pajamas?

This is permitted if the pajamas cannot be seen.

156. May a sick person *daven* while wearing pajamas?

Yes.

157. What if a person cannot obtain dignified clothes, e.g. while traveling?

In extenuating circumstances, one may *daven* without dignified clothes, as long as the body is fully covered according to the rules of modest dress.

158. Is it better to *daven* alone with dignified clothes, or with a minyan while not wearing so dignified clothes?

It is better to *daven* with a minyan while wearing not so dignified clothes, e.g. work clothes.

159. Is it better to *daven shacharis* before a third of the day with not so dignified clothes, or after this time with dignified clothes?

It is better to *daven* before a third of the day with not so dignified clothes, e.g. a woman wearing a robe who will miss this time if she dresses.

Chapter Seven
Personal Hygiene

160. Is there a requirement to wash one's hands before prayer?

Throughout the day, a person may recite *brachos* and *tehillim* and study Torah without washing his hands, and may assume that he did not absent-mindedly make them *tamei*. However, this is not sufficient for *tefillah*, and there is a positive requirement to wash the hands before *davening*.

161. What is the reason for this?

The verse says, "I wash my hands in purity and circle around Your altar, Hashem" (*Tehillim* 26:6). The Sages derive from this that a person should wash his hands before prayer, just as the *cohanim* did before beginning the service in the holy Temple.

162. Does this apply only to *shacharis*?

No. One must wash the hands before each *tefillah*, whether *shacharis*, *mincha*, or *ma'ariv*.

163. What if one remains in shul between *mincha* and *ma'ariv*?

If he thinks that his hands are still clean, he is not required to wash them again for *ma'ariv*. According to some opinions, it is praiseworthy to wash them again.

164. Must one wash the hands before *mussaf*?

This is not required, unless there is a break between *shacharis* and *mussaf* for kiddush or some other activity.

165. What if one does not *daven shacharis* immediately after dressing?

If a person is involved in any time-consuming activity between dressing and *davening*, he is required to wash hands again before beginning *shacharis*. Common situations are:

- A man who attends a *shiur*.
- A woman who attends to her husband, children, or the home.
- A girl who travels to school or seminary.
- A woman or girl who eats breakfast after reciting a few *brachos* (see question 334).

166. Must the hands be washed with a cup?

Preferably, one should use a cup.

167. How much of the hand should be washed?

The entire hand up to the wrist.

168. What if one does not have any water (e.g. when traveling)?

- If he thinks that his hands are not *tamei*, it is sufficient to rub the hands with a cloth or similar item. The entire area of the hands should be rubbed, including between the fingers.
- If he knows that his hands are *tamei*, he must make an effort to obtain water.

169. May a person *daven* if he needs to use the bathroom?

In order to pray, a person must be clean both externally and internally. It is therefore an obligation to use the bathroom before beginning to *daven*, if necessary.

170. What if he will miss the minyan by doing so?

He must use the bathroom even if this will cause him to miss the minyan. This applies even if the need is only slight.

171. What if he will miss the latest permitted time to *daven*?

- If his need is only slight, he should *daven*.
- If his need is strong, he must not *daven*. He should make up the lost *davening* at the next *tefillah* (see chapter three).

172. What is considered a slight need?

If he is able to wait seventy-two minutes.

173. What if a person feels the need to relieve himself but is unable to do so due to constipation?

He is permitted to *daven*.

174. Are the laws the same for all sections of *davening*?

The above laws apply to *shemoneh esrei*. Regarding other sections such as morning *brachos*, shema, hallel, etc., the laws are as follows:

- If one's need is strong, it is forbidden to say any words of Torah or *tefillah*.

- If one's need is slight, opinions differ whether the restriction applies. One may be lenient in extenuating circumstances.

See also questions 181, 282, and 293 regarding *asher yatzar*.

175. What if one feels the need to use the bathroom in the middle of *davening*?

If this occurs at any time except during *shemoneh esrei*, he should do as follows:

- If the need is extremely strong, he must stop *davening* immediately.
- If the need is not extremely strong, he may either stop or continue until the end of that section of *davening*. He may not begin a new section.

176. What is considered a new section?

The following are considered independent sections:
- *Pesukei dezimra.*
- From *barchu* until *shemoneh esrei.*
- *Shemoneh esrei.*
- Hallel.

177. What if one needs to use the bathroom during *shemoneh esrei*?

Even if the need is extremely strong, he must attempt to finish *shemoneh esrei*, if this is physically possible.

178. What if this is impossible?

He should go to the bathroom without speaking.

179. Should he begin *shemoneh esrei* again?

• If the break is as long as he usually takes to say the entire *shemoneh esrei*, he must begin again. The verse *Hashem sefasai* is not repeated.

• If the break is shorter, he should continue from where he left off (compare question 650).

180. Should he return to his original place?

Yes.

181. When should he recite the *b'racha asher yatzar*?

After *shemoneh esrei*.

182. What if the chazan needs to use the bathroom before beginning the repetition?

If his need is only slight, he may say the repetition, since it would be embarrassing to leave the shul.

Summary

		To begin	To conclude
Shemoneh Esrei	Strong need	Forbidden	Must conclude if possible
	Slight need	Forbidden, unless deadline is approaching	Must conclude
Other sections	Strong need	Forbidden	Forbidden
	Slight need	Questionable	May conclude or stop

Chapter Eight
Prayer with a Minyan

183. Is there an obligation to pray with a minyan?

Unfortunately, some men regard this as an optional mitzvah and regularly *daven* alone at home or at work, especially for *mincha* and *ma'ariv*. This is an error, since men are obligated to make every effort to *daven* always with a minyan. However, women are certainly not required to *daven* with a minyan, although it is praiseworthy for them to do so (see question 93).

184. Why is it so important to pray with a minyan?

The verse says, "Behold, Hashem is mighty and does not despise" (*Iyov* 36:5). This is interpreted by the Sages to refer to the prayers of a minyan, which are not despised but always accepted by Hashem, even if they are recited without the correct degree of concentration. On the other hand, the prayer of an individual is scrutinized by Hashem to determine whether it was said with sufficient concentration and whether the person has enough merits. In addition, by praying with a minyan, one is able to participate in the great mitzvos of *kaddish*, *kedusha*, etc.

185. What if a man feels that he can concentrate better when *davening* alone?

He must nevertheless *daven* with a minyan.

186. What if there is no minyan nearby?

A man is obligated to join a minyan if it will take him less than eighteen minutes to get there, whether he is going by foot or by car. If the nearest minyan is further than this, he is not obligated to go there, but it is praiseworthy to do so.

187. May one travel to a place where there is no minyan?

This is incorrect, unless one must inevitably be there for reasons of health, business, or a mitzvah. One should consult a rav before going on vacation to such a place.

188. What should an employee do during work hours?

If possible, he should ask his employer for permission to go to a minyan. If this is not granted, he must *daven* alone. (If he can *daven mincha* with a minyan during the lunch break, he should do so.)

189. What if he must leave for work early in the morning before the minyan starts?

He should *daven* alone before going to work, even if he could leave in the middle of work to *daven* with a minyan.

190. What if one is attending to visitors when it is time to go to shul?

The Sages say that the mitzvah of attending to visitors is greater than speaking to Hashem. Therefore, if a person is occupied with guests who will be upset if he leaves, he is exempt from praying with a minyan, and may pray alone later. However, if possible, he should apologize to his visitors and explain that he must leave for a short time, in order to join the minyan.

191. May a man *daven* alone in order to attend a *bris* or *seudas mitzvah*?

No. He must *daven* with a minyan, even if this will cause him to arrive late or to miss a *bris* or *seudas mitzvah*.

192. If a man is engrossed in Torah study, must he break off to *daven* with a minyan?

Yes. A Torah scholar must be especially careful to attend a minyan, since failure to do so may encourage laymen to be lax in this matter and could cause a *chillul Hashem*, ח"ו.

193. Who is qualified to be included in a minyan?

A minyan must be comprised of ten Jewish males aged thirteen and above.

194. Who does not qualify as one of the ten?

A man is certainly disqualified if he commits any of the following sins:
- Disbelief in the truth of the Torah or the words of the Sages, the coming of Moshiach, the resurrection of the dead, or reward and punishment.
- Marriage to a gentile.

195. What if a man openly desecrates Shabbos?

If possible, such a person should not be counted as one of the ten. However, in extenuating circumstances, he may be included to complete a minyan.

196. What if a man does not eat kosher food?

• If he does so wantonly, with no interest whatsoever to eat kosher, he is disqualified.

• If he understands the need to eat kosher, but is tempted by the taste or cheap price of non-kosher foods, he is not disqualified.

197. May one believe a boy who claims to be thirteen?

Yes.

198. May a boy below thirteen be included in an emergency?

According to most opinions, this is forbidden. According to some opinions, this is permitted in an extreme emergency, e.g. if the continued existence of the minyan is in jeopardy.

199. How should one count the men?

Since it is forbidden to count people verbally, one should count the men mentally to ascertain whether there is a minyan. The custom is to count verbally using the verse *Hoshi'ah es amecha* etc. (*Tehillim* 28:9), which contains ten words.

200. Must all the men be in the same room?

Ideally, at least ten men should be in the same room. In extenuating circumstances, the men may be in adjacent rooms, if the door between them is open and the two groups can see each other.

201. If there are ten men in one room may one *daven* in an adjacent room?

• If the only exit from the adjacent room is via the first room, he may *daven* there, and he is considered to be praying with the minyan.

• If there is another exit from the adjacent room but he can see the minyan, he should preferably move into the first room to join the minyan.

• If there is another exit from the adjacent room and he cannot see the minyan, he must join the minyan.

202. Is a man considered part of the minyan if he prays in the women's section?

• If he can see the minyan, he should preferably move into the men's section to join the minyan.

• If he cannot see the minyan, he must join them.

203. Is a man considered part of the minyan if he prays outside the shul next to a window?

Preferably, he should join the minyan inside.

204. Must ten men in one room be able to see one another?

No. As long as ten men *daven* together in the same room, this constitutes a minyan, even if some cannot see the others. This may occur in an L-shaped room, or if a large bookcase blocks the view.

205. What if the minyan is held outside?

In this situation, the men must be able to see one another and hear the chazan. In addition, there must not be a road or footpath dividing them.

206. Must one *daven* the entire service with the congregation?

Ideally, yes. Men are obligated to make every effort to arrive in shul on time, to enable them to *daven* everything in the correct order together with the minyan. The Sages describe a man who comes late as a negligent and lazy person, and one who does so regularly will receive this description in the World to Come. It is difficult to imagine the eternal shame that he will experience.

207. Is there an advantage in being one of the first ten?

Yes. The Sages say that whoever is numbered among the first ten receives a reward equal to that of the entire congregation. Nevertheless, even after the first ten, whoever arrives earlier than others is more elevated and closer to the Shechina. If one is unable to be among the first ten at *shacharis*, he should make an effort to do so at *mincha* and *ma'ariv*.

208. What if a man arrives late for *shacharis*?

The most essential part of the service that should be said together with the minyan is *shemoneh esrei*. Therefore, a man who arrives late must skip parts of *davening* in order to begin *shemoneh esrei* with the minyan, unless he can join a later minyan (see question 499). Unfortunately, some men are under the impression that it is sufficient to pray in shul, even if they are not *davening* anything with the minyan. They incorrectly *daven* everything in order from the beginning of *shacharis* and lose out on the important mitzvah of praying with a minyan.

209. Which parts of *shacharis* may he skip?

If necessary, he may omit any parts of *shacharis* except the following, which should be said before *shemoneh esrei*:

- *Al netilas yadayim, asher yatzar, elohai neshamah,* and *birchos hatorah.*
- *Baruch she'amar, ashrei, yishtabach.* On Shabbos and Yom Tov, *nishmas* through *yishtabach* must also be said.
- From *yotzeir ohr* until *shemoneh esrei.*

210. What if this procedure will still not enable him to reach *shemoneh esrei* with the minyan?

If possible he should *daven* with a later minyan. Otherwise, he should *daven* everything in order from the beginning of *shacharis*. See also question 499.

211. If time allows, which additional sections have priority?

See questions 502 and 504.

212. What if he arrives on time but *davens* more slowly than the congregation?

- He should *daven* with a slower minyan, or make an effort to arrive early for this minyan.
- If this is not possible, he may *daven* everything in order at his own pace if he wishes, although he will thereby lose the mitzvah of *davening* with the minyan. If he prefers, he may omit parts of the *davening* as mentioned above (question

209), in order to reach *shemoneh esrei* with the minyan. See also question 893 regarding *ma'ariv*.

213. Must one begin *shemoneh esrei* exactly with the minyan?

• It is forbidden to begin *shemoneh esrei* before the congregation.
• Ideally, one should begin *shemoneh esrei* at precisely the same moment as the congregation.
• Even if one begins after the congregation, it is nevertheless considered as if he is praying with the minyan.

214. What if one reaches *shemoneh esrei* considerably after the congregation has begun?

He may begin *shemoneh esrei* only if he is certain that he will reach *elohai netzor* before the chazan reaches *kedusha*. Otherwise, he must wait at *shira chadasha* in order to respond to *kedusha*.

215. How long must he wait at *shira chadasha*?

When he sees that the chazan is preparing to begin the repetition, he should continue *davening* in order to begin *shemoneh esrei* together with the chazan. He must then make an effort to say *shemoneh esrei* word for word with the chazan until *kedusha*, and preferably do so for the entire *shemoneh esrei*. This is almost equivalent to praying with a minyan.

216. What should he do when the chazan reaches *kedusha*?

He should say the entire *kedusha* together with the chazan.

217. Should he raise his heels during *kedusha*?

Yes, this should be done as usual (see question 727).

218. Should he say *ata kadosh* or *ledor vador*?

He should say the same as the chazan. Therefore, if he is *davening* with an Ashkenaz minyan, he should say *ledor vador*.

219. Which version of *modim* should he say?

He should say the version of the quiet *shemoneh esrei* together with the chazan. *Modim de'rabbanan* should not be said in this situation.

220. What should he do during the blessings of the *cohanim*?

- If the chazan recites the blessings (*Eloheinu veilohei avoseinu* etc.), he should wait silently until the chazan continues *sim shalom*.
- If the *cohanim* are blessing the congregation, he should listen to the blessings and respond amen after each of the three verses. He should then continue *sim shalom* with the chazan.

221. What should he do at the conclusion of *sim shalom*?

He should continue *shemoneh esrei* as usual with (*yihyu leratzon* and) the paragraph *elohai netzor*.

222. Should a woman skip sections of *shacharis* in order to *daven shemoneh esrei* with the congregation?

• According to some opinions, she should do so, following the same rules as men.

• According to other opinions, a woman has no obligation to *daven shemoneh esrei* with the congregation, and therefore should not skip sections to do so.

223. What if a man arrives a little late for *mincha* in shul?

If the congregation is about to begin *shemoneh esrei*, he should join them immediately for *shemoneh esrei*. After *mincha* he should recite *ashrei* as though he is reading Torah, but not with the intention of fulfilling an obligation.

224. What if he arrives for *mincha* during the quiet *shemoneh esrei*?

He may begin *shemoneh esrei* only if he is certain that he will reach *elohai netzor* before the chazan reaches *kedusha*. Otherwise, he should start *shemoneh esrei* when the chazan begins the repetition, and must make an effort to say the entire *shemoneh esrei* with the chazan.

225. What if a man arrives late for *ma'ariv*?

See question 890.

226. What if a man is unable to *daven* with a minyan?

In exceptional circumstances, when *davening* with a minyan is impossible, a man should attempt to *daven* at the same time as the minyan in that town.

227. What if there are several minyanim in town?

He may *daven* at the same time as any one of the minyanim. However, he must select a particular minyan with which to synchronize and may not assume that he is *davening* at the same time as some minyan.

228. Which part of the service should be said at the same time?

He should try to begin *shemoneh esrei* at the same time as the minyan does.

229. Should he skip parts of *davening* to achieve this?

No. It is better to *daven* everything in order, rather than skip parts for this purpose.

230. Is it better to *daven* alone in shul, or at home at the same time as the minyan?

It is better to *daven* at home at the same time as the shul.

Chapter Nine

Laws of the Chazan

231. What is the meaning of the word chazan?

It is derived from the Aramaic word *chaza*, meaning "saw". This is to indicate that the chazan is obligated to see that he *davens* correctly. See also question 240.

232. Who is eligible to be the chazan?

In some communities a permanent chazan is appointed to lead the services on a regular basis. Such a person must be chosen carefully and should have the following qualifications:

- He is fully Torah observant.
- He has never had a bad name.
- He is humble, and is pleasing to the congregation.
- He has a pleasant voice.
- He can *daven* fluently.

It is a grave sin to appoint a chazan who is not worthy of the position.

233. Who may be the chazan for a single occasion?

In communities where there is no permanent chazan, or if the permanent chazan is not present, any male over bar mitzvah may lead the service. Nevertheless, a person who commits serious sins openly should not be the chazan even occasionally.

234. Which sins are considered to be serious?

• Disbelief in the truth of the Torah, or the words of the Sages, the coming of Moshiach, the resurrection of the dead, or reward and punishment.

• Desecration of the Shabbos.

• Shaving with a razor.

235. Are there any special rules of dress for the chazan?

Every person who *davens* is required to dress in a dignified manner (see chapter six). A chazan must be especially careful to fulfill all the necessary requirements, since he must show respect to the congregation.

236. Must the chazan wear a tallis?

• In some communities, the chazan wears a tallis for all prayers, and this is the correct practice. However, in many communities the chazan wears a tallis only for *shacharis* and on special occasions (e.g. Shabbos and Yom Tov, fast days, *selichos*). The local custom should be followed.

• If the chazan is not wearing a jacket, he should wear a tallis.

237. Is it correct to refuse the honor of being chazan?

• Initially, a person should decline the offer in order to show that he does not feel worthy of such honor. At the second request he should prepare himself to accept, and at the third request he should step forward to lead the service.

• If the request comes from an important person, e.g. the rav, he should accept immediately.

- If there is no one else capable of being chazan, he should step forward without even being asked.

238. What if the chazan is accustomed to a different *nusach* from the congregation?

He must use the *nusach* of the congregation. However, he may recite the quiet *shemoneh esrei* in the *nusach* to which he is accustomed.

239. What if his *nusach* is the same but his pronunciation is different?

He should not take the position of chazan on a regular basis, but may do so occasionally, e.g. on a *yahrzeit*. When acting as chazan, he should try to *daven* with the pronunciation of the congregation. If this is difficult and will cause him to mix the two pronunciations, he may use his own pronunciation.

240. May the chazan *daven* by heart?

Ideally, he should use a siddur, in order not to err out of fear of the congregation (see also question 231).

241. At what speed should the chazan *daven*?

Each community has its own set pace, and it is important for the chazan to adhere to a speed that is acceptable to the congregation. A pace that is too slow is a burden to the congregation, and to *daven* at a pace that is too fast is completely irresponsible. Generally speaking, the speed should be such that all the words can be said clearly and correctly.

242. May the chazan repeat words?

No. Although some chazanim have a custom to repeat certain words when singing, the Rabbis are very unhappy about this practice.

243. May he sing lengthy tunes?

He must be careful not to be a burden to the congregation and should not sing lengthy tunes even on Shabbos and Yom Tov, unless this is pleasing to the congregation. In any event, whoever sings solely in order to show off his voice is to be despised. However, one who is gifted with a pleasant voice and sings to Hashem with joy and gratitude is to be blessed.

244. How much of the *davening* should he say aloud?

The guiding rule is that everyone in shul should know where the chazan is up to. Therefore, he must say the last line of each paragraph in a loud voice, so that even people *davening* at the back of the shul will be able to follow without having to use guesswork. If the chazan has a weak voice, he should wait for the congregation to become quiet before concluding any section (or perhaps even refrain from being the chazan). Similarly, he should say the opening words of the next paragraph aloud, especially when reading sections that are sometimes omitted, so that the congregation will know what to say next. For example, *lamnatze'ach* on weekdays, and *av harachamim* on Shabbos.

245. Which specific sections should he take care to say aloud?

• The opening words of the paragraph *yishtabach*. This will enable people to join the chazan at this point by skipping parts of *pesukei dezimra* (see question 510). It is incorrect to begin aloud from *brachos ve'hodaos* (or further), since this would not give sufficient time to catch up.

• The verse *shema yisroel*. This is in order for the entire congregation to unite in accepting the Kingship of Hashem.

• After quietly concluding the final paragraph of shema (up to and including the word *emes*) he must repeat aloud the last three words - *Hashem Eloheichem emes*.

• In the paragraph *uva le'tziyon* the two lines *kadosh* and *baruch* should be said aloud by the entire congregation in unison. Therefore, the chazan should say aloud the few words preceding these phrases.

246. Should the words *ga'al yisroel* be said aloud at *shacharis*?

In most communities the custom is to say this quietly, since there is a dispute whether the congregation should respond amen to this *b'racha*. According to some opinions, the chazan should say the words aloud and the congregation should say the words together with the chazan, thereby exempting them from responding amen. Alternatively, they should begin *shemoneh esrei* a second or two before the chazan.

Repetition of Shemoneh Esrei

247. May the chazan say the repetition if he did not say the quiet *shemoneh esrei*?

In normal circumstances, the chazan must not say the repetition unless he said the quiet *shemoneh esrei* together with the congregation. However, in exceptional circumstances, he may say the repetition even if he did not say the quiet *shemoneh esrei.* For example, if a mourner or one who has *yahrzeit* arrives late for *mincha* and does not have enough time to say the quiet *shemoneh esrei,* he may begin the repetition immediately. Similarly, if nine men *daven* together and a tenth man arrives after they have finished *shemoneh esrei,* he may begin the repetition immediately.

248. What if the chazan omitted something essential from his quiet *shemoneh esrei*?

If he omitted something like *mashiv harua'ch, ya'aleh veyavo,* etc. from his quiet *shemoneh esrei,* and did not realize until he concluded *shemoneh esrei,* he may rely on the repetition to fulfill his obligation.

249. In this situation must he say *elohai netzor*?

No. The same applies in the exceptional situations mentioned in question 247.

250. Must the chazan take three steps back after finishing the quiet *shemoneh esrei*?

Yes. In normal circumstances, he may not begin the repetition until he has taken three steps back at the conclusion of his quiet *shemoneh esrei.* After doing so, he should wait until he is ready to begin the repetition and should then take three steps forward.

251. What if someone is still *davening shemoneh esrei* behind the chazan?

He may not take three steps back towards that person, but should take three steps sideways before beginning the repetition. If this is not possible, he may begin the repetition without taking three steps.

252. May the chazan speak while waiting to begin the repetition?

He may *daven* sections of *shacharis* that he omitted, or recite *tehillim*. He may not speak words of Torah, and certainly not mundane talk.

253. When should the chazan begin the repetition?

He must wait for at least nine other men to finish their *shemoneh esrei* before beginning the repetition. If possible, it is preferable to wait until most of the congregation have finished *shemoneh esrei*, in order that they can join in *kedusha*. People who bang on the table to hurry the chazan to begin before most of the congregation have finished, will face Heavenly judgment for this. Nevertheless, the chazan should not be lengthy with his quiet *shemoneh esrei*, in order not to keep the congregation waiting for the repetition.

254. Must the chazan wait for the rav?

In many communities it is the custom to do so, but if the rav wishes he may waive his rights and indicate to the chazan not to wait.

255. Must the chazan place his two feet together during the repetition?

Yes, he must stand in the same posture as for the quiet *shemoneh esrei*.

256. Should he say the verse *ki sheim* at the repetition of *mussaf* and *mincha*?

There is no obligation, but if he wishes he may say it quietly before beginning the repetition.

257. Should he say the verse *Hashem sefasai tiftach*?

Yes, but it is preferable to say this quietly.

258. How much time should the chazan wait between *brachos*?

He must wait until most of the congregation have finished answering amen. Unfortunately, some chazanim are negligent about this, and quickly begin the next *b'racha* immediately after concluding the previous one. In this situation, the congregation should not answer amen to such *brachos*. The chazan must also pause while the congregation says *baruch hu uvaruch shemo* at the end of each *b'racha*, so that they can hear the concluding words.

259. Should the chazan say the entire *kedusha* aloud?

Certainly! Unfortunately, some ignorant people are under the mistaken impression that the chazan should recite the three central lines of the *kedusha* (*kadosh*, *baruch*, and *yimloch*) quietly. The exact opposite is true. These lines in particular must be said aloud for the sake of those who are still in the middle of the quiet *shemoneh esrei*. Such people may not respond to *kedusha* (see question 667), but fulfill a mitzvah by listening carefully to the recital of these essential lines by the chazan.

260. When should the chazan say these three lines?

• According to most opinions, he should begin them before the congregation has finished saying them, since these lines must be recited with a minyan.

• According to some opinions, he should wait until the congregation has become quiet.

261. Should the chazan raise his heels when saying these lines?

Yes. (See question 727.)

262. Should the chazan recite the entire paragraph of *modim* aloud?

Certainly! Since this is part of *shemoneh esrei*, the entire paragraph should be said aloud, and the custom of some chazanim to recite part of it quietly is mistaken.

263. Should he wait until the congregation has finished *modim de'rabbanan*?

He is not required to do so, but may begin *modim* together with the congregation and continue aloud at his regular pace. Although most of the congregation who are reciting *modim de'rabbanan* will not be able to hear the chazan, it is sufficient for ten men nearby to hear him.

264. When should the chazan say the paragraph containing the *birchos cohanim*?

• In *Eretz Yisroel* the main custom is for the *cohanim* to bless the congregation at every *shacharis* and *mussaf*, and at *mincha ketana* on fast days. (Tisha b'Av and Yom Kippur have different laws.) Therefore, this paragraph is recited by the chazan only when no *cohanim* are present.

• In *chutz la'aretz* the Ashkenazic custom is for the *cohanim* to bless the congregation only at *mussaf* on Yom Tov. Therefore, this paragraph is recited by the chazan at every *shacharis*, at *mussaf* on Shabbos, *rosh chodesh*, and *chol hamoed*, and at *mincha* on fast days.

265. Should the chazan bow while reciting the *birchos cohanim*?

No, but he should turn to the sides at two points:
• When saying *ve'yishmerecha* turn to the right.
• When saying *panav eilecha viychuneka* turn to the left.

266. What should the chazan say after concluding the repetition?

According to the main opinion, he should recite the verse *yihyu leratzon* before continuing with the service. According to other opinions, he may continue immediately with the next section.

267. Must he take three steps back after the repetition?

No. This is unnecessary, since he will eventually take three steps back at the end of *kaddish tiskabeil*. However, due to this, he must be careful not to speak anything that is not connected to the prayers until after *kaddish tiskabeil*.

268. What if a different chazan will continue the service before *kaddish tiskabeil*?

In this situation, the first chazan should take three steps back after the repetition of the *shemoneh esrei* or after *tachanun*.

The same applies in the exceptional circumstances mentioned in questions 247 and 248.

269. May the chazan speak after concluding the repetition?

• If he does not take three steps back, he may not say anything that is not connected to the *tefillah* until after *kaddish tiskabeil*. During this entire time, he is compared to an individual who has finished *shemoneh esrei* but has not yet taken three steps back (see question 683).

• If he takes three steps back, he is permitted to talk when necessary (see also question 646).

Chapter Ten

Responses during Davening

When *davening* in shul, a person is sometimes not up to the same section as the congregation, e.g. after arriving late. Responding to the different prayers that are heard, e.g. *kaddish*, *kedusha*, may or may not be permitted. The laws that apply are numerous and complex, and much effort is required to master the details. A summary chart is found at the end of the chapter.

270. Are all responses equally important?

No. The responses are divided into three different levels. For example, a regular amen is more important than *baruch hu uvaruch shemo*, and *barchu* is more important than both of them.

271. Are the laws the same wherever a person is up to in *davening*?

No. *Shacharis* is divided into four sections of successively increasing importance. They are:

- First section - until *pesukei dezimra*.
- Second section - *pesukei dezimra*.
- Third section - shema and its *brachos*.
- Fourth section - *shemoneh esrei*.

The laws of responses are correspondingly stricter as one progresses through the different sections.

272. What about the sections of *shacharis* after *shemoneh esrei*?

These have the same laws as the first section of *shacharis*.

273. Which responses are permitted during the first section of *shacharis* (i.e. until *pesukei dezimra*)?

All responses are permitted (but see question 276).

274. Is there an obligation to respond?

Since one is permitted to respond, there is an obligation to do so. Failure to respond would appear to be disregard of the congregation. However, a person who is *davening* is not usually obligated to respond to a different minyan that he happens to overhear, but may respond if he wishes. See also questions 735 and 842.

275. What if one is in the middle of a verse or phrase?

Ideally, one should try to finish the verse or phrase before responding. However, if necessary one may respond even in the middle of a verse, and then return to the beginning of the verse. With a little foresight this situation can be avoided by waiting at a suitable point in order to respond.

276. What if one is in the middle of a *b'racha*?

• During a short *b'racha* all responses are forbidden.
• During a long *b'racha*, only major responses are permitted (see question 288).

277. What is meant by a short or long *b'racha*?

• A short *b'racha* is one that does not conclude with *baruch ata Hashem*. E.g. *al netilas yadayim, malbish arumim*.

- A long *b'racha* is one that concludes with *baruch ata Hashem*. E.g. *asher yatzar, hama'avir sheina*.

278. Which responses are permitted during *pesukei dezimra*?

- *Barchu.*
- The following three lines of *kedusha*:
    1. *Kadosh kadosh kadosh...*
    2. *Baruch kevod...*
    3. *Yimloch Hashem...*
- The following three responses of *kaddish*:
    1. The first amen (after *yisgadal ve'yiskadash shmei rabba*).
    2. *Amen, yehei shmei rabba...* (excluding the word *yisbarach*).
    3. The amen following *da'amiran be'alma*.
- Amen after any *b'racha*.
- *Modim de'rabbanan* (in its entirety).

279. Which responses are forbidden during *pesukei dezimra*?

- All parts of *kedusha* besides the three main responses.
- The following responses of *kaddish*:
    1. Amen after *veyatzmach purkanei* in *nusach* Sephard.
    2. *B'rich hu.*
    3. Any subsequent amen after *da'amiran be'alma ve'imru amen*.
- Any amen that is only a custom to say, e.g. during *ya'aleh veyavo*.
- *Baruch hu uvaruch shemo*.

280. What if the congregation reaches shema while one is saying *pesukei dezimra*?

He must join them and recite the first two lines, i.e. shema and *baruch sheim*. This does not apply to the shema that is recited when taking out the *sefer Torah* or during the *kedusha* of *mussaf*.

281. May one respond to the blessings of the *cohanim* during *pesukei dezimra*?

• When the blessings are recited by the *cohanim*, one may respond amen to their introductory *b'racha* and to each of the three verses of the blessings.

• When the blessings are recited by the chazan, one may not respond to them.

282. May one recite *asher yatzar* during *pesukei dezimra*?

Yes, but one should recite it only between paragraphs.

283. What if a man is called to the Torah during *pesukei dezimra*?

He should go up and recite the *brachos* and read the Torah together with the *ba'al koreh* as usual. If possible, he should attempt to finish the paragraph on his way up to the Torah. Ideally, such a person should not be called to the Torah, unless he is the only *cohen* or *levi* in shul.

284. May a man recite *brachos* on tallis and *tefillin* during *pesukei dezimra*?

Yes, but he should do so between paragraphs. If he has already reached *yishtabach*, he should say this paragraph before putting on the tallis or *tefillin*.

285. Do all the above rules apply in the middle of *baruch she'amar*?

No.

• During the first half (before the *b'racha*) all responses are permitted.

• During the second half (from the *b'racha* onwards) the rules of *pesukei dezimra* apply. However, one may not answer amen if he hears another person concluding *baruch she'amar* or *yishtabach*. According to some opinions, one may only answer to the responses that are permitted during shema.

286. Do the same rules apply in the middle of *yishtabach*?

No.

• During the first half (before the *b'racha*), one may not answer amen to *baruch she'amar* or *yishtabach*, and according to some opinions to any *b'racha*.

• During the second half (from the *b'racha* onwards), one may not respond to anything.

287. Which responses are permitted between *yishtabach* and *barchu*?

All the responses that are permitted during *pesukei dezimra*. In addition one may respond *b'rich hu*.

288. Which responses are permitted during shema and its *brachos*?

From *yotzeir ohr* until *ga'al yisroel* one may respond only to the following:

- *Barchu.*
- The following two lines of *kedusha*:
    1. *Kadosh kadosh kadosh...*
    2. *Baruch kevod...*
- The following two responses of *kaddish*:
    1. *Amen, yehei shmei rabba...* (excluding the word *yisbarach*).
    2. The amen following *da'amiran be'alma.*
- Amen after *ha'eil hakadosh* and *shomei'a tefillah.*
- The first three words of *modim de'rabbanan* (i.e. *modim anachnu lach*).
- Amen after each of the three verses of blessings by the *cohanim* (when recited by the *cohanim*).

289. Do the same laws apply if one is between *brachos* or paragraphs of shema?

Basically, yes. However, in addition to the above responses one may also answer amen to any *b'racha*.

290. Which places are considered to be the end of a paragraph?

There are four places as follows:

- After *yotzeir hame'oros.*
- After *habocher be'amo yisroel be'ahava.*
- Between the first and second paragraphs of shema.
- Between the second and third paragraphs of shema (i.e. after *al ha'aretz*).

It should be noted that *emes* and *ga'al yisroel* are not considered to be the end of a paragraph.

291. May one respond to anything during the verse *shema yisroel*?

No, all responses are forbidden. The same applies at the following points:

- Between *echad* and *baruch sheim*.
- During the phrase *baruch sheim*.
- At the end of shema, between *Eloheichem* and *emes*.

292. What if the congregation reaches shema while one is saying the *brachos* before shema?

He should act as if he is joining them by covering his eyes. However, he must not say shema with them, but may continue his own *davening*.

293. May one recite *asher yatzar* during shema and its *brachos*?

No, it should be postponed until after *shemoneh esrei*. One must take care to remember to recite it.

294. What if a man is called to the Torah during this section?

He shoud go up and recite the *brachos*. However, he should not read the Torah together with the *ba'al koreh*, but just listen attentively. If possible, he should attempt to finish the paragraph on his way up to the Torah, or at least say until a reasonable stopping point. Ideally, such a person should not be called to the Torah, even if he is the only *cohen* or *levi* in shul.

If he suspects that he may be called, he should leave the shul before the Torah reading begins.

295. Are any responses permitted after *ga'al yisroel*?
See question 586.

296. Are any responses permitted during *shemoneh esrei*?
See questions 667-674.

Summary of Permitted Responses

	During Pesukei Dezimra[1]	During Shema and its Brachos[2]
Barchu	Yes	Yes
Kedusha	Kadosh, Baruch, Yimloch	Kadosh, Baruch
Kaddish	First amen, amen yehei shmei rabba, amen after da'amiran be'alma	Amen yehei shmei rabba, amen after da'amiran be'alma
Amen of ha'eil hakadosh and shomei'a tefillah	Yes	Yes
Amen of other brachos	Yes	Only between paragraphs
Other Amens	No	No
Baruch hu uvaruch shemo	No	No
Modim de'rabbanan	Yes	Only modim anachnu lach
Shema	First two lines	Just cover eyes
Asher yatzar	Between paragraphs	After shemoneh esrei

---

[1] Except during *baruch she'amar* and *yishtabach* (see questions 285 and 286).

[2] Except during *shema yisroel* and *baruch sheim* (see question 291).

Chapter Eleven

Activities before Shacharis

297. Are any activities forbidden before *shacharis*?

The following activities are usually forbidden:

- Greeting others.
- Working.
- Eating.
- Studying Torah.
- Traveling.

Greetings

298. Why is it forbidden to greet others before *shacharis*?

It is disrespectful to honor another person before one shows honor to Hashem. According to the Sages, whoever greets another before *davening* is considered as if he is bringing an offering on a foreign altar. This applies when one specifically goes over to another person to greet him, whether to his house or in shul.

299. From what time is it forbidden to greet others?

From *halachic* dawn.

300. Are all expressions forbidden?

Although the main prohibition is to say "Shalom", since this is one of the names of Hashem, other expressions such as "Good morning" are also forbidden.

301. What if one happens to meet a friend?

- The custom is to refrain from saying "Shalom".
- It is permitted to say "Good morning", etc. According to some opinions, one should use a different expression from usual. For example, if he would usually say "Good morning", he should say *boker tov*.

302. What if one has already recited some of the morning *brachos*?

- He may go to another and use the greeting "Good morning", but not "Shalom".
- If he happens to meet a friend, he may even say "Shalom".

303. May one respond to another person's greeting?

Yes. One may reply "Shalom" or any other response to another's greeting, even if one has not recited any *brachos*. In this vein, after *davening* one may say "Shalom" to another person who has not yet *davened*, although this will cause him to reply.

304. If a relative or friend is going on a journey early in the morning, may one call him to say "Goodbye"?

Yes, but if one wishes to say "Shalom", he should preferably recite some morning *brachos* beforehand.

305. May one go to comfort a mourner before *shacharis*?

Yes.

306. May one bow to a friend as a sign of greeting?

This is forbidden, but if one has recited some *brachos*, he may bow when he happens to meet a friend in the street.

307. Is a handshake permitted before *davening*?

This has the same law as saying "Good morning". Therefore, it is permitted if one happens to meet a person, but one may not go and shake his hand (e.g. to go across the shul).

308. May one give or send a gift before *davening*?

No.

309. May one kiss one's children before *davening*?

No.

310. May one have a friendly conversation before *davening*?

This is permitted, but care must be taken to be brief, since lengthy conversations may cause one to be late for shul or to miss the deadline for shema or *shacharis*.

Working

311. From what time is work forbidden?

From *halachic* dawn. However, since some opinions forbid work from half-an-hour before dawn, it is preferable to recite morning *brachos* before starting work during this half-hour.

(The *b'racha asher nasan lasechvi vina* should not be said until dawn, see question 423.)

312. Which type of work is forbidden?

Any activity that takes more than a few moments. For example:

- Household chores such as laundry, ironing, cleaning, cooking, washing dishes, etc.
- Office work.
- Repairs (car, house, etc.).
- Shopping.

313. What is the reason for this?

The verse says, "Righteousness shall walk before him, and he will set his footsteps on the way" (*Tehillim* 85:14). The Sages interpret this to mean that before a person sets out to attend to his own affairs - "his footsteps", he should occupy himself with prayer - "righteousness".

314. What if one has already recited some of the morning *brachos*?

Although some opinions permit engaging in work after reciting *brachos*, it is preferable not to do so.

315. Are there any exceptions?

It is permitted to do mitzvah activities that cannot be postponed until after *davening*. For example, one may do shopping on Friday morning for Shabbos items, if he is concerned that they may not be available later.

316. May one wash the dishes on Shabbos morning?

This is permitted if the dishes are needed immediately after *shacharis*, and there is no other time to wash them.

317. May a woman prepare food for her husband or children?

Yes, since this is a mitzvah that cannot be postponed. Similarly, she may take the children to school, if necessary.

318. May she do housework while she is waiting for the children to finish breakfast?

If she already recited some morning *brachos*, she may do household chores, if necessary (see question 314).

319. May one make the beds?

It is permitted to quickly straighten one or two beds, but one may not make all the beds of the house since this is time consuming. Contrary to a common misconception, one may *daven* in a bedroom where the beds have not been made.

320. May one switch on the washing machine?

Yes. It is also permitted to load the laundry into the machine if it has already been sorted. However, it is forbidden to sort the different types of laundry, since this is time consuming.

321. May one dispose of the garbage on the way to shul?

Yes.

322. May one read the newspaper before *davening*?

It is permitted to take a quick glance.

323. Is exercising permitted before *davening*?

This is permitted if the intention is not for pleasure but to strengthen oneself for the day's service of Hashem, and it is not possible to exercise after *davening*. Similarly, a person may exercise to invigorate himself for *davening*. Care must be taken not to miss the minyan or the deadline for shema or *tefillah*.

324. May one take a shower before *davening*?

According to most opinions, this is permitted.

325. May one shave before *davening*?

No. In extenuating circumstances, one may shave after reciting some morning *brachos*.

Eating

326. Why is it forbidden to eat before *shacharis*?

This prohibition is based upon two verses:
• "You shall not eat by the blood" (*Vayikra* 19:26). One of the many interpretations given by the Sages is that one should not eat before praying for his own blood, i.e. his well-being.
• "You have cast Me behind your back" (*Melachim* I 14:9). This is understood to be a complaint by Hashem about a person who first eats and drinks and feels haughty, and only then accepts upon himself the yoke of Heaven.

327. From what time is eating forbidden?

• Within half-an-hour of *halachic* dawn, a man may not begin to eat more than a *kebeitza* of bread or *mezonos*, but may have drinks and other foods. A woman is not restricted during this half-hour.

- From dawn, all foods and most drinks are forbidden (see next question).
- According to the Zohar, if a person slept at night, he may not eat any food after *halachic* midnight. Ideally, one should follow this opinion, unless he wishes to eat in order to have strength to learn Torah.

328. May one drink before *davening*?

It is permitted to drink water, tea, or coffee, in order to be able to *daven* with more concentration. One may add milk or sugar to the tea or coffee.

329. Must one recite any of the morning *brachos* before having any of these drinks?

No.

330. May one have milk, fruit juice, herbal tea, or cola?

No, these are all forbidden.

331. Do these restrictions apply to an ill or elderly person?

No, such a person may eat a proper breakfast before *davening*. However, he should preferably say *birchos hatorah* and the first paragraph of shema before eating. He should repeat shema later when *davening shacharis*.

332. What if a person is feeling extremely weak or hungry?

If he will not be able to *daven* with concentration, he may eat first. He should say *birchos hatorah* and the first paragraph of shema before eating. According to some opinions, it is better to *daven* alone at home before eating, than to eat before going to *daven* in shul. After *davening* at home he should go to shul to hear *kaddish, kedusha*, etc.

333. May one take medicine or vitamins before *davening*?

Yes. It is also permitted to eat or drink with the medicine, if this is necessary. He should preferably say *birchos hatorah* and the first paragraph of shema before eating.

334. Do all these laws apply to women?

Basically, yes, except for two differences:
- They are permitted to eat bread or *mezonos* during the half-hour before dawn.
- If their routine does not enable them to *daven* until later in the morning, they may eat breakfast after reciting *birchos hatorah* and the first paragraph of shema. This also applies to girls who must travel to school or seminary before *davening*. They should repeat shema later when *davening shacharis*.

335. Do the same laws apply on Shabbos and Yom Tov?

Basically, yes. Although it is forbidden to eat or drink anything before kiddush, this restriction does not usually apply until after *shacharis*. Therefore:
- A woman who intends to *daven shemoneh esrei* and feels that she must eat first, may do so after reciting *birchos hatorah* and the first paragraph of shema. If possible, she should eat anything except bread or *mezonos*. If she must eat bread or *mezonos* due to sickness or extreme weakness, she

may do so, but must recite kiddush first according to most opinions (see next question). In any event, she should repeat shema later when *davening shacharis*.

• A woman who does not intend to *daven shemoneh esrei* but relies on saying a short prayer (see question 8), may not eat or drink anything after this prayer until she recites kiddush.

336. May a man eat before *shacharis* on Shabbos or Yom Tov?

According to most opinions, this is forbidden, unless he feels extremely weak or will feel weak by the end of *davening*. In this case, he should recite *birchos hatorah* and the first paragraph of shema, and then eat anything except bread or *mezonos*. In extenuating circumstances when he must eat bread or *mezonos*, he must recite kiddush first. According to some opinions, he is not required to recite kiddush, even if he feels it necessary to eat *mezonos*.

337. Do these laws apply to children?

No. Children below bar/bas mitzvah may eat breakfast before reciting any part of *shacharis*. On Shabbos or Yom Tov they may eat anything before kiddush.

Studying Torah

338. From what time is it forbidden to study Torah?

From *halachic* dawn. According to some opinions, the prohibition does not begin until close to sunrise.

339. What if one began to study before this time?

He may continue, but he should take care not to miss the times of shema and *tefillah*.

340. When may a man study Torah before *shacharis*?

- If he studies in shul.
- If he usually *davens shacharis* with a minyan at a fixed time, he may study Torah at home beforehand.
- If he *davens shacharis* with a minyan but at no fixed time, or he sometimes *davens* alone, he may not study Torah at home before *shacharis*. The reason is that he may become engrossed in his learning and miss the times of shema and *tefillah*.

341. Would it help to ask someone else to remind him to *daven*?

Yes, but the other person must not also be studying Torah.

342. Would an alarm clock be a sufficient reminder?

Yes.

Traveling

343. From what time is it forbidden to travel?

One may not set out to travel out of town from *halachic* dawn.

344. What is the reason for this?

Travel is included in the category of work, since a person travels in order to attend to his affairs (see question 313).

345. What if he will be able to *daven* with a minyan after he arrives at his destination?

The prohibition still applies.

346. Are there any exceptions?

One may travel before *davening* in the following cases:
- If he *davens* first, he will miss his transportation and he has no other alternative.
- If he *davens* first, he will have to travel alone in dangerous locations.
- He is traveling for a mitzvah purpose.

Nevertheless, even in these situations, he should recite the morning *brachos* before traveling.

347. Are any other activities forbidden before *shacharis*?

If a person stayed awake all night, he may not go to sleep from half-an-hour before dawn. This is out of fear that he may sleep beyond the permitted times for shema and *tefillah*.

348. Would it help to ask someone else to wake him in time?

Yes, provided that the other person will remain awake the entire time.

349. Would setting an alarm clock be sufficient?

No, since he may be tempted to go back to sleep after switching off the alarm.

350. What if he cannot stay awake any longer but cannot find someone to wake him later?

He should recite *birchos hatorah* and shema after dawn, and he may then go to sleep. Care should be taken to arise in time to *daven shacharis*.

351. What if a person slept at night, but awoke around dawn?

He may go back to sleep again, since in this case we are not afraid that he will oversleep the time of *shacharis*.

Chapter Twelve

Prayers on Arising

352. What is the significance of *modeh ani*?

Modeh ani is based on the verse, "They are new every morning; great is Your faithfulness!" (*Eicha* 3:23). A Jew begins each day with these words, expressing his gratitude to Hashem for faithfully returning his soul in a refreshed condition, ready for another day of service to Him. In addition, the Sages explain that when a person's soul rises to Heaven each night, it must stand in judgment for all that it has done during the previous day. Despite the numerous failures and mistakes, Hashem in His infinite mercy faithfully gives a person another chance to correct his faults, and devote himself wholeheartedly to the ways of the Torah.

353. When should one say *modeh ani*?

As soon as he wakes up and does not wish to sleep more. Care should be taken to pause between the words *bechemla* and *rabba*.

354. What if one falls asleep again?

He is not required to repeat *modeh ani*, but he may do so if he wishes.

355. Should a woman say *modeh* or *modah*?

Although grammatically *modah* is the correct feminine form, the custom is to say *modeh* without change (see also question 428).

356. May one speak before saying *modeh ani*?

Yes. However, it is praiseworthy to devote the very first words of the day to thanking Hashem.

357. May one say *modeh ani* before washing *nagel vasser*?

Yes.

358. May one say any other verses before *nagel vasser*?

No. Since the hands are *tamei*, one should not say any *brachos* or verses.

359. What is the reason for *nagel vasser*?

There are three principal reasons:
•   The hands inevitably touch parts of the body while one is asleep, and clean hands are required for prayer.
•   Before beginning a new day of service to Hashem, a person must sanctify himself by washing his hands, just as the *cohanim* did before starting the service in the holy Temple.
•   To remove the *ruach ra'ah* (unclean spirit) that comes upon the hands when sleeping at night.

360. Exactly how should one wash *nagel vasser*?

•   Take the cup of water in the right hand.

- Transfer the cup to the left hand and pour some water over the right hand up to the wrist.
- Transfer the cup to the right hand and pour some water over the left hand up to the wrist.
- Repeat the alternating washing until each hand has been washed three times. Some have the custom to wash each hand four times.

361. Should a left-handed person reverse the procedure?

No, he should follow the same order as a right-handed person.

362. Should women and children wash *nagel vasser*?

Yes. Strictly speaking, children do not need to be trained to wash the hands in the morning until the age of five or six. Many have the custom to begin when the children start touching food. Nevertheless, it is praiseworthy to wash the hands of even a newborn baby, since this brings holiness and purity to the child.

363. What are the main laws of *nagel vasser*?

- Ideally, a person should wash *nagel vasser* before he walks four steps. Therefore, a cup of water and basin should be left next to the bed at night, if possible. The water does not need to be covered, but should not be kept under the bed. According to some opinions, one is not required to prepare *nagel vasser* next to the bed.
- Before washing *nagel vasser* one should not touch any of the orifices of the body, e.g. eyes, nose, ears, mouth.

- Before washing *nagel vasser* one should not touch any food. According to some opinions, one should also not touch clothing.
- Ideally, there should be no interventions on the hands. Therefore, women should remove their rings before washing.
- The hands should be washed as soon as possible, even if one wishes to remain in bed a little while.

364. May one wash *nagel vasser* over dishes in the sink?

Yes, since the *tamei* water will be rinsed off when the dishes are washed.

365. After *nagel vasser* should one say the verses *Torah tziva* etc.?

The custom is to recite these verses with young children, in order to familiarize them with words of Torah. An adult is not required to say these verses, but when he is ready to start *shacharis* he should say:

מודה אני לפניך ה' אלהי ואלהי אבותי שהוצאתני מאפלה לאורה

I thank You Hashem, my G-d and the G-d of my fathers, that You have taken me out of darkness into light.

366. When should one recite the *b'racha al netilas yadayim*?

There are two equally acceptable customs:

- At the first opportunity. This is usually after using the bathroom and washing the hands again, as one may not recite a *b'racha* when one needs to use the bathroom. See also question 169.

- Together with the other morning *brachos* at the start of *shacharis*.

In any event, the *b'racha* should not be recited twice.

367. According to the first custom, may the *b'racha* be recited while wearing pajamas?

Yes, provided that the body is adequately covered.

368. What if a person arises before dawn?

He should recite the *b'racha al netilas yadayim* as usual. It is permitted to recite all the morning *brachos* before dawn, except for the *b'racha asher nasan lasechvi vina*. At dawn, he should wash *nagel vasser* again without reciting a *b'racha*.

369. When should one recite the *b'racha asher yatzar*?

Immediately after *al netilas yadayim*. According to the first custom, care should be taken not to repeat the *b'racha* at the start of *shacharis*, unless one used the bathroom again. According to the second opinion, if a person anticipates the need to use the bathroom again before *shacharis*, he should recite the *b'racha* after the first use of the bathroom and again at the start of *shacharis*.

370. What if a person does not need to use the bathroom in the morning?

He should nevertheless say *asher yatzar* at the start of *shacharis*.

371. When should one recite the *b'racha elohai neshamah*?

Ideally it should be said immediately after *asher yatzar*, but some have the custom to say it after *birchos hatorah*. Care should be taken to pause after the word *elohai*.

372. May the *b'racha elohai neshamah* be recited if one was awake all night?

No. If possible he should listen to another person who is reciting this *b'racha* and have in mind to be included.

373. When should one recite *birchos hatorah*?

The prevalent custom is to recite them after *elohai neshamah* (see question 371).

374. Why are there two *brachos* for the study of Torah?

The first *b'racha* is for the mitzvah of studying Torah, and parallels similar *brachos* that are recited before the performance of a mitzvah (e.g. shofar, lulav, mezuzah). According to most opinions, the sentence *veha'arev na* is not a second *b'racha* but a continuation of the first, and is a request for Hashem's assistance in understanding the Torah. The second *b'racha* - *asher bachar banu* - is a special praise and thanksgiving for being chosen as Hashem's unique nation, and for receiving His precious gift - the holy Torah.

375. What should one think about when reciting the *birchos hatorah*?

Extreme care should be taken when reciting the *birchos hatorah*. The Sages say that one of the reasons for the destruction of the first holy Temple was the neglect of *birchos hatorah*. Although the people studied Torah, it was not important enough in their eyes to warrant a *b'racha*. It was not studied for pure motives, but simply to accumulate knowledge and even to arrogantly flaunt their wisdom. Rather a person should have the following thoughts:

• To fulfill the mitzvah of reciting *birchos hatorah*, which according to many opinions is a Torah obligation.

• To pray fervently that one's children should cling to the path of the Torah, become great scholars, and acquire good character traits.

• To remember the outstanding event of the giving of the Torah at *Har Sinai* in the midst of fire.

• To feel great joy in being one of Hashem's chosen people, and for the privilege of receiving the infinitely holy and precious gift of the Torah.

376. Should the *birchos hatorah* be recited standing?

Opinions differ about this, but the prevalent custom is to stand.

377. Must one study Torah after reciting *birchos hatorah*?

Yes, and therefore the custom is to say immediately after *birchos hatorah* the *birchos cohanim* and the paragraph *eilu devarim*, which are quotations from both the Written and the Oral Law.

378. May a man study Torah before reciting *birchos hatorah*?

It is forbidden for him to say words of Torah or to listen to them before reciting *birchos hatorah*, but he may think about topics of Torah according to most opinions.

379. May a man write words of Torah before *birchos hatorah*?

Opinions differ about this and it is correct to recite *birchos hatorah* first.

380. May a man give a *halachic* ruling before *birchos hatorah*?

Yes, but he must not give an explanation for the ruling.

381. May one say *tehillim* before *birchos hatorah*?

Although *tehillim* are said as prayers and not as Torah study, it is preferable to recite *birchos hatorah* first. Similarly, one should recite *birchos hatorah* before saying *selichos*, since they contain verses from *Tanach*.

382. May one respond to *kaddish, kedusha, barchu,* etc. before *birchos hatorah*?

Yes. Similarly, a man may recite *kaddish*.

383. Are women obligated to recite *birchos hatorah*?

Although opinions differ about this, it is correct for them to recite *birchos hatorah* and this is the custom.

384. May a woman study Torah before *birchos hatorah*?

It is preferable for her to recite *birchos hatorah* before studying Torah.

385. What if a man is unsure if he recited *birchos hatorah*?

• If he wishes to study Torah before *davening*, he should listen to another man reciting *birchos hatorah* and ask him to be included.

• If he cannot find another man, he should recite the second *b'racha* only (*asher bachar banu*).

• If he wishes to *daven shacharis*, he should have in mind to fulfill the mitzvah of *birchos hatorah* when reciting the *b'racha ahava rabba*, and should study some Torah immediately after *shacharis*.

386. What if a woman is unsure if she recited *birchos hatorah*?

She should not recite them.

387. May one recite *birchos hatorah* if he was awake all night?

See question 463.

Chapter Thirteen
Tallis and Tefillin

388. Who should wear a tallis when *davening*?

Married men. In most *Ashkenazic* communities single boys and men do not wear a tallis, but they may wear one if they wish (provided that this does not violate the local custom).

389. At which prayers should it be worn?

- At *shacharis* and *mussaf.*
- On Tisha b'Av it is worn at *mincha* instead of *shacharis.*
- On Yom Kippur it is worn at all *tefillos.*

390. What if a man does not have his tallis with him?

He should borrow one from the shul. However, the tzitzis must be inspected carefully, since it is not unusual for such a tallis to be invalid due to broken strings.

391. Should he recite a *b'racha* on the shul tallis?

Yes.

392. What if he cannot obtain any tallis?

He should *daven* nevertheless. Even if he can obtain a tallis later, it is better to *daven* with the congregation without a tallis than to *daven* alone with a tallis.

393. What if he obtains a tallis during *davening*?

• If he did not begin *pesukei dezimra* he should recite the *b'racha* on the tallis and wear it.

• If he is in the middle of *pesukei dezimra* he should continue until he is between paragraphs. He may then recite the *b'racha* on the tallis and wear it.

• If he is about to say *yishtabach* he should do so. He may then recite the *b'racha* on the tallis and wear it, but he should take care not to miss *kaddish* or *barchu*.

• If the chazan began *kaddish*, he should wear the tallis after responding to *barchu*, but should not recite the *b'racha* until after *shemoneh esrei*. In this case, he should manipulate the tzitzis before reciting the *b'racha*.

• He must not put on the tallis during the first paragraph of shema, nor during *shemoneh esrei*.

394. Should the tallis be worn over one's head?

It is correct to do so, since this is conducive to humility and fear of Hashem. Nevertheless, single boys and men who wish to wear a tallis should not wear it over the head. It is important to point out that some men mistakenly fold the tallis and wear it around the neck like a scarf. This is totally incorrect and renders the *b'racha* recited on the tallis a blessing in vain. Even if a man does not wish to wear the tallis over his head, he must at least ensure that it covers his back. (Care should be taken when purchasing a tallis to ensure that it is large enough to cover the back.)

395. Must one wear a tallis if he is called up to the Torah?

Although it is correct to do so, especially if he is not wearing a hat, one should follow the custom of the shul, since customs vary regarding this.

396. Should a *b'racha* be recited if a tallis is worn in this case?

- If he wears his own tallis, he should recite a *b'racha*.
- If he borrows another man's tallis, he should not recite a *b'racha*.
- If he borrows a shul tallis, he should not recite a *b'racha*. It is correct for him to intend that he is wearing it solely in honor of the congregation.

397. Must the chazan wear a tallis for every *tefillah*?

- In some communities, the chazan wears a tallis for all prayers. However, in many communities the chazan wears a tallis only for *shacharis* and on special occasions (e.g. Shabbos and Yom Tov, fast days, *selichos*). The local custom should be followed.
- If the chazan is not wearing a jacket, he must wear a tallis.

398. Should a *b'racha* be recited if a tallis is worn in this case?

- If he wears his own tallis, he should recite a *b'racha*.
- If he borrows another man's tallis, he should not recite a *b'racha*.
- If he borrows a shul tallis, he should not recite a *b'racha*. It is correct for him to intend that he is wearing it solely in honor of the congregation.

399. From what time in the morning may the tallis be worn?

The tallis may be worn at all times. However, the *b'racha* should not be recited until a time known as *misheyakir*, which is somewhere between dawn and sunrise. In *Eretz Yisroel*, the custom is to consider this time to be fifty minutes before sunrise. In *chutz la'aretz*, other calculations may be used, and one should follow the local custom. If a man wears his tallis before the time of *misheyakir*, he should manipulate the tzitzis and recite the *b'racha* at a suitable point in the *davening* after this time arrives (see question 284).

400. If one's tallis falls off during *davening*, should the *b'racha* be repeated when putting it back on?

No.

401. What if it falls off during *shemoneh esrei*?

See question 664.

402. Who should wear *tefillin* when *davening*?

All men, and boys over bar mitzvah. Whoever deliberately neglects to wear *tefillin* even for one day is considered to be a grave sinner, and is liable to punishment of extreme severity, ח"ו. Care must also be taken to wear the *tefillin* in the correct position, since failure to do so is equivalent to not wearing them at all. A person who fulfills the mitzvah of *tefillin* meticulously will be blessed with long life and is assured of a portion in the World to Come.

403. At which prayers should they be worn?

* At *shacharis* on weekdays.

- On Tisha b'Av they are worn at *mincha* instead of *shacharis*.

404. Should they be worn on *chol hamoed*?

- In *Eretz Yisroel* they should not be worn.
- In *chutz la'aretz* the prevalent custom is to wear them without reciting the *brachos*, but some do not wear them. A person should follow the local custom, and members of each congregation should uniformly adhere to one opinion.

405. What about a visitor from *chutz la'aretz* in *Eretz Yisroel*?

If he is accustomed to wear *tefillin* on *chol hamoed* he should wear them in private. The *brachos* should not be recited.

406. From what time in the morning may *tefillin* be worn?

From a time known as *misheyakir* (see question 399). In extenuating circumstances, one may put on the *tefillin* before this time, but the *brachos* must not be recited. When the time of *misheyakir* arrives, he should manipulate the *tefillin* and recite the *brachos* at a suitable point in the *davening* (see question 284).

407. Should the *tefillin* be put on before or after the tallis?

The tallis should be put on first.

408. What if a man accidentally took hold of the *tefillin* first?

He should put on the *tefillin*, followed by the tallis, as it would be disrespectful to reject the *tefillin*. Since the common practice is to keep the tallis and *tefillin* in one bag, care should be taken to position them in such a way that one's hand will meet the tallis first.

409. What if he has *tefillin* but will not obtain a tallis until later?

He should wear the *tefillin* and is not required to wait until he obtains a tallis.

410. What if he does not have his *tefillin* with him?

He should borrow a pair from another man and make an effort to *daven* with an earlier or later minyan. Care should be taken to adjust the knot of the *shel rosh*, if necessary, so that the *tefillin* are worn correctly.

411. What if there is no other minyan?

He should *daven* alone with *tefillin*, rather than *daven* with the minyan without *tefillin*. If possible he should attend the minyan to hear *kaddish*, *kedusha*, etc.

412. What if waiting for *tefillin* will cause him to miss the deadline for *shacharis*?

He should *daven* without *tefillin*. When he is later able to obtain *tefillin* he should wear them and recite shema again.

413. May one respond to *kaddish*, *kedusha*, etc. while putting on *tefillin*?

After reciting the first *b'racha le'haniach tefillin*, it is forbidden to talk or to respond to anything until after reciting the second *b'racha al mitzvas tefillin*. If he hears *kaddish*, *kedusha*, or *barchu*, he should listen attentively but not respond.

414. What if he accidentally responded between the two *brachos*?

He should recite the second *b'racha* on the *tefillin shel rosh* as usual.

415. When may one take off his *tefillin*?

Ideally, one should not take them off until after the mourner's *kaddish* that follows *aleinu*. If necessary, one may take them off after *kedusha de'sidra* during *uva le'tziyon*.

416. May one put them away while listening to *kaddish*?

One must answer *amen yehei shmei rabba* with intense concentration (see question 836). It is therefore improper to fold one's tallis or put away one's *tefillin* during *kaddish*, since this is likely to disturb one's concentration. This applies even more to one who is reciting *kaddish*.

Chapter Fourteen
Morning Brachos

417. When should one say the paragraph *ma tovu*?

While standing outside the door of the shul, one should say, *be'veis Elohim ne'haleich be'ragesh* ("In the house of Hashem we will walk with enthusiasm" - *Tehillim* 55:15). One should then recite the first two verses of *ma tovu*, enter shul, and say the remaining verses. According to some opinions, one should enter shul while saying the second verse and bow towards the Ark at the word *eshtachaveh*.

418. Should one say *ma tovu* when *davening* at home?

This is not necessary.

419. Must one say *adon olam* and *yigdal*?

The custom is to say them, but there is no obligation. There is a tradition from the time of the *Geonim* that whoever says *adon olam* with proper concentration is assured that his prayers will be heard and will not be opposed by the Satan.

420. Why are there so many morning *brachos*?

There are two apparently contradictory verses in *Tehillim*. One says, "To Hashem belongs the earth and all that fills it" (24:1), whereas the other says, "The heavens belong to Hashem, but He has given the earth to man" (115:16). The Sages explain that the first verse applies before one recites a *b'racha*, when

Hashem's creations may not be used, and a person who enjoys the pleasures of this world without a *b'racha* is a thief and is committing sacrilege. The second verse applies after one recites a *b'racha*, granting him permission to use Hashem's creations. At the beginning of each day we recite *brachos* and thank Hashem for all the general gifts that have been bestowed upon us for our benefit and pleasure. It is tragic that these *brachos* are often recited thoughtlessly and by rote (see question 2). A person can greatly elevate the quality of his *tefillah* by devoting a few seconds' thought to each of these *brachos*, and expressing his heartfelt thanks for Hashem's wonderful gifts.

421. Are women obligated to recite the morning *brachos*?

Yes.

422. When is the correct time to recite the morning *brachos*?

Ideally, they should be recited at the beginning of *shacharis*. However, if one is pressed for time he may postpone saying them until after *shacharis*.

423. What is the earliest time for the morning *brachos*?

It is permitted to recite them after *halachic* midnight. The exception is the *b'racha asher nasan lasechvi vina*, which must be said after dawn.

424. What is the latest time for the morning *brachos*?

- Ideally, they should be recited before one third of the day.

- If this time passed, one should make every effort to recite them before *halachic* noon.
- If this time passed, they may be said all day.

425. Should the *brachos* be recited while standing?

It is preferable to stand, and this is the custom.

426. May a person recite the *brachos* if he was awake all night?

He may recite all except the last one, *hama'avir sheina*. Regarding this *b'racha*, see question 466.

427. What if one of the *brachos* does not apply to a particular person?

All the *brachos* should be recited by everyone. Even if a *b'racha* does not apply to someone, he must thank Hashem for creating all the needs of mankind. Therefore, even a person who cannot see or walk (ח"ו) must recite all the *brachos*.

428. Should women say *shelo asani goyah* and *shelo asani shifcha*?

Although some opinions suggest such versions as the correct feminine form, the custom is not to alter the standard text, i.e. *shelo asani goy* and *shelo asani aved*. See also question 355.

429. Should one say *shelo asani goy* or *shelo asani nochri*?

Although some have the custom to say *shelo asani nochri*, the prevalent custom is to say *shelo asani goy*.

430. Should one say *hameichin mitz'adei gaver* **or** *asher heichin mitz'adei gaver?*

Both versions are acceptable.

431. Should a man put on *tefillin* **before reciting the** *b'racha oteir yisroel besif'arah?*

Although this *b'racha* does include a praise for the *tefillin*, it is not essential to wear them beforehand. Some have the custom to kiss the *tefillin* when they recite this *b'racha*.

432. May one speak between the *b'racha hama'avir sheina* **and the paragraph** *viyhi ratzon?*

No. This is considered to be one long *b'racha* and it is forbidden to speak in the middle. If one hears another person reciting this *b'racha*, one must not say amen at this point, but should wait until the concluding words *le'amo yisroel*.

433. Must the *brachos* **be said in the correct order?**

With a few exceptions, the order of the *brachos* is not important. A person who began a *b'racha* intending to conclude it in a particular way, should not change his mind and alter the ending. If he accidentally skipped a *b'racha*, he may return to it after finishing the next *b'racha*.

434. Which *brachos* **are exceptions?**

• Ideally, the *brachos shelo asani goy/aved/isha* should be recited in the correct order. However, if a person accidentally skipped one of them, he may still recite it later.

• The *brachos matir asurim* and *zokeif kefufim* must be said in this order. If a person accidentally skipped *matir asurim* he may not recite it after *zokeif kefufim*. If possible, he should listen to another person reciting it and ask to be included.

435. What if one began the *b'racha zokeif kefufim* and realized before the end that he had skipped *matir asurim*?

He should not change his mind, but should conclude *zokeif kefufim*, even though this will cause him to lose the *b'racha matir asurim*.

436. What if by the slip of the tongue one said a different conclusion than was intended?

• If the *b'racha* that was actually said had not yet been recited, he should leave it without attempting a correction.

• If that *b'racha* had already been recited, he should immediately correct himself and say the intended conclusion.

437. Aren't these rules rather complex?

Yes. This demonstrates the importance of thinking about *brachos* and not reciting them by rote.

438. What if a person is unsure whether he recited one of the *brachos*?

He should ask another person to include him when reciting the *b'racha*, and listen carefully. If he cannot find someone, he should not recite it.

439. Should one skip the morning *brachos* in order to say more of *pesukei dezimra*?

See question 507.

440. How important is the section that begins *le'olam yehei adam*?

It is a well-established custom to recite this section after the morning *brachos* in order to accept upon oneself the yoke of Heaven at the beginning of *shacharis*. It may be omitted by women, and by a man who is pressed for time.

441. How much of shema should be recited in this section?

• If one expects to reach shema before *shemoneh esrei* in good time, he should say only the first two lines (*shema yisroel* and *baruch sheim*). He should have in mind not to fulfill the mitzvah of shema at this point.

• If he suspects that he may not reach shema before the deadline, he should recite the entire shema at this point, having in mind to fulfill his obligation. (See questions 533-535.)

442. Should the name of Hashem be included in the conclusion of the *b'racha*?

According to most opinions it is included, and this is the standard custom.

443. What is the correct text for the conclusion of the *b'racha*?

There are two acceptable versions:
• *Ham'kadeish shemo barabim.*
• *Mekadeish [es] shimcha barabim.*

444. How important is the section of *korbanos*?

Our Sages relate that when *Avraham Avinu* was promised countless descendants who would inherit *Eretz Yisroel*, he was afraid that they may sin and would be punished heavily. Hashem reassured him that as long as they would bring offerings in the holy Temple, their sins would be forgiven. *Avraham Avinu* continued to query what would happen after the destruction of the holy Temple, whereupon Hashem replied, "I have already established the order of *korbanos*. When they will recite these verses, I shall reckon it as though they have brought the offerings, and I will forgive all their sins." It is sad to note that this precious offer is ignored by many people, who in the morning rush often skip the entire section of *korbanos*.

445. Is there an obligation to say *korbanos*?

Men are obligated to say at least *parshas hatamid*. If time allows, they should say the additional sections that are found in the standard siddur. See also questions 452-458.

446. Are women obligated to say *parshas hatamid*?

According to some opinions they are obligated, but the widespread custom is to omit it. It is certainly praiseworthy for them to say it, if time allows.

447. What is *parshas hatamid*?

It is the section of the Torah that describes the communal offering that was brought twice daily in the holy Temple on behalf of the entire nation. It is found in *Bamidbar* 28:1-8, and the custom is to conclude with an additional verse from *Vayikra* 1:11 (*ve'shachat*). The section can be found in any standard siddur. There are also short prayers that precede and follow the *parshas hatamid* in which we ask Hashem to forgive our sins, and accept this recital as if we have actually brought the offering. Although *parshas hatamid* is recited on Shabbos and Yom Tov, the additional prayers are omitted.

448. Should one stand when reciting *parshas hatamid?*

It is preferable to stand.

449. What if one does not understand the words?

The recital is equivalent to bringing the offering only if its meaning is fully understood. It is therefore worthwhile studying the text when one has some spare time, in order to reap the full benefit. Nevertheless, the section should be said even if one does not understand the words (see question 3).

450. May one say *parshas hatamid* after *shacharis?*

If *parshas hatamid* was omitted before *shacharis* due to lack of time, it is correct to say it after *shacharis*. According to some opinions, it is better to say *parshas hatamid* before *shacharis* and skip one section from *pesukei dezimra* than to say all *pesukei dezimra* and say *parshas hatamid* after *shacharis*.

451. May *parshas hatamid* be said after one third of the day?

Ideally, it should be said before one third of the day, in order to parallel the *tamid* offering that was always brought before this time. However, if this time passed one may say *parshas hatamid* until *halachic* noon.

452. What is the second most important section of *korbanos*?

The section that describes the preparation and burning of the incense (*pitum haketores*). This consists of a quotation from the Torah (*Shemos* 30:34-36, 7-8), followed by sections from the Talmud.

453. What is the significance of this section?

According to the Zohar, whoever recites daily the *pitum haketores* with concentration will be saved from all harsh decrees, accidents, and mishaps, and cannot be harmed by the forces of evil. If people would know how precious this is to Hashem, they would take each word and treat it like a crown of gold. Hashem cherishes the *ketores* more than any other form of service to him.

454. Is there an obligation to say this section?

No, but it is praiseworthy to say it. If a man is pressed for time, he should say the verses from the Torah and omit the sections from the Talmud.

455. May one say *pitum haketores* after *shacharis*?

If *pitum haketores* was omitted before *shacharis* due to lack of time, it is correct to say it after *shacharis*. In *Eretz Yisroel* the custom is to say *pitum haketores* daily at the end of *shacharis*. In *chutz la'aretz*, most communities recite it only at the end of *mussaf* on Shabbos and Yom Tov. It is very praiseworthy to say it daily before and after *shacharis*.

456. Is it permitted to recite *pitum haketores* by heart?

Yes. Some are particular not to do so out of fear of missing one of the eleven ingredients, since the Talmud states that whoever misses an ingredient is liable to the death penalty. However, one need not be concerned about this, since the Talmud is referring to the *cohen* who burns the *ketores,* and not to one who recites *pitum haketores.* According to some opinions, a person who recites it only on Shabbos and Yom Tov should say it from a siddur.

457. What is the significance of *eizehu mekoman*?

These are Mishnayos that describe in detail the laws of the various sacrifices that were offered in the holy Temple. If one recites this section with concentration, it is considered as if he brought the offerings. It is followed by the *beraisa* of Rabbi Yishmael, which lists the principles by which the Torah is expounded. Both sections are included in *shacharis* to ensure that every man will learn some Mishna and Gemara daily. It is therefore vital to understand the words, otherwise it cannot be considered as Torah study.

458. Is there an obligation to say these sections?

No, but the custom is to say them unless one is pressed for time. It is correct to say them after *shacharis* if they were omitted beforehand. Women are certainly not required to say them.

Chapter Fifteen

Awake all Night

459. If a person was awake all night, should he wash *nagel vasser* in the morning?

Yes, after dawn he should wash *nagel vasser*.

460. Must he wash immediately at dawn?

No, he may wait until he is ready to *daven shacharis*.

461. Should he recite the *brachos al netilas yadayim* and *asher yatzar*?

- Preferably, he should use the bathroom, wash *nagel vasser*, and recite the *brachos al netilas yadayim* and *asher yatzar*.

- If he has no need to use the bathroom, he may not recite the *brachos al netilas yadayim* or *asher yatzar*. If possible, he should listen to another person who is reciting these *brachos* and have in mind to be included.

462. Should he recite the *b'racha elohai neshamah*?

No. If possible he should listen to another person who is reciting this *b'racha* and have in mind to be included.

463. Should he recite *birchos hatorah*?

- If he slept for at least half-an-hour during the previous day, he should recite *birchos hatorah*.

- If he did not sleep for half-an-hour during the previous day, he should not recite *birchos hatorah*. If possible, he should listen to another person who is reciting these *brachos* and have in mind to be included. When doing this, he should answer amen to the two *brachos* (see question 374) and then immediately say *birchos cohanim* and the paragraph *eilu devarim*.

464. What if he cannot find another person to listen to?

When reciting the *b'racha ahava rabba* in *shacharis*, he should have in mind to fulfill through this the mitzvah of *birchos hatorah*, and immediately after *shacharis* he should say some words of Torah.

465. What if he forgot to have this in mind when reciting *ahava rabba*?

It can nevertheless be regarded as if he said *birchos hatorah*, and he should say some words of Torah immediately after *shacharis*.

466. Should he recite all the morning *brachos*?

He should say all the morning *brachos* except the last one - *hama'avir sheina*. If possible, he should listen to a person who is reciting this *b'racha* and have in mind to be included. When doing this, he should answer amen after the words *le'amo yisroel*, but not after the words *usnuma mei'afapai*, since this is one long *b'racha* (see question 432).

467. Do the above laws apply to a person who slept for a short time during the night?

• If he slept for less than half-an-hour, he should follow all the above laws.

• If he slept for half-an-hour between *halachic* midnight and dawn, he should recite all the morning *brachos* as usual.

• If he slept for half-an-hour before midnight, he should follow the above laws regarding *al netilas yadayim* and *asher yatzar*. The *brachos elohai neshamah*, *birchos hatorah*, and *hama'avir sheina* should be recited as usual.

468. What if he fell asleep at the table or in an armchair?

Even if he slept for half-an-hour or more this is not considered to be a proper form of sleep, and he should follow the above laws for a person who did not sleep.

469. What if he slept on a bed while wearing his clothes?

• If his intention was to sleep for several hours, this is considered a proper sleep and he should recite all the morning *brachos* as usual.

• If he lay down for a short nap, this is not considered to be a proper form of sleep even if he slept for several hours. In this case, he should follow the laws for a person who did not sleep.

470. What if a person slept his night's sleep in an airplane?

See Volume Two.

Chapter Sixteen
Pesukei Dezimra

471. What is *pesukei dezimra?*

This section of *shacharis* consists of a collection of verses, mainly from *Tehillim*, whose main theme is the praise of Hashem for His glorious creations, control of the universe, and kindnesses to mankind. This is to satisfy the requirement to relate the praises of Hashem before beseeching Him with requests (see question 5). In this context, the phrase *pesukei dezimra* means verses of praise. On a deeper level, the commentators explain that by reciting these verses, one severs and silences the spiritual forces that attempt to block one's prayers. In this sense, the word *zimra* means pruning or chopping off. *Pesukei dezimra* opens with the *b'racha baruch she'amar* and closes with the *b'racha yishtabach.*

472. Are women obligated to say *pesukei dezimra?*

Although opinions differ about this, it is correct for them to say at least *baruch she'amar, ashrei,* and *yishtabach.* On Shabbos and Yom Tov they should also say from *nishmas* until *yishtabach.* If they wish to say additional sections of *pesukei dezimra,* they should follow the order of priorities listed in question 502.

473. Must a man say the entire *pesukei dezimra?*

Ideally, yes. Men must make every effort to arrive in shul with sufficient time to recite morning *brachos, korbanos,* and the entire *pesukei dezimra*, since the laws of skipping sections should only be used in an emergency (see question 497). This is particularly relevant when *davening* in a shul that rushes the *tefillah*, or for a person who reads Hebrew slowly.

474. How much time should be devoted to *pesukei dezimra*?

As much time as is necessary to say everything without rushing. Every word should be pronounced slowly and clearly, as if one was counting money.

475. Is it better to say everything with less concentration or say less with more concentration?

It is better to say less with more concentration, and this is an important rule for women. A man must try to find a shul in which he can *daven* everything without rushing, but if necessary he may also skip sections of *pesukei dezimra* in order to *daven* more slowly.

476. Why is *mizmor shir chanukas* recited before *pesukei dezimra*?

This psalm was added by the *Arizal* as an appropriate introduction to *pesukei dezimra*. It was recited by *Shlomo Hamelech* at the inauguration of the holy Temple, invoking the merit of his righteous father *Dovid Hamelech*. Although most communities recite it, some omit it. A person who is pressed for time may omit it.

477. Must one stand for *pesukei dezimra*?

The custom is to stand for *baruch she'amar*, from *vayevarech David* until after the words *ata hu Hashem ha'elohim*, and for *yishtabach*. Many people stand for *mizmor le'sodah* and *az yashir*. The remaining sections may be said sitting or standing.

478. May one cross one's legs while *davening*?

No, this is disrespectful.

479. May one hold a child during *pesukei dezimra*?

It is forbidden to hold a child or any object except a siddur from the beginning of *pesukei dezimra* until after *shemoneh esrei*. A woman who suspects that a child may cry or need attention while she *davens* should not attempt to *daven*. In this situation, she is exempt from regular *tefillah*, and should say a short prayer comprising a praise, request, and thanksgiving (see question 10). If she is able to *daven shemoneh esrei* while the child is sleeping she should do so (see question 8).

480. May one speak during *pesukei dezimra*?

No. It is forbidden to speak from the beginning of *baruch she'amar* until after *shemoneh esrei*, and until after *tachanun* on days that it is recited.

481. May one write during *davening*?

If necessary this is permitted, except during *shemoneh esrei* and the first paragraph of shema.

482. What if a person accidentally spoke?

He should continue *davening* from where he stopped. If the interruption was made in the middle of a verse, he should begin the verse again. Extreme care should be taken not to talk immediately after *baruch she'amar*, since this may obligate him to repeat it. Ideally, he should not even pause between *baruch she'amar* and the section that follows it.

483. May one respond to *kaddish, kedusha,* etc., during *pesukei dezimra*?

See question 278.

484. What if a man is called to the Torah during *pesukei dezimra*?

He should go up and recite the *brachos* and read the Torah together with the *ba'al koreh* as usual. If possible, he should attempt to finish the paragraph on his way up to the Torah. Ideally, such a person should not be called to the Torah, unless he is the only *cohen* or *levi* in shul.

485. May a man recite *brachos* on tallis and *tefillin* during *pesukei dezimra*?

Yes, but he should do so between paragraphs. If he has already reached *yishtabach*, he should say this paragraph before putting on the tallis or *tefillin*.

486. What if a man realizes in the middle of *pesukei dezimra* that the deadline for shema will soon pass?

He should say the entire shema in the middle of *pesukei dezimra*.

487. Should one hold his tzitzis when reciting *baruch she'amar*?

Men have the custom to hold the front two tzitzis of the tallis while reciting *baruch she'amar* and kiss them after the conclusion. If one is not wearing a tallis, he should kiss the tzitzis of his tallis *katan*. This is not done on Tisha b'Av.

488. On which days is *mizmor le'sodah* omitted?
- Shabbos and Yom Tov.
- *Erev* Yom Kippur.
- *Erev* Pesach.
- *Chol hamoed* Pesach.

It is recited on *chol hamoed* Succos, including *Hoshana Rabba*.

489. What if one accidentally began to say *mizmor le'sodah* on one of these days?
He should complete the paragraph.

490. Must one stand for *ki le'olam chasdo* (Psalm 136) recited on Shabbos and Yom Tov?
There is no obligation, but many have the custom to stand.

491. Why is *ashrei* so important?
The Sages say that whoever recites *ashrei* every day with concentration is assured of a portion in the World to Come. The significance of this psalm is two-fold:
- Each verse begins with a different letter of the *aleph-beis*. This alludes to the supreme mitzvah of studying Torah, which comprises the twenty-two letters of the *aleph-beis*.
- It contains the vitally important verse - *Posei'ach es yadecha*. This describes the infinite kindness of Hashem, who constantly provides sustenance for every living creature, from the gigantic beasts to the tiniest of insects. It is essential to recite this verse with concentration.

492. What if a person said this verse without concentration?

He must repeat it.

493. What if he already said further?

- If he did not begin the next psalm, he should go back to *posei'ach* and repeat from there.
- If he began the next psalm, he should finish that psalm and then repeat the verses from *posei'ach* until the end of *ashrei*.
- If he started *yishtabach*, he should repeat these verses after *shacharis*.

494. Should a man kiss his *tefillin* when reciting the verse *posei'ach*?

There is no obligation, but some have the custom to do so. This reminds us that we require sustenance solely in order to be able to fulfill mitzvos, and not for our physical enjoyment.

495. Should one give charity while reciting *vayevarech David*?

It is praiseworthy to give charity before *davening*. This is based on the verse, "I will behold Your face with righteousness" (*Tehillim* 17:15). In addition, some have the custom to give charity during *vayevarech David* when reaching the phrase *ve'ata mosheil bakol*.

496. How important is *az yashir* (the song of the sea)?

This section was not originally included in *pesukei dezimra* and was inserted only by custom at some later date. Nevertheless, the Zohar guarantees that whoever recites the song of the sea with proper concentration will merit to recite it in the days of Moshiach and the World to Come. According to the Sages, if a person sings it with joy, and imagines that he has just crossed the sea, he will receive forgiveness for all his sins.

497. Must one stand for *nishmas*?

There is no obligation, but many have the custom to stand.

498. When is it permitted to skip parts of *pesukei dezimra*?

• If a man accidentally arrived late in shul and will not be able to reach the start of *shemoneh esrei* with everyone. It is better to skip parts of *pesukei dezimra* and begin *shemoneh esrei* with the congregation than to say all of *pesukei dezimra* and miss *shemoneh esrei* with the congregation.

• A woman is permitted to do this on a regular basis, since she is not obligated to say the entire *pesukei dezimra* (see question 472).

499. If a man arrives late, should he wait for another minyan?

If there is another minyan that he can join without difficulty, he is required to *daven* with them, rather than skip some of *pesukei dezimra*.

500. What if he will be able to *daven* in his regular seat with the present minyan but not with the next minyan?

It is better to skip parts of *pesukei dezimra* and *daven* in his regular place than to say all of *pesukei dezimra* and not *daven* in his regular place.

501. If necessary, may one skip all *pesukei dezimra* in order to *daven shemoneh esrei* with the minyan?

No. One should *daven* all *pesukei dezimra* and forfeit *davening shemoneh esrei* with the minyan. It is certainly forbidden to begin from *yishtabach* and continue to *daven* with the congregation.

502. What has priority when skipping sections?

The following is the list of sections in order of importance for weekdays:

1. *Baruch she'amar, ashrei, yishtabach*. These must be recited.
2. The last halleluyah (psalm 150).
3. The third halleluyah (psalm 148).
4. The remaining three chapters of halleluyah (psalms 146, 147, 149).
5. The section *vayevarech David* until *tif'artecha*.
6. *Hodu lashem* until *ki kadosh Hashem Eloheinu* (*nusach Ashkenaz*).
7. The remaining sections of *pesukei dezimra* (according to some opinions, *az yashir* has priority over the remaining sections).

Important note: This is not the order in which to recite *pesukei dezimra*. A person who wishes to skip part of *pesukei dezimra* should estimate how much time is available, and say as many sections as possible in the order that they are printed in the siddur.

503. Is there a different order for *nusach Sephard*?
All the sections that are recited after *baruch she'amar* have priority over those that are recited before *baruch she'amar*. Therefore, *hodu lashem* has less importance than the entire *pesukei dezimra*.

504. What is the order of priority for Shabbos and Yom Tov?
1. *Baruch she'amar, ashrei, nishmas, yishtabach*.
2. The entire weekday *pesukei dezimra* in the order listed above.
3. *Lamnatze'ach mizmor le'david* (psalm 19), *le'david beshanoso* (psalm 34), *tefillah le'moshe* (psalm 90). (For *nusach Sephard, ranenu tzaddikim* - psalm 33).
4. The remaining additional sections.

505. What if one finds that he has more time than he estimated?
If he did not yet say *yishtabach* he may go back and say additional sections of *pesukei dezimra*, even though he is not following the order of the siddur. (See also question 515.)

506. Must a man say all the skipped sections after *shacharis*?
Yes.

507. Should one skip the morning *brachos* in order to say more of *pesukei dezimra*?

Opinions differ about this. According to many opinions, all the morning *brachos* should be said as usual, even if this will necessitate skipping some of *pesukei dezimra*. According to some opinions, one may skip from *asher nasan lasechvi vina* until *baruch she'amar* in order to say all *pesukei dezimra*. The omitted sections should be recited after *shacharis*.

508. What if one forgot to say *baruch she'amar*?

• If he remembered in the middle of *pesukei dezimra*, he should say *baruch she'amar* and continue.
• If he reached *yishtabach* he may not say *baruch she'amar*, but should say *yishtabach* nevertheless.

509. What if one forgot to say *yishtabach*?

Once he has begun the *b'racha yotzeir ohr* he may not go back to *yishtabach*. This mistake could easily happen in shul if one responds to *barchu* before saying *yishtabach*. Care must then be taken not to begin *yotzeir ohr* with the congregation.

510. Should one skip part of *pesukei dezimra* in order to begin *yotzeir ohr* with the shul?

According to some opinions, it is preferable to do this.

511. What if one forgot to say *nishmas* on Shabbos or Yom Tov?

• If he did not yet say Hashem's name at the conclusion of *yishtabach* (*baruch ata Hashem*), he should go back to *nishmas*.

- If he said Hashem's name he should conclude *yishtabach* and not say *nishmas*.

512. If one finished *pesukei dezimra* before the congregation, should he wait to say *yishtabach* with the chazan?

No. He should recite *yishtabach* immediately after concluding *pesukei dezimra* and then wait for the chazan.

513. Does the same apply on Shabbos and Yom Tov?

Yes. One should conclude *nishmas* and *yishtabach* and not wait for the chazan at *shochein ad* (on Shabbos), or *ha'eil* (on Yom Tov).

514. How should the last few words of *yishtabach* be grouped?

The concluding words of this paragraph - *melech, eil, chei ha'olamim* - mean "King, Almighty, life-giver of the worlds". Therefore, one should pause after the word *melech*, and again after the word *eil*, but the words *chei ha'olamim* should be said together. It is totally wrong and meaningless to join the words *eil chei*.

515. After *yishtabach* may one recite *tehillim* or other sections of *shacharis* while waiting for the chazan?

No, but one may look into a *sefer* and study Torah while waiting.

Chapter Seventeen

Shema and its Brachos

516. What are the laws of *kaddish* following *yishtabach*?

See chapter twenty-four.

517. Should one respond to *barchu* if he did not hear the chazan?

- If he did not hear the chazan but heard the congregation responding, he should respond with them.
- If he did not hear the congregation responding but heard the chazan repeating the response, he may not respond with the chazan, but should say amen.

518. At which point may one sit?

After responding to *barchu*. It is not necessary to remain standing while the chazan repeats the response.

519. Should one bow when responding to *barchu*?

Yes, but one should bow only while saying the word *baruch* and straighten up before saying Hashem's name. (See question 613.) Similarly, the chazan should bow only while saying the words *barchu es*, and straighten up before saying Hashem's name.

520. May one say *barchu* when *davening* alone?

No, this may only be recited in the presence of a minyan.

521. What is the structure of this section of *shacharis*?

- There are two *brachos* preceding shema:

  1. *Yotzeir ohr* until *yotzeir hame'oros*. Although this section comprises many paragraphs, it is one long *b'racha* and must be said in its entirety (including the lines *kadosh kadosh* and *baruch kevod*). This applies on both weekdays and Shabbos. (See also question 34.)

  2. *Ahava rabba* (or *ahavas olam* in *nusach Sephard*) until *habocher be'amo yisroel be'ahava*.

- This is followed by the three paragraphs of shema until *emes*.

- This is followed by a third *b'racha* - *emes veyatziv* until *ga'al yisroel*.

522. Is there a time limit for these *brachos*?

The three *brachos* of shema must be recited before one third of the day. Men must be extremely careful about this, since according to most opinions it is forbidden to recite these *brachos* after this time. See also questions 25 and 26. If a man missed this time by sheer accident but not by negligence, he may recite these *brachos* until *halachic* noon.

523. Is a woman obligated to say these *brachos*?

- She is exempt from the two *brachos* before shema.

- According to some opinions, she is obligated to recite the *b'racha* after shema - *emes veyatziv* (see question 33).

524. May a woman recite these *brachos* after a third of the day?

According to many opinions this is forbidden. If she reaches this part of *shacharis* after a third of the day she should skip to shema, and after shema she should skip to *shemoneh esrei*. See also question 36.

525. May she recite these *brachos* omitting their opening and conclusions?

Yes, but she must take great care not to say the entire *b'racha* out of habit. In effect, this means that she may say the following:

- From *hame'ir la'aretz* (or *hakol yoducha* on Shabbos) until *meheira le'oro*.
- From *ahava rabba* (or *ahavas olam*) until *ul'yachedcha be'ahava*.
- The entire shema.
- From *emes veyatziv* until *kedosh yisroel*.

526. What if she accidentally started the *b'racha yotzeir ohr*?

She should finish that *b'racha* with its conclusion.

527. Should a man kiss his *tefillin* at the beginning of the *b'racha yotzeir ohr*?

There is no obligation, but some have the custom to do so. Some kiss the *shel yad* when saying *yotzeir ohr*, and the *shel rosh* when saying *u'vorei choshech*, but others kiss only the *shel yad* at *yotzeir ohr* and the *shel rosh* before commencing *shemoneh esrei*.

528. Why do some people conclude the *b'racha* before shema together with the chazan?

Opinions differ whether one may answer amen to this *b'racha*. In order to avoid the problem, this procedure is used, whereby there is no requirement to answer amen.

529. What if a person concluded the *b'racha* before the chazan?

He should answer amen to the chazan's *b'racha*.

530. Is there a time limit for shema?

A man must recite shema before the end of three *halachic* hours (one quarter of the day). This is a Torah obligation and extreme care must be taken not to miss this deadline on any day of the year. If this time passed, he may still recite shema (in *shacharis*) but the mitzvah has been lost. It is forbidden for a man to willfully delay recital of shema until close to the deadline, and one who regularly does so demonstrates his complete disdain for Hashem's mitzvos.

531. How is this time calculated?

There are two main opinions:
• According to the *Magen Avraham* the day is reckoned from dawn until nightfall.
• According to the *Vilna Gaon* the day is reckoned from sunrise until sunset.
The deadline for shema according to the *Magen Avraham* is considerably earlier than according to the *Vilna Gaon*.

532. Which opinion should a man follow?

The widespread custom is to follow the opinion of the *Vilna Gaon*, which gives a later deadline. It is praiseworthy to *daven* with a minyan that reaches shema before the deadline of the *Magen Avraham*.

533. What if the minyan will not reach shema before the deadline of the *Vilna Gaon*?

He must recite the entire shema before *shacharis*. (See also questions 441 and 486.)

534. What if he is in doubt whether the minyan will reach shema in time?

He should recite shema before *shacharis* and make the following stipulation: "If I will not reach shema in time with the minyan, it is my intention to fulfill the mitzvah now; but if I reach shema in time with the minyan, my intention now is only to read verses from the Torah without fulfilling the mitzvah". The reason for this stipulation is that it is far better to fulfill the mitzvah of shema together with its *brachos* during *shacharis*, if time allows.

535. What if the minyan will reach shema before the time of the *Vilna Gaon*, but he is particular to follow the time of the *Magen Avraham*?

He should do the same as in the previous question.

536. What if the minyan will not reach the *brachos* of shema before one third of the day?

If he cannot find an earlier minyan, he should *daven* alone before one third of the day. Ideally, he should *daven* alone before one quarter of the day, in order to recite shema with its *brachos* before the deadline for shema.

537. Is a woman obligated to recite shema?

Strictly speaking she is exempt, since this is a time-bound mitzvah. However, since the concept of accepting the yoke of Heaven is so fundamental, it is correct for her to recite shema, and this is the widespread custom.

538. Must she be careful to recite shema before the deadline?

No, she may recite shema even after the deadline. Nevertheless, she performs a greater mitzvah if she recites it before the deadline.

539. How much of shema should she recite?

- The minimum is the first two lines (*shema yisroel* and *baruch sheim*).
- It is preferable to read the first paragraph (until *uvish'arecha*).
- It is praiseworthy to read the entire shema (until *emes*).

540. When should one say the introductory words *eil melech ne'eman*?

When reciting shema alone.

541. What is the reason for this?

The verse says, "It [the Torah] is a remedy to your stomach and an elixir to your bones" (*Mishlei* 3:8). The Sages explain that each word of shema corresponds to one of the limbs of a person's body, and if recited properly will bring health to that limb. However, there are 248 limbs in the body, but only 245 words in shema, leaving a shortfall of three words. When shema is read in shul, the chazan repeats the last three words on behalf of everyone in order to complete the total. When a person is *davening* alone, he should make up the missing three words by saying *eil melech ne'eman* at the start.

542. What if one is *davening* in shul but the congregation is far ahead of him?

• If he is in the middle of shema when the chazan repeats the last three words, he should stop and listen.
• If he is about to start shema, he should listen to the chazan and begin shema without saying *eil melech ne'eman*.
• If he is anywhere earlier, he should say *eil melech ne'eman* before starting shema.

543. Should a woman say *eil melech ne'eman*?

She should say it in the same situations that a man says it. If she is not saying all three paragraphs of shema, she should omit *eil melech ne'eman*, since saying this phrase will not help her to reach 248 words.

544. Why is the custom to cover one's eyes for *shema yisroel*?

In order to enhance one's concentration.

545. Which hand should one use?

The right hand. This also applies to a left-handed person.

546. If one wears glasses should he remove them?

He may put his hand over the glasses if he wishes.

547. Should a man hold his tzitzis while reciting shema?

The custom is to hold either the front two or all four tzitzis throughout shema. They should be gathered together before shema when saying the words *vehavi'einu le'shalom*, and held in the left hand between the ring finger and the little finger. See also question 573.

548. Should shema be recited sitting or standing?

It may be said either sitting or standing. However, if a person was previously sitting, he may not stand to recite the morning shema (compare question 896).

549. What should one think when reciting shema?

• Before beginning shema, one should intend to fulfill the Torah mitzvah of reciting shema (only when reciting it before the deadline).
• While reciting shema, one should think about the meaning of the words.
• While reciting the verse *ve'ahavta*, one should arouse in his heart deep feelings of love towards Hashem.

550. What if one does not understand the words?

The minimum essential requirement is to understand the first two lines - *shema yisroel* and *baruch sheim*. A person who does not understand the meaning of these lines cannot fulfill the mitzvah of shema.

551. What is the meaning of *shema yisroel*?

This line, which is undoubtedly the most famous verse of the entire Torah, holds within it endless layers of meanings, from the simple to the sublimely profound. Basically, it is a declaration of one's belief in the following fundamental principles of Jewish faith:

- Hashem exists.
- He is one, i.e. there is no other God.
- He is eternal.
- He is all-powerful.
- He created and is the Master of all that exists.
- He watches over the Jewish people with special Divine providence.
- He will ultimately be acknowledged by all mankind.
- Also included is one's acceptance of the yoke of Heaven to the degree that he would sacrifice his life in order to sanctify Hashem's name. This indicates complete subordination to Hashem's will and subservience to the Torah.

552. How should these concepts be incorporated into the individual words of *shema yisroel*?

One should concentrate on the words in the following way:
- *Shema yisroel* - (as if addressing all the Jewish people) Listen *Yisroel*, I testify to and believe in the following:
- Hashem - God always was, is, and will be; and He is the Master of all creation.
- *Eloheinu* - Is all-powerful and watches over the Jewish people with Divine providence.
- Hashem - God always was, is, and will be; and He is the Master of all creation.
- *Echad* - Is one, and will ultimately be acknowledged by all mankind. I completely accept His sovereignty and will sacrifice my life to sanctify His name, if so required.

553. Is it essential to think of all these concepts?

Ideally, one should think of all the above. Although initially a person may feel overburdened by the number of thoughts included, he will gradually become accustomed to the correct intentions if he persists for a few days. Nevertheless, if he is overwhelmed by this, it is sufficient for him to have the following minimum thoughts: Listen *Yisroel*, Hashem is our God and we accept His rulership, Hashem is the one and only God.

554. Should one think of the meaning of each word before, after, or while reciting it?

All three ways are acceptable.

555. Why is the custom to draw out the word *echad*?

Ideally, while saying this word one should think that each letter symbolizes a different concept. The letter *aleph* (=1) indicates that there is only one God. The *ches* (=8) indicates that Hashem rules over the seven heavens and this earth. The *dalet* (=4) indicates that Hashem rules over the four corners of the world. The custom is to draw out the word in order to have time for these thoughts.

556. Doesn't this stretching spoil the structure of the word?

This can easily happen if one does not take care. For example, one should not make a break during the vocalizing of the *kametz* vowel, since this would divide the word into two – *echa-ad*. Nor should one create a *sheva* sound under the *dalet* – *echadeh*. For these reasons, some opinions contend that one should say the word without any stretching at all, but should simply continue with the correct thoughts after the word has been said.

557. What if a man forgot to have in mind to fulfill his obligation?

• If he was reciting shema before *shacharis*, he has not fulfilled his obligation and must repeat shema with the correct intention.

• If he was reciting shema during *shacharis*, he has fulfilled his obligation.

558. What if one did not think about the meaning of the words of the first verse?

He has not fulfilled his obligation and must repeat shema with the proper concentration. If he is alone he may repeat it aloud, but if other people will hear him he must repeat it quietly.

559. What if he is in doubt whether he concentrated on the words?

He must recite shema again.

560. What is the meaning of the line *baruch sheim*?

This is a prayer that the glory of Hashem's sovereignty shall be revealed to the entire world forever. In this context, the word *baruch* means to become increased, and the word *sheim* means the revelation. Therefore the line means: May the revelation of the glory of His kingdom be increased forever.

561. Why is this line said quietly?

The Sages give the following two reasons:

- It does not appear in the paragraph of shema as written in the Torah (*Devarim* 6:4-9).
- It is one of the praises sung by the angels, and we are not entitled to equate ourselves with them. Only on Yom Kippur the Jewish people are compared to angels, and are then permitted to join them in saying it aloud.

562. What if one did not think about the meaning of *baruch sheim*?

- If he has not started the next verse, he should repeat *baruch sheim* with the proper concentration.
- If he has started the next verse, he should continue.

563. Why do many people recite shema very slowly?

- Great care should be taken when reciting shema to pronounce each word clearly and correctly. Letters should not be swallowed or slurred, and words should not be run together. For example, one must pause for a moment between the words *bechol levavecha*, in order not to fuse them into one word. Similarly, the words *vesamtem es* must be kept apart. In the word *tizkeru* the letter *zayin* should be pronounced clearly, so that the word does not sound like *tiskeru*. (There are many more similar examples throughout shema.)
- Ideally, one should concentrate on the meaning of every word.
- Shema should be read as if one is reading it for the first time, like a letter that one has just received from the king. It should therefore be read with fear and reverence, paying attention to each instruction and warning.

564. During shema may one indicate something to another person by means of a sign?

Since shema must be read with intense concentration, this is forbidden even if one pauses when making the sign. One may indicate something for a mitzvah purpose during the second and third paragraphs, but not during the first.

565. What if a child is making a noise during shema?

• If the noise is disturbing one's concentration or that of other people, he may quieten the child without speaking, even during the first paragraph.

• If the noise is not disturbing anyone, he may not attend to the child until after the first paragraph.

566. May one give charity during shema?

• During the first paragraph it is forbidden to interrupt and give charity.

• After the first paragraph a person may give charity if he wishes, but there is no obligation to do so.

567. Should one stand up for a rav or elderly person during shema?

• During the first paragraph one should not stand.

• During the second and third paragraphs one may stand if he wishes.

• Between paragraphs one should stand.

568. May one respond to *kaddish*, *kedusha*, etc. during shema and its *brachos*?

See question 288.

569. What if one's mind wandered during shema and he lost his place?

He should go back to the last place where he knows that he said and continue from there.

570. What if he is unsure whether he is in the middle of the first or second paragraph?

He should assume that he is in the middle of the first paragraph.

571. What if he omitted a verse and realized later?

He must go back to the omitted verse and continue again from there. It is not sufficient to insert the missing verse, since the entire shema must be recited in the correct order.

572. Should a man kiss his *tefillin* during shema?

The custom is to kiss the *tefillin shel yad* when saying *le'os al yadecha/yedchem*, and the *tefillin shel rosh* when saying *bein einecha/eineichem*. These words appear in the first and second paragraphs.

573. What should be done with the tzitzis during shema?

• The tzitzis should be held in both hands when reciting the third paragraph.
• The custom is to kiss them each time the word 'tzitzis' is said.
• Some have the custom to pass them across the eyes and kiss them when saying *ur'isem oso*.
• Many have a custom to kiss them at *emes*.

574. When should he release the tzitzis from his hands?

After the phrase *ve'nechemadim la'ad* he should kiss the tzitzis and release them.

575. What if a person is up to a different part of *shacharis* when the congregation is saying shema?

- If he has not yet started the *brachos* of shema, he must join them and recite the first two lines, i.e. *shema yisroel* and *baruch sheim*.
- If he has started the *brachos* of shema, he should act as if he is joining them by covering his eyes. However, he must not say shema with them, but may continue his own *davening*.

576. What if a man is learning Torah in shul when the congregation is saying shema?

He should say the lines *shema yisroel* and *baruch sheim* with the congregation. It is praiseworthy to recite the entire shema with them. (Compare questions 734 and 841).

Chapter Eighteen

Shemoneh Esrei

577. When should one stand in preparation for *shemoneh esrei*?

At *tehilos le'eil elyon*.

578. When should one take three steps back?

There is actually no obligation to take three steps back, but the custom is to do so if there is sufficient room. This is also done at *tehilos le'eil elyon*. If a person is not up to this point when the congregation stands, he should nevertheless stand and take three steps back, in order not to disturb others when he begins *shemoneh esrei*.

579. With which foot should one begin to step back?

With the right foot. A left-handed person should begin with the left foot.

580. When should one take three steps forward?

The custom is to do this after saying *ga'al yisroel*. Some take three steps forward while saying *ga'al yisroel*, or even before saying it. It is certainly incorrect to go forward while saying *Hashem sefasai tiftach*, since this verse is part of *shemoneh esrei*.

581. With which foot should one begin to step forward?

With the right foot. A left-handed person should begin with the left foot. By beginning with the stronger foot one demonstrates his enthusiasm to enter the presence of Hashem.

582. How large should each step be?
- The first step should be the length of one's foot.
- The second step should be twice the length of one's foot.
- The third step should be the length of one's foot, thereby bringing the two feet side by side.

583. What if there is not enough room to do this?

Effort should be made to take paces that are the correct length. If there is not enough room, one may walk backwards and return to one's place in a sideways direction. If this is also impossible, one should take three small steps.

584. Is it better to take one or two correct paces or three small ones?

It is better to take three small paces.

585. May one answer amen after the chazan says *ga'al yisroel*?

Opinions differ whether one may answer amen to this *b'racha*. In order to avoid the problem, the widespread custom is for the chazan to say the words quietly, so that people will not be able to answer amen. Some opinions question this practice and maintain that the chazan should say it aloud. In this case, one should say the words *ga'al yisroel* together with the chazan, and not answer amen. Another option is to begin *shemoneh esrei* a second or two before the chazan.

586. May one respond to *kaddish, kedusha,* etc. after *ga'al yisroel?*

On weekdays and Yom Tov it is forbidden to say any responses between *ga'al yisroel* and *shemoneh esrei,* and ideally one should not pause there for more than a second. The Sages say that whoever begins *shemoneh esrei* after *ga'al yisroel* is assured of a share in the World to Come. The reason is that Hashem redeemed the Jewish nation from Egypt in order that they should become His servants, and one of the greatest forms of service to Hashem is prayer (see question 1). By beginning *shemoneh esrei* immediately after describing the redemption from Egypt, one demonstrates his readiness to serve Hashem and fulfill all of His commandments.

587. What if one wishes to respond to *kaddish, kedusha,* etc.?

He should wait at *shira chadasha* and respond at that point before continuing. See question 288.

588. Is the rule the same for Shabbos?

On Shabbos one should ideally begin *shemoneh esrei* immediately after *ga'al yisroel,* and therefore one should wait at *shira chadasha* to respond to *kaddish* and *kedusha.* However, if one concluded *ga'al yisroel,* and then realized that the congregation is saying *kaddish* or *kedusha,* he should respond according to the rules of interruptions during shema. (See question 288.)

589. What if one accidentally began to say *ki sheim Hashem*?

He should stop immediately even in the middle of the verse, since this does not belong in *shacharis*.

590. Which direction should one face?

- In *chutz la'aretz* one should face *Eretz Yisroel*.
- In *Eretz Yisroel* one should face *Yerushalayim*.
- In *Yerushalayim* one should face the site of the Temple.

Wherever a person is *davening*, he should direct his thoughts toward the holy Temple, and imagine that he is standing inside the Holy of Holies.

591. What if one does not know the correct direction?

If possible, he should try to estimate the direction from the position of the sun, which is in the east in the morning and in the west in the afternoon. If he is still in doubt, he should face any direction and focus his attention on Hashem.

592. What if the Ark in shul is not facing the correct direction?

- If he is *davening* alone, he should stand facing the correct direction.
- If he is *davening* with a minyan, he should stand in the same direction as everyone else. If possible, he should turn his face toward the correct direction.

593. Which direction should one face when traveling?

See Volume Two.

594. May one lean on a *shtender* during *shemoneh esrei*?

• A healthy person may not lean on any object such as a *shtender*, table, or chair. This is forbidden even if one leans lightly and would not fall over if the object were removed.

• An elderly or ill person may lean on an object even heavily, if necessary. If this is also difficult, he may *daven* sitting down, but if he is able to stand for the first *b'racha*, he should.

595. How should the body be positioned when *davening shemoneh esrei* seated?

The two feet should be placed together as usual. He must sit up straight without leaning his back on the chair.

596. What should one think about when *davening shemoneh esrei*?

There are two areas on which to concentrate:

• To think about the meaning of the words as they are being said.

• To realize that one is standing before the Holy Shechinah.

A person is required to make extreme effort to remove all foreign thoughts from the mind during *shemoneh esrei* until he can focus his attention solely on the words of the *tefillah*. A person must remember that Hashem can read his mind, and if his thoughts wander to other topics such as business, food, or what has to be done today, this is a disgrace to Hashem, ו"ח. How embarrassing it is to conclude *shemoneh esrei* with the verse, "Let the words of my mouth and the thoughts of my heart be pleasing before You". This immense task is the greatest challenge of prayer, and it is for this reason that *tefillah* is referred to as "service of the heart" (see also questions 1 and 2).

597. What can a person do to enhance his concentration?

• One should imagine himself to be the *cohen gadol* standing in the Temple in the Holy of Holies.

• One should think about the exaltedness of Hashem and the lowliness of man.

• One should remove all thoughts about the pleasures of this world.

• One should feel like a pauper begging at the door for assistance.

• One should not feel as though prayer is a burden that one must be rid of.

• One should not think that his prayers deserve to be answered. Rather one should feel lowly and unworthy to request anything, if not for the great kindness that Hashem bestows upon His creatures.

• One should not *daven* while he is troubled, angry, or upset about something.

• One should not *daven* immediately after laughter or light-headed conversation.

• One should not *daven* after studying a complex Torah issue, since he may continue to think about it during *davening*.

598. What if a person knows that he will not be able to concentrate?

• If he is able to concentrate on at least the first *b'racha* he should *daven*.

- If he cannot concentrate on the first *b'racha*, he should wait a while and *daven* later when his mind is at ease. Nevertheless, he should *daven* before the deadline for *shacharis*.
- A woman who cannot concentrate on the first *b'racha* is exempt from *davening shemoneh esrei*.

599. What if a person's mind wandered throughout the first *b'racha*?

- If he did not say the name of Hashem at the conclusion of the *b'racha*, he should go back to *Elohei Avraham* and repeat from there.
- If he said the name of Hashem at the conclusion of the *b'racha*, he should conclude the *b'racha* and do the following:
  1. Repeat from the start of *shemoneh esrei* in his mind without saying the words, but thinking about their meaning.
  2. Concentrate as much as possible at the *b'racha modim*.

600. What if he concentrated on most of the first *b'racha* but his mind wandered for a few words?

He should repeat from the place where his mind began to wander, provided that he did not yet say the name of Hashem at the conclusion of the *b'racha*.

601. What if his mind wandered during a part of another *b'racha*?

He is not obligated to repeat anything. However, he may do so if he wishes, provided that he did not yet say the name of Hashem at the conclusion of the *b'racha*.

602. Why is *shemoneh esrei* said quietly?

This is learned from Channah's prayer, about which it is written that her lips moved but her voice could not be heard (*Shmuel* I, 1:13). Whoever *davens shemoneh esrei* loudly apparently does not believe that Hashem can hear a silent prayer, and is following the ways of the false prophets who used to scream to their idols.

603. How quietly must one *daven*?

Ideally, the voice should be loud enough to hear oneself, but not to be heard by others. If it is difficult to concentrate at this volume, one may *daven* a little louder, but care should be taken not to disturb other people.

604. What if a person *davened* so quietly that he could not hear himself?

As long as his lips were moving, he has fulfilled his obligation. However, if he just read the words with his eyes and did not move his lips, he did not fulfill the mitzvah of praying. Unfortunately, some people mistakenly think that it is sufficient to pray with their eyes and mind. They may *daven* this way for years, and tragically do not fulfill their obligation even once.

605. May one *daven* loudly when alone?

This is also forbidden, unless it is impossible for him to concentrate when *davening* in a whisper. As long as he can concentrate somewhat when whispering he may not raise his voice, even if this will enhance his concentration.

606. May a person in shul say the words *ya'aleh veyavo* loudly during *shemoneh esrei* in order to remind others?

Although such intentions are praiseworthy, this practice is not approved.

607. If one overhears the *shemoneh esrei* of another person, should he answer amen to his *brachos*?

No.

608. Should one *daven* with eyes closed?

One may *daven* either with eyes closed, or looking into a siddur, whichever enables him to concentrate better. It is forbidden to look anywhere except into a siddur during *shemoneh esrei*, and whoever looks out will not merit to see the Shechinah when his soul leaves this world.

609. At which points should one bow during *shemoneh esrei*?

At the start and conclusion of the first *b'racha*, and at the start and conclusion of the *b'racha modim*.

610. How should one bow?

At the three places where one says *baruch ata Hashem*, one should bow as follows:

- When saying *baruch* bend the knees.
- When saying *ata* bend the body forward.

At the beginning of *modim*, one should bend the body forward without bending the knees.

611. How far forward should one bow?

It is sufficient to bow slightly (approx. 45°), until the bones of the spine begin to protrude. It is wrong to bow until the body is horizontal (90°).

612. Should one bow quickly or slowly?

Quickly.

613. At which point should one straighten up?

Before saying the name of Hashem. The name of Hashem should not be said until one is standing straight.

614. How should one straighten up?

First one should straighten the head and then the body. This is a more difficult way of straightening than one would naturally do, and is intended to demonstrate that bowing is not a burden. One should straighten up slowly.

615. What if one is unable to bend the body?

He should bow his head.

616. May one bow at other places in *shemoneh esrei*?

It is forbidden to bow at the start or conclusion of any *b'racha* except the first and *modim*, but it is permitted to bow elsewhere. Some have the custom to bend the body throughout *shemoneh esrei* on Rosh Hashanah and Yom Kippur in order to instill feelings of fear and humility. In this case, the body must be straightened at the beginning and end of each *b'racha*. The best way to pray is with a straight body and a bent heart.

617. May one add personal requests during *shemoneh esrei*?

• During the first three and last three *brachos* it is forbidden to add personal requests, but one may think about them at appropriate places.

• During the other *brachos* it is permitted to verbally add personal or communal requests of the same subject matter as the *b'racha*.

• During *shema koleinu* and *elohai netzor*, one may verbally add a request about any topic.

618. Where in the *b'racha* should the request be inserted?

• A request for an individual should be inserted at a suitable point in the middle of the *b'racha*.

• A request for a group of people should be inserted before the words *baruch ata* at the conclusion of the *b'racha*.

619. May any type of request be added?

• During most of the *brachos*, one may only add a request concerning a present need, but not for future protection. For example, a person who is in financial difficulties may add a prayer for sustenance during *barech aleinu*. But a person who is earning a sufficient livelihood may not insert a prayer that he should not suffer poverty.

• During *shema koleinu* and *elohai netzor*, one may include any type of request, including future protection.

620. Must the request be said in Hebrew?

No, one may add a request in any language.

621. Is it better to add personal requests in *elohai netzor*?

• When *davening* with a minyan it is better to add requests in *elohai netzor*, in order not to miss *kedusha* or *kaddish*. (See questions 288 and 679.)

• When *davening* alone, it is better to add them during the appropriate *brachos* of *shemoneh esrei*.

622. May one pray for any sick person during *refa'einu*?

Some opinions suggest the following guidelines:

• During *refa'einu*, one should pray for seriously ill people who are known personally.

• During *shema koleinu*, one should pray for other sick people who are known personally.

• During *elohai netzor*, one should pray for sick people who are not known personally.

623. With which name should the patient be mentioned?

One should mention the name of the patient and that of his mother. If the mother's name is not known, one should use the father's name. If neither are known, one may mention the family name of the patient.

624. What if one does not know the patient's or the parent's Hebrew name?

One should use the name by which the person is called, even if this is an English name.

625. May one pray for a person's recovery in every *shemoneh esrei*?

This should preferably not be done, for several reasons:

- It may appear like a vow, which must be continued always.
- It could become monotonous and might be said without feeling.
- It appears to be a fixed part of *shemoneh esrei*, instead of a voluntary addition.

Therefore, the prayer should be omitted occasionally.

626. For how long may one continue to mention a person's name?

As long as one thinks that the person is still sick and needs *tefillos*. If one has not heard about the patient for some time and he may have recovered, the name should not be mentioned.

627. When should one begin to say *vesein tal u'matar*?

Although *mashiv haru'ach* is said from *Shemini Atzeres*, the request for rain with *tal u'matar* is not said until the 7th of Cheshvan in *Eretz Yisroel*. In *chutz la'aretz*, it is said from the 5th of December, but if the following year is a civil leap year, it is said from the 6th of December. In all cases, *tal u'matar* is said starting from *ma'ariv* of the previous evening.

628. May one say confession during *shema koleinu*?

If one has recently sinned, it is appropriate to confess in *shema koleinu* during the next *tefillah*. If one wishes, he may say confession during *shema koleinu* at any time. In any event, confession should only be recited if one can say it sincerely and with humility. A person who confesses without feelings of remorse arouses the prosecuting angels against himself, ו"ח.

629. Should one say the verse *yihyu leratzon* before *elohai netzor*?

It is preferable to do so.

630. Where in *elohai netzor* should one add personal requests?

Once one has said the verse *yihyu leratzon* before *elohai netzor*, one may add any requests. Many have the custom to add requests before the second *yihyu leratzon*. A person should pray regularly for his livelihood and other needs, and that his children and all his descendants shall become true servants of Hashem. This may be said in any language.

631. Why do many people say a special verse before *yihyu leratzon*?

There is a custom to say at this point a verse whose first and last letters are the same as the first and last letters of one's name. This is intended to be a merit and protection on the day of judgment in the next world. Some siddurim have a list of appropriate verses for common names.

632. What if a person has more than one name?

He should say a separate verse for each name.

633. When should one take three steps back?

After the verse *yihyu leratzon* and before saying *oseh shalom*. Nothing is said while stepping back.

634. How should the steps be made?

- Bow forward as in *modim* and step back while maintaining the bowed posture.
- Move the left foot back the length of one's foot.
- Move the right foot back twice the length of one's foot.
- Move the left foot back the length of one's foot, bringing the two feet side by side.

635. How should a left-handed person step back?

He should reverse the above procedure, i.e. begin to step back with the right foot. By beginning with the weaker foot one demonstrates his reluctance to leave the presence of Hashem.

636. What if there is not enough room to do this?

See questions 583 and 584.

637. What if the person behind has not yet finished *shemoneh esrei*?

It is forbidden to take three steps back in this situation, and one must wait for the other person to finish *shemoneh esrei*. It is therefore imperative to glance behind before taking the three steps, in order to ascertain whether the person behind has finished. (See Volume Two for more details.)

638. How should one continue after taking three steps back?

- While still in a bowed posture one should turn to the left and say *oseh shalom bimromav.*
- Then turn to the right and say *hu ya'aseh shalom aleinu.*
- Then face forward and say *ve'al kol yisroel ve'imru amen.*

- One should then straighten up and say the paragraph *yehi ratzon milfanecha* before returning to one's place.

Care should be taken to divide the verse *oseh shalom* as described above, since some people mistakenly do otherwise.

639. How soon may one return to his original place?

- If a person is *davening* alone, he should wait a few moments before returning.
- If he is *davening shacharis, mussaf,* or *mincha* in shul, he should not return until the chazan reaches *kedusha*.
- If he is *davening ma'ariv* in shul, he should not return until the chazan begins *kaddish*.

640. What if there are additions to the chazan's *shemoneh esrei* before *kedusha*?

When this happens, e.g. on Rosh Hashanah and Yom Kippur, one may return to his place when the chazan begins the repetition of *shemoneh esrei*. This may also be done on a regular day if the place in shul is cramped and it is difficult to wait until *kedusha*.

641. When may one return to his place in shul on Friday night?

When the chazan begins *vay'chulu*.

642. Should one be concerned about other people walking in front of him before he has returned to his place?

Since nothing is lost by this, one should remain still until the correct time, and not be concerned. Many people are mistaken about this and incorrectly rush back to their place.

643. What if the chazan reaches *kedusha* before one has said *yehi ratzon milfanecha*?

He may return to his place immediately.

644. With which foot should one begin to return to his place?

With the right foot. A left-handed person should begin with his left foot.

645. Why do some people raise their heels three times after taking three steps forward?

There is no known source for this. It probably arose in error, by confusion with the laws of *kedusha* (see question 726).

646. May one talk after concluding *shemoneh esrei*?

• On days when *tachanun* is recited, one may not talk even words of Torah until after *tachanun*. Nevertheless, one may say any sections of *shacharis* that he omitted, or recite *tehillim*, until the chazan begins the repetition. One must stop immediately when the repetition begins (see question 713).

• On days when *tachanun* is not recited, talking is permitted when it is associated with a mitzvah, until the chazan begins the repetition (see question 711). However, mundane talk is forbidden in shul at all times.

Chapter Nineteen

Interruptions during Shemoneh Esrei

647. Which types of interruptions are forbidden during *shemoneh esrei*?

In normal circumstances, the following are forbidden:

- Moving from one's place.
- Talking.
- Signalling to someone.
- Yawning or belching.

648. What if one must move due to an emergency?

If an emergency arises, such as an imminent danger or a bad odor, he may move to another location. Care must be taken not to talk, unless this is essential. See also question 129.

649. Should he take three steps backwards before moving?

No.

650. Must he begin *shemoneh esrei* again?

- If the interruption was as long as it takes him to say the entire *shemoneh esrei* at his regular pace, he must begin again. The verse *Hashem sefasai* is not repeated.
- If the interruption was shorter than this, he should continue from where he left off (compare question 179).

651. What if the telephone is ringing continually and disturbing one's concentration?

He may walk over to the telephone and disconnect it. This should be done between *brachos*. It is a good idea to disconnect the telephone (and cellphone) before beginning to *daven*.

652. Should he continue *shemoneh esrei* there or return to his original place?

He should return to his original place.

653. What if the doorbell is ringing continually and disturbing one's concentration?

He may open the door without talking.

654. What if a child is continually disturbing?

Without moving from his place, he may indicate to the child to be quiet. If this does not help, he may move to another place, or go to the child to quieten him.

655. What if one's child is crying continually in shul?

The child should be taken out of shul in order not to disturb the congregation. The parent who is in the middle of *shemoneh esrei* must not talk, and should continue *shemoneh esrei* outside. See also question 94.

656. What if the child needs to use the bathroom?

If the child will not go alone, the parent may accompany him without talking.

657. May a parent correct his child who is making an error in his *tefillah*?

• If possible he should ignore it and continue *shemoneh esrei*.

• If the parent is very disturbed, he may indicate to the child how to *daven* correctly. This should preferably be done between *brachos*.

658. What if a child asks his parent what to *daven*?

• If possible, the parent should ignore the child.

• If the child persists, the parent may indicate to the child what to say.

Since this situation is common, it is important for the parent to show the child what to say before beginning *shemoneh esrei*. This should be done even if it will cause the parent to miss beginning *shemoneh esrei* with the congregation.

659. What if a page in the siddur is torn or missing and one does not know how to continue?

If possible, he should indicate to someone to bring him another siddur. Otherwise, he may go himself to look for another siddur. The same applies if he began to *daven* by heart and became confused during *shemoneh esrei*.

660. What if he erred in *shemoneh esrei* (e.g. forgot *ya'aleh veyavo*) and does not know how to continue?

He should go to look in a *sefer* to clarify the issue. After doing so, he should return to his original place to continue *shemoneh esrei*.

661. What if he cannot find the relevant law?

He should ask someone what to do.

662. What if he is alone at home?

He should call a rav, and present the question concisely.

663. What should one do if a *sefer* falls on the floor?

- If possible, he should ignore it and continue *shemoneh esrei*.
- If he is very disturbed, he may indicate to someone to pick it up, or if necessary go and pick it up himself between *brachos*.

664. What if one's *tallis* falls off?

- If it has not fallen off completely, he may put it on properly.
- If it has fallen off completely, he may not put it on again during *shemoneh esrei*, even if he is still holding it. If he is very disturbed, he may put it on again between *brachos*.

665. May a person yawn or belch if necessary?

He must make an effort to suppress this, but if his efforts are failing he may do so. Before yawning, he should place his hand in front of his mouth, even if he is alone.

666. What if he needs to use the bathroom?

See question 177.

667. May a person respond to *kedusha* in the middle of *shemoneh esrei*?

No, it is forbidden to respond to any part of *davening* during *shemoneh esrei*. He should stop and listen to the chazan reciting the main lines of *kedusha*, i.e. *kadosh*, *baruch*, and *yimloch*.

668. May he continue *shemoneh esrei* between these lines?

Yes.

669. What if he cannot hear the chazan?

He should ignore *kedusha* and continue *shemoneh esrei*.

670. What if a person hears *kaddish* during *shemoneh esrei*?

He should stop and listen from the beginning of *kaddish* until *yisbarach*.

671. What if he hears *barchu*?

He should stop and listen to the chazan and to the response of the congregation.

672. Should he bow with the congregation?

He should bow if he is at any of the following points in *shemoneh esrei*:

- One of the four places where it is an obligation to bow.
- Between *brachos*.
- In the middle of a *b'racha*.
- During *elohai netzor*.

He should not bow if he is at the beginning or end of a *b'racha* (except the first and *modim*).

673. What if the chazan reaches *modim*?

He should bow with the congregation according to the rules in the previous question.

674. What should he do when the *cohanim* bless the congregation?

He should stop *davening* and listen to the blessings. If the chazan recites the blessings, he should ignore him and continue *shemoneh esrei*.

675. What if he accidentally began responding to *kedusha*, *kaddish*, etc.?

He must stop immediately, even in the middle of a verse. If he was in the middle of a *b'racha*, he must start the *b'racha* again.

676. May one stop and listen to the Torah reading during *shemoneh esrei*?

No, one should continue *shemoneh esrei*.

677. What if a man was called to the Torah during *shemoneh esrei*?

He may not move from his place and should continue *shemoneh esrei*.

678. Do all the laws of this chapter apply when one has reached *elohai netzor*?

All the laws apply until one has taken three steps back, except for the laws regarding responses to *kaddish*, *kedusha*, etc.

679. May one respond to *kaddish*, *kedusha* etc. during *elohai netzor*?

One may respond to whatever is permitted when he is in the middle of shema (see question 288). If possible, he should say the verse *yihyu leratzon* before saying any responses.

680. Is it better to omit *elohai netzor* in this situation?

Yes. It is better to omit or cut short *elohai netzor* rather than respond before or during *elohai netzor*. If possible, he should also take three steps back before responding, and if time allows he should also say *oseh shalom* before responding.

681. What if a man was called to the Torah during *elohai netzor*?

He should go up to the Torah, but he must say the verse *yihyu leratzon* before moving.

682. When should he take three steps back?

After reading the Torah, he should return to his place and take three steps back. He should then say *oseh shalom* and *yehi ratzon*.

683. May one speak if he has finished *shemoneh esrei* but cannot take three steps back due to another person behind him?

He may continue to *daven*, make all responses in shul, recite *tehillim*, or speak words of Torah study. He may not talk about mundane matters.

Chapter Twenty
Mistakes in Shemoneh Esrei

684. What if a person forgot to say the verse *ki sheim* at *mussaf* or *mincha*?

He should continue *shemoneh esrei*.

685. What if a person forgot to say the opening verse *Hashem sefasai tiftach*?

He should continue *shemoneh esrei*.

686. What if he accidentally omitted one of the *brachos*?

- If he omitted one of the first three *brachos*, he must start *shemoneh esrei* again. The verse *Hashem sefasai* is not repeated.
- If he omitted one of the last three *brachos*, he must go back to *retzei*.
- If he omitted one of the middle *brachos*, he must go back to that *b'racha*.

In all cases, after returning to the correct place, he must continue again from there, even if this necessitates repeating some *brachos*.

687. What if he realized his error in the middle of a *b'racha*?

He must stop immediately and should not conclude that *b'racha*.

688. What if he omitted a phrase from the middle of a b'racha?

• If he did not conclude the b'racha he should go back to the correct place.

• If he concluded the b'racha he should continue shemoneh esrei, and should insert the omitted phrase in the b'racha shema koleinu if he has not yet reached there.

689. What if he concluded a b'racha incorrectly (e.g. he said chonain hada'as instead of ha'eil hakadosh)?

• If he realized within one second **and** did not yet begin the next b'racha, he should correct himself immediately.

• If he realized after one second **or** after beginning the next b'racha, he should follow these rules:

   • If this occurred in the first three brachos, he must start shemoneh esrei again.

   • If this occurred in the last three brachos, he must go back to retzei.

   • If this occurred in one of the middle brachos, he must go back to the beginning of that b'racha.

690. What if he lost his place in shemoneh esrei?

• If this occurred in the first three brachos he must start shemoneh esrei again.

• If this occurred in the last three brachos he must go back to retzei.

• If this occurred in one of the middle brachos, he must start again from the first b'racha that he is unsure if he said.

691. What if he realized in the middle of *shemoneh esrei* that he had already *davened*?

He must stop immediately and say *baruch sheim kevod malchuso le'olam va'ed*.

692. What if one began to say *shalom rav* instead of *sim shalom*?

• If he did not say the name of Hashem at the conclusion of the *b'racha*, he should begin again from *sim shalom*.

• If he said the name of Hashem, he should continue.

693. What if one began to say *sim shalom* instead of *shalom rav*?

He should continue the *b'racha sim shalom*.

694. What if he forgot to say *mashiv haru'ach* during the winter?

• If he did not yet say *vene'eman ata*, he should insert *mashiv haru'ach* between phrases and does not need to repeat anything.

• If he said *vene'eman ata* but did not yet say *baruch*, he should say *mashiv haru'ach u'morid hageshem* and repeat from *vene'eman ata*.

• If he said *baruch*, or *baruch ata*, he should go back to *mashiv haru'ach* and continue *mechalkeil chaim*.

• If he said the name of Hashem, there are different rules for varying customs:

> • If he said *morid hatal*, as he is accustomed during the summer, he should conclude the *b'racha mechayei hameisim* and continue *shemoneh esrei*.

- If he did not say *morid hatal*, he should say *lamdeini chukecha* and go back to *mashiv haru'ach, mechalkeil chaim*, etc.
- If he concluded the *b'racha*:
  - If he said *morid hatal*, he should continue *shemoneh esrei*.
  - If he did not say *morid hatal*, he should immediately say *mashiv haru'ach umorid hageshem*, and continue *shemoneh esrei*.
- If he began the next *b'racha*:
  - If he said *morid hatal*, he should continue *shemoneh esrei*.
  - If he did not say *morid hatal*, he must go back to the beginning of *shemoneh esrei*.

See also question 437.

695. What if he said *mashiv haru'ach* during the summer?

- If he said only the words *mashiv haru'ach*, he should continue *shemoneh esrei*.
- If he said *mashiv har'uach umorid*, he should say *hatal* and continue *shemoneh esrei*.
- If he said the word *hageshem*, he should begin the *b'racha* again (*ata gibor*), provided he did not yet say the name of Hashem at the conclusion of the *b'racha*.
- If he said the name of Hashem, he should say *lamdeini chukecha* and go back to the beginning of the *b'racha* (*ata gibor*).
- If he said the name of Hashem and the word *mechayei*, he must go back to the beginning of *shemoneh esrei*.

696. What if he is in doubt whether he said *mashiv haru'ach*?

• For the first thirty days of the new winter or summer season, a person is not yet accustomed to alter the text. It must therefore be assumed that he said the wrong version, and he should follow the rules in the previous two questions.

• After thirty days, he may assume that he said the correct text.

697. Does it matter when the doubt entered his mind?

Yes. The above rules apply only if the doubt arose during *shemoneh esrei* or immediately afterwards. However, if the doubt arose some time after concluding *shemoneh esrei*, he need not repeat *shemoneh esrei* if he definitely had intention to say the correct text.

698. What if he forgot to say *vesein tal u'matar* during the winter?

• If he did not yet say the name of Hashem at the conclusion of the *b'racha*, he should go back to *vesein tal u'matar* and continue from there.

• If he said the name of Hashem, he should continue *shemoneh esrei*, and insert the phrase *vesein tal u'matar livracha* in the middle of *shema koleinu*.

• If he forgot to insert it in *shema koleinu* and remembered after saying the name of Hashem at the conclusion of *shomei'a tefillah*, he should say *lamdeini chukecha*, insert the phrase *vesein tal u'mater livracha*, and continue *ki ata shomei'a*, etc.

• If he concluded *shomei'a tefillah*, he should insert the phrase *vesein tal u'matar livracha* and continue with *retzei*.

- If he began *retzei*, he must go back to *bareich aleinu* and repeat everything from there.
- If he said the verse *yihyu leratzon* at the conclusion of *shemoneh esrei*, he must repeat *shemoneh esrei*. This is true even if he did not yet take three steps back.

699. What if he said *vesein tal u'matar* during the summer?

- If he did not yet say the name of Hashem at the conclusion of the *b'racha*, he should go back to the beginning of the *b'racha*.
- If he said the name of Hashem, he should say *lamdeini chukecha* and go back to the beginning of the *b'racha*.
- If he said further, he should go back to *bareich aleinu* and repeat from there.
- If he said the verse *yihyu leratzon* at the conclusion of *shemoneh esrei*, he must repeat *shemoneh esrei*. This is true even if he did not yet take three steps back.

700. What if he said *vesein tal u'matar* after *Shemini Atzeres*?

Care must be taken not to begin saying *vesein tal u'matar* before the correct day. Although *mashiv haru'ach* is said from *Shemini Atzeres*, the request for rain with *vesein tal u'matar* is not said until the 7th of Cheshvan in *Eretz Yisroel* and the 5th of December in *chutz la'aretz* (see also question 627.) If one said *tal u'matar* before the appropriate date, he should correct the mistake, unless he said the name of Hashem at the conclusion of the *b'racha*.

701. What if he is in doubt whether he said *vesein tal u'matar*?

See questions 696 and 697.

702. What if he forgot to say *ya'aleh veyavo* on *rosh chodesh*?

• If this occurred in *ma'ariv* and he already said the name of Hashem at the conclusion of the *b'racha*, he should continue *shemoneh esrei*, and the mistake does not require correction.

• If this occurred in *shacharis* or *mincha*, the rules are as follows:

> • If he did not yet say the name of Hashem at the conclusion of the *b'racha*, he should go back to *ya'aleh veyavo*.

> • If he said the name of Hashem, he should say *lamdeini chukecha* and go back to *ya'aleh veyavo*.

> • If he concluded the *b'racha*, he should say *ya'aleh veyavo* and continue with *modim*.

> • If he began *modim*, he should go back to *retzei*.

> • If he said the verse *yihyu leratzon* at the conclusion of *shemoneh esrei*, he must repeat *shemoneh esrei*. This is true even if he did not yet take three steps back.

703. What if he forgot to say *ya'aleh veyavo* on *chol hamoed*?

The mistake must be corrected at all *tefillos*, including *ma'ariv*, and the above rules should be used.

704. What if he began to say *ya'aleh veyavo* on a regular day?

- If he did not yet say *rosh hachodesh hazeh* (or *chag hamatzos/hasuccos*), he should stop immediately and continue *vesechezena*.
- If he said *rosh hachodesh hazeh* (or *chag hamatzos/hasuccos*), he should go back to *retzei*.

705. What if he forgot to say *al hanissim* on Chanukah or Purim?

- If he did not yet say the name of Hashem at the conclusion of the *b'racha*, he should go back to *al hanissim* and continue from there.
- If he said the name of Hashem, he should continue *shemoneh esrei*. At the end of the paragraph *elohai netzor* before saying the verse *yihyu leratzon* he should add a special prayer:

יהי רצון מלפניך שתעשה לנו נסים ונפלאות כשם שעשית לאבותינו בימים ההם בזמן הזה.

He should then continue *biymei Mordechai* or *biymei Matisyahu*. If he forgot to say this prayer, he should not repeat *shemoneh esrei*.

706. What if he forgot to say *aneinu* on a fast day?

If he said the name of Hashem at the conclusion of the *b'racha* of *shema koleinu*, he should continue and say *aneinu* just before the verse *yihyu leratzon* at the end of *shemoneh esrei*. If he forgot there also, he should not repeat *shemoneh esrei*.

707. What if he forgot to say *ata chonantanu* on *motzai Shabbos*?

- If he said the name of Hashem at the conclusion of the *b'racha*, he should continue *shemoneh esrei*, and say *ata chonantanu* before the verse *yihyu leratzon* at the end of *shemoneh esrei*.

- If he forgot there also, he should not repeat *shemoneh esrei*. However, he may not do any *melacha* until he says *baruch hamavdil bein kodesh lechol* or recites (or hears) *havdalah*.

Chapter Twenty-one

Repetition of Shemoneh Esrei

708. Why is *shemoneh esrei* repeated by the chazan?

- For the sake of people who do not know how to *daven* themselves. By listening to the entire repetition of the *shemoneh esrei*, such people can fulfill the mitzvah of prayer. Although this reason is not applicable today, the Sages instituted the repetition of *shemoneh esrei* as a fixed part of communal prayer to cover the eventuality that may arise.

- In order to say *kedusha* and for the *cohanim* to bless the people.

709. How attentive must the congregation be during the repetition?

Each person is obligated to give his full attention to the repetition, answering amen to each *b'racha*. If there are not nine men listening to the chazan, his *brachos* are considered to be almost in vain. Therefore, each person should think that without him there will not be nine people listening. If he pays attention to the entire repetition, he will receive reward as if he *davened* the *shemoneh esrei* himself a second time. It is recommended that one looks into the siddur in order to follow the repetition word for word. It is sad to note how many times a chazan has made an error in the repetition and not a single person in the congregation noticed the mistake.

710. What if the chazan suspects that there will not be nine men listening?

He should stipulate before beginning that if this occurs, his *shemoneh esrei* should be a voluntary prayer. This should not be done on Shabbos or Yom Tov, nor at any *mussaf*.

711. May one talk during the repetition?

Talking during the repetition is an extremely severe transgression, and in the words of the *Shulchan Aruch*, "the sin is too great to be forgiven". It is worth noting that such a condemnation is not found anywhere else in the *Shulchan Aruch*. The *Chofetz Chaim* writes that he saw many shuls that were destroyed due to this iniquity.

712. May one learn Torah during the repetition?

This is also forbidden. Even if he half listens and answers amen to the *brachos*, such behavior may encourage others to ignore the repetition entirely and engage in conversation. He will thereby be guilty of causing others to sin.

713. May one say parts of *shacharis* that he omitted?

No. During the repetition one must be completely silent and listen to the chazan.

714. Should one say *baruch hu uvaruch shemo* at the end of each *b'racha*?

The main custom is to do so, provided this does not cause one to miss answering amen after the conclusion of the *b'racha* (see question 258). Some refrain from answering *baruch hu uvaruch shemo* due to this concern. In any event, this response should not be drawn out or said too loudly, since this would disturb the chazan.

715. Exactly when should one answer amen?

Immediately after the chazan has concluded the last word of the *b'racha*. One must take care not to answer amen too hastily, before the *chazan* has completed the final syllable, since this is forbidden. Many people are at fault in this matter.

716. How long after the *b'racha* may one still answer amen?

Until most of the congregation have finished saying amen.

717. What if one did not hear the end of the *b'racha*?

He may answer amen together with the congregation, provided that he knows which *b'racha* the chazan has just concluded. It is forbidden to answer amen without knowing to what it applies.

718. Why is this forbidden?

The word amen should be said with the proper intent, according to the type of *b'racha* that was recited.
- For a *b'racha* of praise (e.g. *magen Avraham*), one should think that the praise is true and he believes so.
- For a *b'racha* of praise and request (e.g. *chonein hada'as*) one should think that the praise is true and he hopes that the request will be answered.

719. How loudly may one answer amen?

It is usually forbidden to answer amen more loudly than the chazan. However, it is permitted to do so if one's intention is to encourage others to answer amen. In any event, one should not draw out the word amen, since this would cause a disturbance to the chazan (see question 258).

720. Must a person stand during the repetition?

• It is forbidden to sit down within four *amos* of the chazan during the repetition.

• One must stand from the beginning of *kedusha* until *ha'eil hakadosh*, while reciting *modim derabbonon*, and when the *cohanim* bless the congregation.

• During the rest of the repetition it is preferable to stand, but one may sit if necessary. One should refrain from walking around the shul during the repetition.

721. If one prefers to stand may he lean on a *shtender*?

If he leans on the *shtender* to the degree that he would fall if it were removed, he is considered to be sitting.

722. Is it better to stand during the repetition or during the reading of the Torah?

If a person does not have the strength for both, it is better to stand for the repetition of *shemoneh esrei*.

723. What is the significance of *kedusha*?

The theme of *kedusha* is the sanctification of Hashem by mortals on earth, imitating the way in which the angels on high exalt Hashem and sing his praises. According to the Sages, Hashem prefers the song of men over that of the angels, and has no greater pleasure than to listen to our recitation of *kedusha*. At that time, Hashem (so to speak) embraces and kisses the image of *Ya'akov Avinu* that is engraved on His Holy

Throne, and remembering the Jewish people's merits hastens to bring the redemption.

724. What should one think during *kedusha*?

He should have in mind to fulfill the verse, "And I shall be sanctified among the children of Israel" (*Vayikra* 22:32). If a person recites *kedusha* with proper concentration, Hashem will bestow holiness upon him from above.

725. What should be one's posture?

The feet should be placed together as one stands for *shemoneh esrei*, and the eyes should be turned towards Heaven.

726. Why is there a custom to raise one's heels?

This is to imitate the angels who fly upwards when singing the praises of Hashem.

727. When should a person raise his heels?

- Three times when saying *kadosh, kadosh, kadosh*.
- Once when saying *baruch kevod*.
- Once when saying *yimloch Hashem*.

728. Why do some people turn to the right and left when saying *vekara zeh el zeh ve'amar*?

There is no known source for this custom.

729. Should the congregation say all parts of *kedusha*?

Strictly speaking, it is sufficient for the congregation to say the three lines *kadosh, baruch,* and *yimloch*. However, the widespread custom is to say also the first line of *kedusha*, and the intermediary lines on Shabbos and Yom Tov.

730. May one recite *kedusha* during *pesukei dezimra*?
See question 278.

731. May one recite *kedusha* during shema and its *brachos*?
See question 288.

732. May one recite *kedusha* during *shemoneh esrei*?
See question 667.

733. May one recite *kedusha* while putting on *tefillin*?
See question 413.

734. If a man is learning Torah in the same room as a minyan, must he respond to *kedusha*?
Yes. (Compare questions 576 and 841).

735. If one is *davening* or studying Torah and overhears *kedusha* from another room, must he respond?
He may respond, but there is no obligation. (Compare question 842.)

736. If one is walking in the street and overhears *kedusha* from a nearby shul, must he respond?
He may respond, but there is no obligation. (Compare question 843.)

737. If one is saying *tehillim* at the *Kosel* and overhears *kaddish* or *kedusha* from one of the *minyanim*, must he respond?

He may respond, but there is no obligation.

738. What should be done during *aseres yemei teshuvah* if the chazan forgot to say *hamelech hakadosh* and was not corrected?

He must begin the repetition again, and *kedusha* must also be repeated.

739. Should the chazan strike his chest during the *b'racha selach lanu*?

Yes.

740. What if the chazan forgot to say *aneinu* on a fast day?

Although individuals insert the paragraph *aneinu* in the *b'racha shema koleinu*, the chazan adds *aneinu* as a complete *b'racha* before the *b'racha refa'einu*. If he mistakenly began *refa'einu*, he must stop immediately and say *aneinu*. If he said the name of Hashem at the conclusion of the *b'racha*, he should continue, and insert *aneinu* in *shema koleinu*.

741. What is the significance of *modim de'rabbanan*?

The Talmud reports that when the chazan came to *modim*, each Sage would say his own private prayer of thanksgiving. These prayers were subsequently combined to become what is now known as *modim de'rabbanan* (literally, the *modim* of the Sages).

742. When should the congregation begin to say *modim de'rabbanan*?

They should answer amen to the previous *b'racha*, pause a moment, and then begin *modim de'rabbanan*. It is incorrect to begin *modim* immediately following amen, since these are two different concepts.

743. Should one stand when saying *modim de'rabbanan*?

Yes.

744. Must one bow when saying *modim de'rabbanan*?

Yes. He should bow until the name of Hashem, as is done during the quiet *shemoneh esrei* (see question 613). Some have the custom to bow again at the concluding words *al she'anachnu modim lach*.

745. Must one bow towards the front of the shul?

Yes. Some people bow in whichever direction they happen to be facing, but this is incorrect and they should turn towards the front of the shul when bowing.

746. Should one say *modim de'rabbanan* **during** *pesukei dezimra*?

See question 278.

747. Should one say *modim de'rabbanan* **during** shema and its *brachos*?

See question 288.

748. May one say *modim de'rabbanan* during *shemoneh esrei*?

See question 673.

749. May one say *modim de'rabbanan* while putting on *tefillin*?

See question 413.

750. If a man is studying Torah in shul, must he say *modim de'rabbanan*?

Yes. If he is in another room in the shul, he should not respond but should continue learning.

751. If one is walking in the street and overhears *modim* from a nearby shul, must he say *modim de'rabbanan*?

He may respond, but there is no obligation.

752. What should the congregation say during *birchos cohanim*?

• When the *cohanim* give the blessings, the congregation should answer amen after the introductory *b'racha* and after each of the three verses. See Volume Two for further details.

• When the chazan recites the blessings, the congregation should say *kein yehi ratzon* after each of the three verses.

Some congregations have the custom to recite the paragraph *adir bamarom* when the chazan says the *b'racha sim shalom*.

Chapter Twenty-two

Tachanun

753. What is the significance of *tachanun*?

• After the sin of the golden calf, *Moshe Rabbeinu* prayed to Hashem for forgiveness in three different positions: sitting, standing, and falling on his face (*Devarim* 9:9, 10:10, 9:18). Following this precedent we *daven birchos shema* sitting, *shemoneh esrei* standing, and *tachanun* falling on the face.

• According to the Zohar, the recital of *tachanun* is a declaration of one's readiness to sacrifice his life as an atonement for his sins, and one should have this intention when saying this prayer.

• According to the Sages, prayers said while one is falling on one's face during *tachanun*, are more readily answered.

754. Should women say *tachanun*?

The custom is for women to omit *tachanun*.

755. Why do some people recite *viduy* before *tachanun*?

This is also based upon the Zohar, which requires a person to confess his sins before declaring his readiness to sacrifice his life.

756. What if a person's custom is different from the shul's?

• If the congregation is reciting *viduy*, he should do likewise, even if his custom is not so.

• If the congregation omits *viduy*, he may only recite *viduy* if this is done inconspicuously (e.g. he should not strike his chest). He must also omit the thirteen attributes of mercy, since these may only be said together with a minyan.

757. Why do some people recite *tachanun* without falling on the face?

This is the custom of Sephardim, who fear the punishment threatened by the Zohar if one falls on the face without the correct intentions. Ashkenazim fall on the face, but avoid this threat by reciting a different paragraph from the one recommended by the Zohar.

758. What if an Ashkenazi is *davening* in a Sephardi shul?

• If there are other Ashkenazim present who are falling on their face, he may do likewise.

• If he is the only Ashkenazi, he should follow the custom of the shul and not fall on his face.

759. Is falling on the face always performed?

Falling on the face is performed only in a room where there is a *sefer Torah*. If there is no *sefer Torah*, *tachanun* is recited without falling on the face. In Yerushalayim, the custom is to fall on the face even where there is no *sefer Torah*, due to the extra holiness of the city.

760. What if one *davens* in the women's section or a side room of a shul?

- If he can see the Ark from there, he should fall on his face.
- If he cannot see the Ark from there, he should not fall on his face, unless he recites *tachanun* together with the congregation (or he is in Yerushalayim).

761. How should one fall on his face?

The head should be turned downward and the face covered with a garment. The custom is to rest the forehead on the sleeve of one's jacket. It is incorrect to rest the forehead on one's hand or one's bare arm.

762. Should one use the left arm or the right?

One should use the left arm, unless he is wearing *tefillin* on this arm, in which case he should use the right arm. The same applies to a left-handed person.

763. Should one cover the face for the entire *tachanun*?

The face should be covered from *rachum vechanun* until *yaivoshu raga*.

764. Should one say the introductory verse *vayomer David*?

The widespread custom is to say it, but some omit it (since it was said by *Dovid Hamelech* at a time of Heavenly punishment).

765. Must *tachanun* be recited sitting?

Ideally, yes (including the chazan). If there are not sufficient chairs, or if one cannot take three steps back after *shemoneh esrei* due to a person behind him, he may say *tachanun* standing. In this situation it is preferable to lean on an object, since this is equivalent to sitting.

766. At which point should one stand?

After saying the words *va'anachnu lo neida*.

767. Why is *tachanun* longer on Monday and Thursday?

After Hashem forgave the Jewish people for the sin of the golden calf, *Moshe Rabbeinu* spent another period of forty days on Mount Sinai in preparation to receive the second *luchos*. Since he ascended the mountain on a Thursday and descended on a Monday, these days were fixed forever as days of mercy. Therefore, the prayer *vehu rachum* is recited, in which we appeal to Hashem to have mercy on the Jewish people and redeem them from all their sufferings.

768. Why is *vehu rachum* so lengthy?

There is a miraculous story behind this prayer. According to the Kol Bo, three pious men who were exiled at the time of the destruction of the holy Temple were captured by a cruel gentile ruler. Upon discovering that they were Jews, he had them cast into a fiery furnace. A great miracle occurred resembling the splitting of the sea, and the three men walked unscathed through a clearing in the fire. As an act of thanksgiving, each one composed a moving prayer for Hashem to protect and help the entire Jewish nation, and the three prayers were combined to form the long *vehu rachum*. Despite its extreme length and repetitiveness, it should be recited slowly and with concentration.

769. What if the congregation rushes this prayer?

One should nevertheless say as much as possible slowly, but join the congregation when they fall on their faces to recite the main section of *tachanun*. The omitted sections of *vehu rachum* should be recited later.

770. May one omit this prayer?

It is a serious transgression to do so. If a person does not have time to say it during *shacharis* he should say it at any time during the day.

771. Should one stand for *vehu rachum*?

Yes, since it contains phrases of confession.

772. Why do some congregations fall on the face before *vehu rachum*?

This is a Sephardic custom based upon the Zohar, which requires one to fall on the face immediately after *shemoneh esrei*.

773. What if one has a custom that differs from the congregation's regarding this?

• If he is the only person in shul with a different custom, he should follow the custom of the shul.

• If there are other people with his custom, he may follow his own custom.

774. May one say *tachanun* while the congregation is saying *aleinu*?

If a person finishes *shemoneh esrei* when the congregation is saying (or is about to say) *aleinu*, he should say *tachanun* and not *aleinu*. Although one is usually required to recite *aleinu* together with the congregation (see question 801), in this situation it is more important to say *tachanun* immediately following *shemoneh esrei*. This applies both at *shacharis* and at *mincha* (see question 871).

775. On which days is *tachanun* omitted?

- Shabbos and *rosh chodesh*.
- *Erev* Rosh Hashanah and Rosh Hashanah.
- From *erev* Yom Kippur until the day after Simchas Torah, inclusive.
- Chanukah.
- The 15th of Shevat.
- The 14th and 15th of Adar (both Adars in a leap year).
- The entire month of Nissan.
- *Lag ba'omer*.
- From *rosh chodesh* Sivan until the day after Shavuos, inclusive.
- The 9th and 15th of Av.

In *Eretz Yisroel* and in some communities in *chutz la'aretz*, the custom is to omit *tachanun* on the following additional days:
- Between Simchas Torah and *rosh chodesh* Cheshvan.
- The 14th of Iyar (*Pesach sheini*).
- Between Shavuos and the 12th of Sivan inclusive.

776. When is *tachanun* omitted at *mincha*?

See question 870.

777. Is *tachanun* recited when a *chosson* is present?

No. This applies from the time of the *chuppah* until the end of seven full days (i.e. 7x24 hours).

778. What if this is the *chosson's* second marriage?

• If either the *chosson* or the *kallah* is marrying for the first time, *tachanun* is omitted for seven days.

• If the *chosson* and *kallah* are both marrying for the second time, *tachanun* is omitted for three days.

779. What about prayers before the *chuppah*?

• If the *chuppah* will take place during the day, the main custom is to omit *tachanun* in the presence of the *chosson* both at *shacharis* and at *mincha* on the day of the wedding.

• If the *chuppah* will take place at night, *tachanun* is recited at *shacharis*, and at *mincha* if it is early afternoon. If *mincha* is said shortly before the *chuppah*, *tachanun* is omitted. In any event, the *chosson* himself should omit *tachanun* at *shacharis* and *mincha*.

780. Is *tachanun* recited when the *kallah* is in the women's section of the shul?

Yes.

781. Is *tachanun* recited in shul when a *bris* is scheduled?

Tachanun is omitted at the *tefillah* preceding the *bris*. Therefore, if the *bris* is scheduled following *mincha*, *tachanun* is recited at *shacharis* but not at *mincha*.

782. Does the exemption also apply to a minyan held in a side room of the shul?

If there is no *aron kodesh* and *bima* in the side room, it is considered to be an extension of the main shul, and *tachanun* is omitted.

783. What if the *bris* is being held in the side room?

Tachanun is omitted in the side room, but recited in the main shul.

784. What if the father of the baby is in shul, but the *bris* will be performed elsewhere?

Tachanun is omitted in the presence of the father, the *mohel*, or the *sandek*, even if the *bris* is held elsewhere. In this situation, *tachanun* is omitted at *shacharis*, even if the *bris* is scheduled following *mincha*.

785. What if *mincha* is said immediately following the *bris*?

Tachanun is omitted only if *mincha* is said before the *seudas mitzvah* and the baby is present. In any event, the father, *mohel*, and *sandek* should omit *tachanun* at *shacharis* and *mincha*, since it is a Yom Tov for them.

786. Is *tachanun* recited when there is a *pidyon haben* or bar mitzvah?

The main custom is to recite *tachanun*. According to some opinions, it is omitted when the *tefillah* is held prior to and in the place of the celebration.

787. Is there any justification for omitting *tachanun* on the *yahrzeit* of a *tzaddik*?

Although this custom is practiced in certain circles, it has no firm *halachic* basis and is criticized by many authorities. It could perhaps be justified when the followers of a particular *tzaddik* assemble to honor his *yahrzeit* by studying his writings, visiting his grave, and holding a festive meal. Otherwise, one could discover *yahrzeits* for almost any day of the year, and the omission of *tachanun* would become a mockery.

788. What if one *davens* in a shul that has this practice?

He should recite *tachanun* even if the shul omits it.

789. What if the congregation began saying *tachanun* on a day that it should be omitted?

They should stop as soon as the mistake is discovered, being careful not to break off in the middle of a phrase in a meaningless way. For example, if one said the opening words of *viduy* - *Eloheinu veilohei avoseinu* - he should continue with the next few words - *tavo lefanecha tefiloseinu* - before stopping.

Chapter Twenty-three
Conclusion of Shacharis

790. Why is *ashrei* repeated after *shemoneh esrei*?

- In order to say it three times daily (see also question 491).
- The first part of *shacharis* until *shemoneh esrei* is intended to bring spiritual enlightenment to one's soul. In the concluding sections of *shacharis*, we pray for our bodily needs, and begin with *ashrei*, which contains the request for physical sustenance.

791. What is the significance of *lamnatze'ach*?

In this paragraph (Psalm 20), we evoke the merit of *Ya'akov Avinu*, who suffered extreme hardship in raising his family and earning a livelihood. In the same way that he was rescued by Hashem from all troubles, so too do we hope and pray to experience His salvation.

792. When is *lamnatze'ach* omitted?

- Shabbos, Yom Tov, *chol hamoed*, and *rosh chodesh*.
- *Erev* Yom Kippur.
- Chanukah.
- The 14th and 15th of Adar (both Adars in a leap year).
- *Erev* Pesach.
- Tisha b'Av.
- There are different opinions regarding *isru chag*, but the main custom is to omit it.

793. What is the importance of *uva le'tziyon*?

The primary section of this prayer is *kedusha de'sidra* - the two essential lines of *kedusha* with a translation into Aramaic. The Sages say that since the destruction of the holy Temple, each day is more cursed than the previous one, and the world endures solely on the merit of *kedusha de'sidra* and the *kaddish* recited after Torah study (see question 827). Since Aramaic was the vernacular during the days of the Sages, a translation into this language was included for the benefit of those who did not understand Hebrew. Care should be taken to recite this *kedusha* with concentration.

794. Should one stand for *kedusha de'sidra*?

Although opinions differ about this, the main custom is to recite it sitting. If a person happens to be standing when he reaches these verses, he should remain standing.

795. Must these verses be recited with a minyan?

It is preferable but not essential to do so. If a person has not yet reached this point when the congregation is about to recite these verses, he should skip to the verse *ve'ata kadosh* and join the congregation.

796. How should he continue after reciting these verses?

He should continue with the congregation until *vehachein levavam eilecha*, and then return to where he left off. When reaching *ve'ata kadosh*, he should not repeat the verses of *kedusha*.

797. Should *kedusha de'sidra* be recited aloud?

- The two phrases *kadosh kadosh* and *baruch kevod* should be said aloud.
- The Aramaic translation should be said quietly if recited with the congregation. Otherwise, it may be said aloud.

798. What is the significance of *aleinu*?

Composed by Yehoshua after entering *Eretz Yisroel*, *aleinu* is a beautiful song of praise to Hashem and a declaration of implicit faith in the Oneness of Hashem's kingship. It condemns idol worship and false beliefs, and concludes with a heartfelt prayer for the day when all mankind will recognize the truth of the Torah and Hashem's sovereignty. The Sages included *aleinu* in the most solemn *mussaf shemoneh esrei* of Rosh Hashanah, and it later became the custom to recite it at the conclusion of all prayers. It should be said with concentration, awe, and respect.

799. Should one stand when saying *aleinu*?

Yes, and when saying the phrase *va'anachnu kor'im u'mishtachavim* one should bow.

800. Should one bend the knees when bowing?

The main custom is not to bend the knees. According to some opinions, one should bend the knees at *kor'im* and bow at *u'mishtachavim*.

801. Must one say *aleinu* together with the congregation?

Customs differ regarding the order of prayers at the conclusion of *shacharis*. Some recite *aleinu* after *uva le'tziyon* while others recite it as the final prayer of *shacharis*. If a person's custom differs from that of the shul, he should nevertheless say *aleinu* together with the congregration. Similarly, if he has not yet concluded *ashrei* and *uva le'tziyon* he should join the congregation for *aleinu*.

802. If a person enters shul as the congregation is about to recite *aleinu*, must he say it with them?

Yes. Similarly, if he is studying Torah in shul, he must join the congregation for *aleinu*.

803. What is the significance of the psalm of the day?

One of the highlights of the service in the holy Temple was the singing of a special psalm by the *Leviyim* after the daily sacrifice. The recital of the daily psalm at the end of *shacharis* is a reminder of that joyous service. In addition, according to some opinions, by saying the introductory line that announces the day of the week one fufills the mitzvah to remember the Shabbos every day.

804. Should one say *pitum haketores* at the end of *shacharis*?

See question 455.

805. Why is *ein keiloheinu* said before *pitum haketores*?

A person who recites *pitum haketores* with intense concentration will be blessed with wealth. Since he may attribute his success to his own skill, *ein keloheinu* is recited as a declaration that everything is in the hands of Hashem.

806. Why is *barchu* repeated after *shacharis*?

This is for the benefit of people who came late to shul and missed the *barchu* following *pesukei dezimra*. In *Eretz Yisroel*, the main custom is to recite it daily, except on days when the Torah is read. In *chutz la'aretz*, many communities do not have the custom to say this *barchu*.

807. What if everyone was present at the earlier *barchu*?

In this case, it is preferable not to repeat *barchu* after *shacharis*.

808. Should women say all the sections that follow *tachanun*?

It is customary for them to say *aleinu*. All the remaining sections are voluntary, but many women have the custom to say some or all of them according to the time available.

809. Which of these sections take precedence for women?

Ashrei is the most important, and *uva le'tziyon* next.

810. When may a man remove his tallis and *tefillin*?

See question 415.

811. Is there an obligation to recite the six remembrances?

No, but according to kabbalistic sources one fulfills a mitzvah by reciting them. According to some opinions there are ten remembrances.

812. Is there an obligation to recite the thirteen principles of faith?

No.

813. May one leave shul before the end of *shacharis*?

- Ideally, one should remain in shul until the end of *shacharis*.
- In times of need one may leave earlier, but one should remain until after the first *kaddish* recited by the mourners, if possible.
- It is forbidden to leave before *kedusha de'sidra*, unless in extenuating circumstances.
- It is forbidden to leave early on a regular basis.

A person who leaves before the end of *davening* because he has no patience to wait a few more minutes is grossly disgracing the service of Hashem. How can he expect his prayers to be answered if he does not appear to believe that the Shechina is present in shul?

814. How should one leave shul?

As he is about to leave he should recite the verse, "*Hashem ne'cheini vetzidkasecha lema'an shoreray, hay'shar le'fanay darkecha*" (*Tehillim* 5:9) and bow towards the Ark. He should not leave with his back to the Ark, but should walk sideways or backwards through the entrance.

Chapter Twenty-four
Kaddish

815. What is the significance of *kaddish*?

Composed (by the Men of the Great Assembly) after the destruction of the first holy Temple, this great and awesome prayer laments the desecration of God's name caused by the loss of the Temple and the dispersion of the Jewish nation to the four corners of the globe. The prayer is a heart-rending appeal to Hashem to speedily reveal Himself to the world, thereby elevating and sanctifying His great name. It is based upon the verse, "And I will magnify and sanctify Myself, and will make Myself known in the eyes of many nations, and they shall know that I am Hashem" (*Yechezkel* 38:23). The Sages say that when the Jewish people enter the synagogue and respond *yehei shmei rabba*, Hashem nods his head and says, "Happy is the King who is praised so in His house. Pained is the Father who exiled His children, and woe to the children who were driven from their Father's table".

816. Why is it recited in Aramaic?

• Since Aramaic was spoken by the common people during the exile in Babylon, the *kaddish* was composed in this langauge so that everyone would understand it.

• Since angels do not understand Aramaic, this language was chosen in order not to arouse their jealousy when such a magnificent prayer is recited.

817. When is *kaddish* recited?

There are three types of *kaddish*:

- Half or whole *kaddish* recited by the chazan at the conclusion of various sections of the prayers.
- Mourner's *kaddish* recited in memory of a departed relative.
- *Kaddish de'rabbanan* recited after Torah study.

818. May a child recite *kaddish*?

The mourner's *kaddish* and *kaddish de'rabbanan* may be recited by a boy below bar mitzvah.

819. Is there a minimum age?

No. Even if the child cannot read the words fluently he may recite the *kaddish* with the assistance of an adult.

820. What is the significance of the mourner's *kaddish*?

When a mourner recites *kaddish* he redeems the soul of the departed relative from the torments of gehinnom. If the soul has entered *Gan Eden*, it is elevated to higher levels by the recital of *kaddish*.

821. What should the mourner think when reciting *kaddish*?

He should not think that he is reciting *kaddish* in order to protect or elevate the soul of the departed. Rather his only intention should be to sanctify the name of Hashem, and in this merit the departed soul will be rescued.

822. Can one *kaddish* serve as a merit for several departed souls?

Yes.

823. May several mourners recite *kaddish* together?

Ideally, only one mourner should recite each *kaddish*. However, in most communites, the custom is to permit all the mourners to recite *kaddish* together. Nevertheless, they must take great care to recite the words in unison, to enable the congregation to respond correctly at the appropriate places. It is grossly incorrect for the mourners to recite *kaddish* at different speeds, as this creates great confusion, and is far from a sanctification of Hashem's name, to say the least.

824. What if a mourner *davens* with a different *nusach* from the shul?

He must recite *kaddish* according to the *nusach* of the shul. See also question 90.

825. What if there are no mourners present?

The *kaddish* after *aleinu* and the *kaddish de'rabbanan* after *pitum haketores*, should be recited by one of the congregants who has lost a parent.

826. May *kaddish* be recited by one whose parents are alive?

• The chazan's *kaddish* and *kaddish de'rabbanan* may be recited.

• The mourner's *kaddish* may be recited only if he knows or thinks that his parents will not be upset.

However, the usual custom is that only the chazan's *kaddish* is recited by one whose parents are alive.

827. What is the significance of *kaddish de'rabbanan*?

The Sages enacted the recital of this *kaddish* following the public study of the oral Torah, and in particular the sections of *aggada*. So great is its recital, that according to the Sages, the world endures solely on the merit of *kedusha de'sidra* and the *kaddish de'rabbanan* (see question 793).

828. Should one bow when reciting *kaddish*?

• According to one opinion, he should bow slightly when saying the following words; *yisgadal, yehei shmei rabba, yisbarach, b'rich hu,* and the amen after *da'amiran be'alma.*
• According to another opinion, he should not bow at all.

829. Should one say *yisgadal veyiskadash* or *yisgadeil veyiskadeish*?

Either version is acceptable, but not a combination. One should take extra care to pronounce the word *yisgadal* correctly, so that it should not sound like *yiskadal.*

830. Should one take three steps back before saying *oseh shalom*?

Yes. The three steps should be taken in the same way as one does at the end of *shemoneh esrei* (see question 634).

831. Must the congregation stand when listening to *kaddish*?

According to the Ashkenazic custom, one should stand when listening to any *kaddish*.

832. May one continue to *daven* during *kaddish*?

This is usually forbidden. As soon as *kaddish* has begun, the congregation must be completely silent and should concentrate fully on the words of *kaddish*. All the more so, one must be extremely careful to avoid the grave sin of talking during the recital of *kaddish*. Some of the most fearful punishments are reserved for this serious transgression, ח"ו.

833. What if one is in the middle of a *b'racha*?

- If it is a short *b'racha*, he should conclude the *b'racha*.
- If it is a long *b'racha*, he should stop to listen to *kaddish*, and respond *amen yehei shmei rabba*, and the amen following *da'amiran be'alma* (see also question 277).

834. What if one is in the middle of *shemoneh esrei*?

He should stop and listen to *amen yehei shmei rabba* until *yisbarach*.

835. May one think about Torah topics during *kaddish*?

No, one must listen to the words with full attention.

836. May a man put away his tallis or *tefillin* during *kaddish*?

One must answer *amen yehei shmei rabba* with intense concentration. It is therefore improper to fold one's tallis or put away one's *tefillin* during *kaddish*, since this is likely to disturb one's concentration. This applies even more to one who is reciting *kaddish*.

837. Is it correct to shout the line *yehei shmei rabba*?

The Sages say that whoever responds to *yehei shmei rabba* with all his might abrogates evil decrees. This involves responding with one's full concentration on the meaning of the words, as well as raising one's voice. Nevertheless, a person should not shout in an exaggerated way, since this may cause others to sin by scorning him.

838. Must one say *yehei shmei rabba* in one breath?

This is not necessary. However, one should not pause during its recital until after the word *mevarach*. One should pause a little between amen and *yehei shmei*.

839. When responding to *yehei shmei rabba*, should one say the word *yisbarach*?

Some have the custom to say it, and some not. Although both customs are acceptable, one must be careful not to say *yisbarach* if he is in the middle of *davening* between *baruch she'amar* and *shemoneh esrei*.

840. What if a person hears the congregation saying *yehei shmei rabba* as he enters shul?

He should join them and respond *yehei shmei rabba*. He should not say the amen before *yehei shmei rabba* unless the congregation is saying amen and he is able to think about the previous phrase to which it refers.

841. If a man is learning Torah in the same room as a minyan, must he respond to *kaddish*?

Yes. (Compare questions 576 and 734).

842. If he is *davening* or studying Torah and overhears *kaddish* from another room, must he respond?

He may respond, but there is no obligation. (Compare question 735.)

843. If one is walking in the street and overhears *kaddish* from a nearby shul, must he respond?

He may respond, but there is no obligation. (Compare question 736.)

Chapter Twenty-five
Mincha

844. What is the importance of *mincha*?

The Sages say that a person should be especially careful with the *mincha* prayer. In the famous episode on Mount Carmel when *Eliyahu Hanavi* disputed the false prophets of the idol worshippers, his fervent prayers for success were accepted at the time of *mincha*. The time for *shacharis* is at the start of the day before a person begins his daily routine, and the time for *ma'ariv* is in the evening when he has completed all his activities. However, the time for *mincha* is in the middle of the day, when a person is deeply involved in his own affairs. When one breaks off from work and devotes some time to the service of Hashem, he is indeed worthy of great reward.

845. Are women obligated to *daven mincha*?

See question 8.

846. What is the correct time for *mincha*?

See questions 39-43.

847. Are there any restrictions on working before *mincha*?

- If a person usually *davens mincha* with a minyan at a fixed time, he may do any type of work beforehand.

- If he *davens mincha* with a minyan but at no fixed time, or sometimes *davens* alone, he may not begin certain types of work before *davening mincha*.

848. From what time does the restriction apply?

From halfway between *halachic* noon and sunset.

849. Which type of work is forbidden?

Any activity that tends to continue for a considerable length of time **or** which is difficult to break off in the middle. In extenuating circumstances, one may begin an activity that tends to continue if it is not difficult to break off in the middle.

850. What if the work cannot be postponed?

Another person should be appointed to remind him to *daven mincha* before sunset. The other person must not be occupied with this type of work (even if he has *davened mincha*), lest he too will forget to act as a reminder. An alarm clock may also be used.

851. May one shave or take a haircut before *mincha*?

Yes. Nowadays, this activity does not take long, and there is no concern that one may miss the time of *mincha*.

852. May one sleep before *mincha*?

Yes, but it is preferable to appoint someone to awaken him and remind him to *daven*.

853. May one study Torah before *mincha*?

There is no limitation before the time of *mincha ketana* (see question 42). After the time of *mincha ketana* the following laws apply:

• If he usually *davens mincha* with a minyan at a fixed time, he may study Torah beforehand.

• If he *davens mincha* with a minyan but at no fixed time, or he sometimes *davens* alone, he may not study Torah before *mincha*. He may study if he appoints someone to remind him to *daven*, sets an alarm clock as a reminder, or studies in shul where *mincha* will be held.

854. May one begin a journey before *mincha*?

This is permitted if all the following conditions are fulfilled:

• He will not forget to *daven*.

• He will be able to *daven* properly on the way or after arriving at his destination.

• He is not forfeiting *davening* with a minyan.

• According to some opinions, he must begin the journey before the time of *mincha ketana*.

855. Are there any restrictions on eating before *mincha*?

From *halachic* noon it is forbidden to begin a major festive meal before *davening mincha*. This includes a wedding, *sheva brachos*, *bris*, *pidyon haben*, and any similar occasions where there is a large gathering of people. Therefore, the assembly should organize a minyan to *daven mincha* before commencing such a meal.

856. What if an individual missed the minyan for *mincha*?

He may not partake of the meal unless he appoints someone to remind him after the meal to *daven mincha*. This other person must not be participating in the meal, lest he will forget to act as a reminder. An alarm clock may also be used.

857. Is a regular Shabbos or Yom Tov meal included in this category?

No, it is considered as a regular meal.

858. Are there any restrictions on eating a regular meal before *mincha*?

- If a person usually *davens mincha* with a minyan at a fixed time, the custom is to allow him to eat a regular meal beforehand. Nevertheless, it is praiseworthy not to do this from halfway between *halachic* noon and sunset unless he asks someone to remind him to *daven*.

- If he *davens mincha* with a minyan but not at a fixed time, or sometimes *davens* alone, he may not begin to eat a regular meal from halfway between noon and sunset unless he asks someone to remind him to *daven*.

859. What is considered to be a meal?

More than a *kebeitza* of bread or a large amount of *mezonos* foods (except rice). According to some opinions more than a *kebeitza* of baked *mezonos* foods (e.g. cake) is also considered to be a meal. Other foods and non-alcoholic drinks are permitted, even in large quantities.

860. Should one wash hands before *davening* *mincha*?

Yes, if water is easily accessible (see also question 168). A *b'racha* is not recited for this washing.

861. Does this apply if one was studying Torah prior to *mincha*?

Yes. Although it is assumed that one's hands are not *tamei* while studying Torah, there is nevertheless a requirement to wash them before *davening* (see question 160). However, if he washed his hands in preparation for *mincha* and spent some time studying Torah before the prayer commenced, he is not required to wash his hands again.

862. What if he washed his hands for a meal prior to *mincha*?

He must wash again for *mincha*.

863. Should one say any *tefillos* before *mincha*?

One should say, מודה אני לפניך ה' אלהי ואלהי אבותי שכשם שזיכתני לראות כשהחמה במזרח כך זכיתי לראותה במערב.
I thank You Hashem, my G-d and the G-d of my fathers, that just as You enabled me to see the sun in the east, so I have merited to see it in the west.
Some have the praiseworthy custom to say the *parshas hatamid*, and it is also praiseworthy to say *pitum haketores* if time allows. Nevertheless, if the recital of *korbanos* will prevent one from completing *shemoneh esrei* before sunset, he should begin *mincha* immediately. If necessary, even *ashrei* should be omitted in order to complete *mincha* before sunset.

864. Should *ashrei* be recited sitting or standing?

It should preferably be said sitting.

865. What if a man arrives a little late for *mincha* in shul?

If the congregation is about to begin *shemoneh esrei*, he should join them immediately for *shemoneh esrei*. After *mincha* he should recite *ashrei* as though he is reading Torah, but not with the intention of fulfilling an obligation.

866. May a minyan *daven* a "short *mincha*"?

Under normal circumstances a minyan should not *daven* a short *mincha*, but should *daven* as usual with a full repetition of the *shemoneh esrei*.

867. What if the repetition would overrun sunset?

• If the repetition can be completed no later than fifteen minutes before nightfall, they should *daven* a regular *mincha* with a complete repetition of *shemoneh esrei*.

• If the repetition cannot be completed within this time, they should *daven* a short *mincha*.

868. What is the procedure for a short *mincha*?

After the recital of *ashrei*, the chazan should say half-*kaddish* and begin to recite *shemoneh esrei* aloud. The congregation should listen to the chazan and join him for the recital of *kedusha*. After the words *ha'el hakadosh*, the chazan should continue *shemoneh esrei* silently, and the congregation should begin the silent *shemoneh esrei*. *Mincha* continues with *tachanun* as usual.

869. May one say *tachanun* after sunset?

Yes, *tachanun* should be said even after sunset. However, the custom in Yerushalayim is not to say it after sunset.

870. On which days is *tachanun* omitted?

- On all the days that it is omitted at *shacharis* (see question 775).
- At *mincha* that precedes all of these days, except for the *mincha* that precedes *erev* Rosh Hashanah, *erev* Yom Kippur, and *Pesach sheini*.

871. Should one skip *tachanun* to join the congregation for *aleinu*?

No. Therefore, if a person finishes *shemoneh esrei* as the congregation is about to say *aleinu*, he should not join them, but should recite *tachanun* first. (See also question 774.)

Chapter Twenty-six
Ma'ariv

872. Are women obligated to *daven ma'ariv*?

See question 13.

873. What is the correct time for *ma'ariv*?

See question 46.

874. Are there any restrictions on activities before *ma'ariv*?

Yes. The same restrictions that apply before *mincha* also apply before *ma'ariv*. This includes working, studying Torah, traveling, and eating (see chapter eleven). In addition, it is forbidden to sleep before *ma'ariv* (compare question 852).

875. From what time do the restrictions apply?

- The restrictions on working, traveling, eating, and sleeping begin from half-an-hour before nightfall.
- The restriction on studying Torah begins at nightfall.

876. Under what conditions may one engage in these activities?

If he appoints someone to remind him to *daven* (see also question 341), or sets an alarm clock as a reminder. It should be noted that having a fixed time to *daven ma'ariv* is not sufficient to permit eating beforehand (compare question 858).

877. What if one is too tired to *daven ma'ariv* properly?

He may sleep first, but he must appoint someone to awaken him and remind him to *daven*.

878. Is it sufficient to set an alarm clock to awaken him?

No. Even if he wakes up from the alarm, he may fall asleep again.

879. Are there any restrictions if one *davens ma'ariv* before nightfall?

A man who *davens ma'ariv* before nightfall (see question 47) must recite shema again after nightfall. Although no restrictions apply before this second recital of shema, it is correct to take care and recite shema as soon as it is night.

880. Should one wash hands before *davening ma'ariv*?

Yes, if water is easily available (see also question 168). A *b'racha* is not recited for this washing.

881. Does this apply if one was studying Torah prior to *ma'ariv*?

Yes. Although it is assumed that one's hands are not *tamei* while studying Torah, there is nevertheless a requirement to wash them before *davening* (see question 160). However, if he washed his hands in preparation for *ma'ariv* and spent some time studying Torah before the prayer commenced, he is not required to wash his hands again.

882. What if he washed his hands before *davening mincha*?

If he knows that his hands did not become *tamei* between *mincha* and *ma'ariv*, he is not required to wash them again.

883. Should one say any *tefillos* before *ma'ariv*?

One should say, יהי רצון מלפניך ה' אלהי ואלהי אבותי כשם שהייתי באפלה והוצאתני לאורה כן תוציאני מאפלה לאורה.

May it be Your will Hashem, my G-d and G-d of my fathers, that just as I was in darkness and You brought me into light, so may You bring me (again) from darkness into light.

884. What is the significance of *vehu rachum* at the beginning of *ma'ariv*?

In the times of the holy Temple, sacrifices were offered during the day to atone for people's sins. Since sacrifices cannot be brought at night, prayers are offered instead to ask Hashem for forgiveness for any sins committed during the day.

885. May one speak after responding to *barchu*?

No. Unfortunately, many people are ignorant about this, and do not realize that after responding to *barchu* one is considered to be in the middle of a *b'racha*.

886. What if the chazan recited *barchu* before one was able to say *vehu rachum*?

He should respond to *barchu* and say *vehu rachum* after *ma'ariv*.

887. What if one used the bathroom before *ma'ariv* but did not have time to say *asher yatzar* before *barchu*?

He should respond to *barchu*, but have the intention that this should not be considered as if he began *ma'ariv*. He should then recite *asher yatzar*, and continue with *ma'ariv*. If he did not have this intention, he must postpone reciting *asher yatzar* until after *shemoneh esrei*.

888. Should one respond to *barchu* if he did not hear the chazan?

• If he did not hear the chazan but heard the congregation responding, he should respond with them.

• If he did not hear the congregation responding but heard the chazan repeating the response, he may not respond with the chazan, but should say amen.

889. What if one missed *barchu*?

If he can easily join another minyan, he should do so. Unfortunately, many men are negligent about this, and do not realize the importance of responding to *barchu* at the start of *ma'ariv*. However, if it is difficult to find or wait for another minyan, he may begin *ma'ariv* immediately.

890. What if one arrived late for *ma'ariv*?

• He should make an effort to *daven* with a later minyan.

• If he cannot *daven* with a later minyan but is only slightly late, he should follow the instructions given in the next question.

• If he cannot *daven* with a later minyan and came considerably late, he should say the last verse of shema and begin *shemoneh esrei* with the minyan. He should then say the entire *ma'ariv*, except *shemoneh esrei*. In communities where *barchu* is repeated after *ma'ariv*, he should preferably begin the first *b'racha* of *ma'ariv* immediately after responding to *barchu*.

891. May one who arrived late omit part of *ma'ariv* in order to begin *shemoneh esrei* with the congregation?

• In *chutz la'aretz*, where the *b'racha baruch Hashem le'olam* is recited before *shemoneh esrei*, this *b'racha* should be omitted in order to begin *shemoneh esrei* with the congregation.

• In *Eretz Yisroel* where the *b'racha baruch Hashem le'olam* is not said (or in *chutz la'aretz* on days when it is omitted) one may not omit other parts of *ma'ariv* in order to begin *shemoneh esrei* with the congregation. Instead, one should follow the procedure outlined at the end of the previous question.

892. May one omit the verses *baruch Hashem le'olam* etc. and say the paragraph *yiru eineinu*?

No. The paragraph *yiru eineinu* may not be recited without the preceding verses *baruch Hashem le'olam*.

893. What if one is not late for *ma'ariv* but cannot keep up with the pace of the minyan?

In this situation too, effort should be made to begin *shemoneh esrei* with the congregation. The following options are available:

• Omit the *b'racha baruch Hashem le'olam*.

- Begin *ma'ariv* before the congregation, respond to *barchu* in the middle of *ma'ariv* (see question 291), and aim to reach *shemoneh esrei* with the congregation.
- Wait until the congregation reaches *shemoneh esrei*, begin *shemoneh esrei* with them, and say the rest of *ma'ariv* after *shemoneh esrei*. However, this should not be done on a regular basis.

894. Why do some people conclude the *b'racha* before shema with the chazan?

See question 528.

895. What important points should one remember when saying shema?

See questions 549-552.

896. Should shema be said standing or sitting?

It may be said either standing or sitting. However, if a person was previously standing, he may not sit to recite the evening shema (compare question 548).

897. What if one said the wrong conclusion to the *b'racha hashkiveinu*?

The *b'racha hashkiveinu* is concluded differently on Shabbos and Yom Tov than on weekdays. If a person said the wrong version and realized within a second, he should immediately correct himself. If more than a second passed, nothing needs to be done.

898. Should *baruch Hashem le'olam* be said standing or sitting?

It is preferable to sit.

899. May one announce to the congregation *ya'aleh veyavo, al hanissim*, etc. before *shemoneh esrei*?

Although such announcements are forbidden before *shemoneh esrei* of *shacharis*, they are permitted at *ma'ariv*. In some communities, the custom is not to announce such additions, but to bang on the table to remind people to make the appropriate changes. This is the custom in Yerushalayim.

900. May one say these words aloud during *shemoneh esrei* in order to remind others?

See question 606.

901. When may the chazan recite the *kaddish* after *shemoneh esrei*?

Strictly speaking, he may begin *kaddish* when nine other men have finished *shemoneh esrei*. However, it is preferable to wait until most of the congregation have finished, so that they can fulfill the mitzvah of responding to *kaddish*.

902. May he say *kaddish* with less than nine other men?

In extenuating circumstances, he may begin if eight other men have finished. According to some opinions, he may even begin if five other men have finished, since this constitutes the majority of a minyan.

Glossary

Aggada - Homiletical teachings of the Sages.

Aleph-beis - The Hebrew alphabet.

Amah (pl. *amos*) - Linear measure (approx. 50cm.).

Amos - The prophet Amos.

Arizal - Rabbi Yitzchak Luria (1534-1572), considered to be one of the greatest Kabbalists.

Aron kodesh - The holy ark, in which the Torah scrolls are kept.

Aseres yemei teshuva - Ten days of penitence.

Asher yatzar - *B'racha* recited after using the bathroom.

Ashkenaz - German or Polish Jewry.

Avraham Avinu - Abraham our patriarch.

Avudraham - Rabbi Dovid Avudraham. Commentator and *halachic* authority (14th century).

Ba'al koreh - The man who reads the Torah.

Bamidbar - The book of Numbers.

Bedieved - *Halachic* compromise in extenuating circumstances (lit. "after the fact").

Beis midrash - House of Torah study.

Beraisa - Statement of the Sages.

Bereishis - The book of Genesis.

Bima - Table upon which the Torah is placed when reading.

Birchos cohanim - The blessings given by the *cohanim*.

Birchos hatorah - The blessings on the Torah.

B'li neder - Without a vow.

Boker tov - Good morning.

B'racha (pl. *brachos*) - A blessing.

Bris - Circumcision.

Chanukah - One of the minor festivals.

Chazan - The man who leads the prayer service.

Chillul Hashem - Profanation of Hashem's name.

Chofetz Chaim - Rav Yisroel Meir HaCohen Kagan (1839-1933), *halachic* authority. See also *Mishna Brura*.

Chol hamoed - The intermediate days of the festival.

Chosson - Bridegroom.

Chovos Halevavos - Duties of the Heart. A classic ethical work (11th century).

Chuppah - Wedding ceremony.

Chutz la'aretz - The Diaspora.

Cohen (pl. *cohanim*) - Priest.

Cohen gadol - The high priest.

Daven - To pray.

Devarim - The book of Deuteronomy.

Dovid Hamelech - King David.

Eicha - The book of Lamentations.

Eliyahu Hanavi - Elijah the prophet.

Eretz Yisroel - The land of Israel.

Erev Pesach - The day before Pesach.

Erev Rosh Hashanah - The day before Rosh Hashanah.

Erev Yom Kippur - The day before Yom Kippur.

Gan Eden - The garden of Eden.

Geonim - Post-talmudic authorities (6th-11th century).

Halacha (pl. *halachos*) - Jewish law.

Hallel - Psalms of praise, recited on festive days.

Har Sinai - Mount Sinai.

Hashem - G-d.

Havdalah - Prayer recited at the conclusion of Shabbos and Yom Tov to divide between a holy day and a weekday.

Hoshana Rabba - The seventh day of the Succos holiday.

Isru chag - The day after Yom Tov.

Iyov - The book of Job.

Kaddish - Prayer that calls for the exultation of G-d.

Kallah - Bride.

Kebeitza - A volume measure (approx. 60ml.).

Kedusha - Section of repeated *shemoneh esrei*.

Ketores - Incense.

Kiddush - Sanctification of Shabbos and Yom Tov, usually recited over a cup of wine.

Kiddush levanah - Sanctification of the new moon.

Kol Bo - *Halachic* work by R. Aharon ben R. Jacob HaCohen of Narbonne, France (14th century).

Korbanos - Sacrifices.

Kosel Hama'aravi - The Western Wall.

Krias hatorah - The Torah reading.

Lag ba'omer - The 33rd day of the *Omer*.

Luchos - Stone tablets on which the Ten Commandments were written.

Lulav - Palm branch, taken on the Succos holiday.

Ma'ariv - The evening prayer service.

Magen Avraham - Rav Avraham HaLevi Gombiner (1637-1683), major *halachic* commentator on the *Shulchan Aruch*.

Maggid shiur - Torah lecturer.

Mechitza - A partition.

Melacha - Activity forbidden on Shabbos.

Melachim - The book of Kings.

Mezonos - Food (except bread) made from primary grains.

Mezuzah (pl. *mezuzos*) - Parchment scroll on which parts of the Torah (including the shema) are written. The scroll is affixed to the doorway of every room.

Mitzvah - Commandment.

Mincha - The afternoon prayer service.

Mincha gedola - Half an hour after *halachic* noon.

Mincha ketana - Two and a half *halachic* hours before sunset.

Minyan - A quorum of ten men required for congregational prayer.

Mishlei - The book of Proverbs.

Mishna Brura - The classic and accepted *halachic* work on the daily and holiday laws, written by Rav Yisroel Meir HaCohen Kagan (1839-1933).

Modeh ani - Thanksgiving said when awakening each morning.

Mohel - The man who performs the *bris*.

Moshe Rabbeinu - Moses our teacher.

Moshiach - The Messiah.

Motzai Shabbos - The evening after Shabbos.

Mussaf - The additional service, recited on Shabbos, Yom Tov, and *rosh chodesh*.

Nagel vasser - Ritual washing of the hands performed upon awakening.

Nusach - Text of prayer.

Pesach - Passover.

Pesach sheini - Minor holiday (14th of Iyar).

Pidyon haben - Redemption of the firstborn.

Plag hamincha - One and a quarter *halachic* hours before sunset.

Posek - *Halachic* authority.

Purim - One of the minor festivals.

Rambam - Maimonides, Rabbi Moshe son of Maimon (1135-1204), author of the first systematic codification of Jewish law. One of the greatest Torah authorities.

Ramban - Nachmanides, Rabbi Moshe son of Nachman (1194-1270). One of the greatest Torah authorities and commentators.

Rav (pl. *Rabbonim*) - Rabbi.

Rosh chodesh - The first day of the new month.

Rosh Hashanah - The first day(s) of the new year.

Sandek - The man who holds the baby at a *bris*.

Sefer - Jewish book.

Sefer Torah - Hand written scroll of the five books of Moses.

Selichos - Penitential prayers.

Sephard - Spanish or Eastern Jewry.

Seudas mitzvah - Meal eaten to celebrate a mitzvah, e.g. wedding, circumcision, redemption of the firstborn.

Shabbos - The Sabbath.

Shacharis - The morning prayer service.

Shalom - Hello.

Shavuos - Pentecost.

Shel rosh - Phylactery of the head.

Shel yad - Phylactery of the hand.

Shema - Prayer recited daily proclaiming the oneness of G-d.

Shemini Atzeres - The eighth day of the Succos holiday.

Shemoneh esrei - Supplication that forms a central part of formal prayer. On a weekday it contains 19 blessings.

Shemos - The book of Exodus.

Sheva brachos - Festive meal held in honor of *chosson* and *kallah*.

Shiur - Torah lesson.

Shlita - May he live long.

Shlomo Hamelech - King Solomon.

Shmuel - The book of Samuel.

Shofar - Ram's horn, blown on Rosh Hashanah.

Shtender - Podium.

Shulchan Aruch - Code of Jewish law.

Siddur - Prayer book.

Simchas Torah - The ninth day of the Succos holiday (in the diaspora).

Succos - Tabernacles.

Tachanun - Prayer recited after *shemoneh esrei*.

Tallis - Prayer shawl.

Tallis katan - Small four cornered garment.

Talmid chacham (pl. *Talmidei chachamim*) - Torah scholar.

Tamei - Unclean, spiritually or physically.

Tanach - The Bible.

Tefach (pl. *tefachim*) - Linear measure (approx. 8cm.)

Tefillah (pl. *tefillos*) - Prayer.

Tefillin - Phylacteries.

Tehillim - Psalms.

Tisha b'Av - The ninth of Av, day of mourning and fasting.

Tzaddik - Righteous person.

Tzitzis - Fringes attached to a man's tallis.

Vayikra - The book of Leviticus.

Viduy - Confession.

Vilna Gaon - Rabbi Eliyahu (1720-1797), genius of Vilna. Author of commentary on the *Shulchan Aruch* and leader of Eastern European Jewry.

Ya'akov Avinu - Jacob our patriarch.

Ya'aleh veyavo - Prayer added to *shemoneh esrei* on *rosh chodesh* and festivals.

Yahrzeit - Hebrew date on which a person passed away.

Yechezkel - The prophet Ezekiel.

Yehoshua - The prophet Joshua.

Yerushalayim - Jerusalem.

Yeshayahu - The prophet Isiah.

Yom Kippur - The Day of Atonement.

Yom Tov (pl. *Yomim Tovim*) - A festival.

Zohar - Kabbalistic work containing secrets of the Torah, authored by Rabbi Shimon bar Yochai.

Index

Hebrew Sources

פרק א - הקדמה

[1] עי׳ רש״י בראשית פרק מח פסוק יא ופירוש הר״ר שמשון רפאל הירש, חובות הלבבות שער חשבון הנפש פרק ג חשבון ט ד״ה וראוי לך אחי, דרך ה׳ ח״ד פ״ה סעיף א, ברכות ו/ב. [2] עי׳ מ״ב סי׳ ה סק״א, תענית ב/א ע״פ דברים יא:יג. [3] הקדמת אבודרהם, הליכות שלמה ח״א פ״ח ס״ק יא, ועיין ספר חסידים סימן תשפה. [4] סי׳ סב סעיף ב מ״ב סק״ג. ועיין ערוה״ש סי׳ קא סעיף ט שחלילה להתפלל בלשון אחר, ועיין שו״ת תשובות והנהגות ח״א סי׳ שנה מש״כ למעשה לבעל תשובה שאינו יודע לשון הקודש. [5] תענית ב/א, רמב״ם הל׳ תפילה ריש פרק א, רמב״ן ספר המצוות מצוה ה׳. [6] רמב״ם שם הל׳ ד׳-ו׳, פרק ב ה״א, פרק ג, מ״ב סי׳ קו סק״ד. [7] מ״ב שם. [8] מ״ב שם בשם שאגת אריה, אשי ישראל פ״ז סעיף ו-ז ובהערות שם, הליכות בת ישראל פ״ב סעיף א-ב וסק״ב, שו״ע סי׳ ע׳ סעיף א, מ״ב סי׳ ס״ו ס״ק יא, שו״ת מחזה אליהו סי׳ יט אות יד בשם החזו״א, מועדים וזמנים ח״ח סי׳ קמו בשם הגר״ח, ועיין גם בתשובות והנהגות ח״א סי׳ עד. [9] אשי ישראל פ״ז ס״ק סט, הליכות בת ישראל פ״ב סק״ב, הגריש״א והגרחפ״ש הובא ברגשי לב עמוד 87 הערה 20. [10] הליכות בת ישראל פ״ב סעיף ב, שו״ת מחזה אליהו סי׳ יט סעיף טו. [11] קובץ תשובות ח״א או״ח סי׳ יד שהן חייבות. ולגבי פרשת התמיד עיין שו״ת מחזה אליהו סי׳ יד שהביא כמה צדדים לפוטרם, ובאשי ישראל פ״ז סעי׳ ט שאינן נוהגות לאמרן. [12] מ״ב סי׳ קו סק״ד ונטיית לשונו משמע שהן חייבות, כף החיים סי׳ רפו אות ז, הליכות בת ישראל פ״ב סעיף כא. [13] מ״ב שם, תפלה כהלכתה פ״א סעיף יא. [14] ביה״ל סי׳ תכב סעיף ב ד״ה הלל, ומ״ש שמוסף עדיף, פשוט מכיון שי״א שחייבת. [15] מ״ב סי׳ ע סק״ו וסי׳ קו סק״ה, חינוך הבנים למצוות להגרי״י נויבירט סעיף כה ס״ק פח, הקטן והלכותיו פי״א סעיף א והערה ג. [16] מ״ב סי׳ סח סק״ד. [17] אגרות משה ח״ב סי׳ כד, הגריש״א הובא בתפלה כהלכתה פ״ד סעיף ב. [18] הליכות שלמה ח״א פ״ה ס״ק לז, תפלה כהלכתה שם סעיף ג בשם הסטייפלר והחזו״א. [19] הליכות שלמה שם. [20] אגרות משה או״ח ח״א סי׳ קנח, תפלה כהלכתה שם סעיף ב בשם הגריש״א, הליכות שלמה ח״א פ״א סעיף ז.

פרק ב - זמני התפילות

[21] סי׳ פט סעיף א, מ״ב סק״א. [22] שם וסק״ד. [23] סי׳ נח ס״ק יח, תפלה כהלכתה פ״ג סעיף ד והערה שם. [24] אשי ישראל פי״ג סק״כ ואבני ישפה פי״ד סעיף א בשם הגריש״א, תפלה כהלכתה פ״ג סעיף כט. ולגבי ללכת לביהכ״נ עיין ביה״ל סי׳ פט סעיף ג ד״ה וכן. [25] שו״ע שם ומ״ב סק״ה. [26] מ״ב סי׳ מו ס״ק לב. [27] סי׳ פט סעיף ח ומ״ב ס״ק לח, וכן שמענו מפי הגר״ח ובר. [28] מ״ב סי׳ פט סק״ו, ולגבי להתפלל בתורת נדבה

בשבת ויו"ט עיין מ"ב סי' קז סק"ה.   [29] לגבי ברכת ענ"י עי' מ"ב סי' ד
סק"א בס"ד. וה"ה שצריך לומר א-להי המתים פוטרת אותו, עיין סי' נב מ"ב סק"ט.
להיכנס לספק אם ברכת מחיה המתים פוטרת אותו, עיין סי' נב מ"ב סק"ט.
לגבי ברכות התורה עי' סי' נא סק"י. לגבי דילוג פסוד"ז הרי עדיף להתפלל
בזמן, כך שמענו מאת הגר"ז ובר. ואינו דומה למש"כ המ"ב סי' נב סק"ו
שאין לדלג פסוד"ז עבור תפלה בציבור.   [30] מ"ב סי' נב סק"ח, ועי' קצה"ש
סי' יד סעיף א לגבי השלמת חלקי התפילה של קודם ברוך שאמר אחר
התפילה, ולגבי השלמת חלקי פסוד"ז עי' חיי אדם כלל יט סעיף ה, ערוה"ש
סי' נב סעיף ד, ועי' בס' ארחות יושר עמ' צה שיש חיוב לאמרם אחרי
התפילה.   [31] כך שמענו מאת הגר"ץ ובר, והטעם כי בכל שאר חלקי
התפילה נחלקו הפוסקים אם נשים חייבות, ואע"פ שאנו מחמירים לחייבן
מ"מ תפלה בזמנה עדיף. ולגבי הפסוק האחרון שבקר"ש, עיין מקורות 37.
[32] הגרחפ"ש הובא ברגשי לב עמוד 148 סעיף 1, רגשי לב עמוד 157 סעיף
14, ולגבי עדיפות אמירת פסוד"ז קודם ברכות השחר עיין אשי ישראל פ"ז
ס"ק סג בשם הגרח"ק.   [33] מ"ב סי' ע סק"ב.   [34] פשוט, ולדאבוננו הרבה
נשים טועות בזה.   [35] מ"ב סי' נב סק"ח, ואינה יכולה לברך ברכת קר"ש
עד חצות כמו איש (עיין 522) שהיתר זה אינו נאמר אלא באונס לאיש שחייב
בהם - הגריש"א הובא ברגשי לב עמוד 159 הערה 29.   [36] הגרשז"א הובא
בהליכות ביתה פ"ה סעיף ה וסק"י, הגריש"א הובא ברגשי לב עמוד 159
הערה 29, ולגבי סוף זמן ברכות קר"ש עיין סי' נח סעיף ו, ומ"ב סי' סז סק"ג.
[37] כנ"ל. ומ"ש פסוק אחרון דשמע הוא כדי לסמוך גאולה לתפילה, וכעין
זה עי' הליכות שלמה ח"א פי"ג סק"כ.   [38] מבואר במ"ב סי' פט סק"ה
שעליו לסיים שמו"ע קודם סוף הזמן, וא"כ אין להתחיל באופן שיסיים אחרי
סוף הזמן. וכ"כ באבני ישפה פ"ח סעיף יג לא להתפלל. ויש שיטות שמותר
להתחיל, עיין בערוה"ש סי' קי סעיף ה ומשמע שמותר אפילו להתחיל בענייין
זה ועיין א"א בוטשאטש סי' רלב ד"ה עוד מצאתי, שערים מצויינים בהלכה
סימן יח קו"א סק"ב. ויש עוד כמה שיטות מובאות באשי ישראל פי"ג סק"ט
ובפסק"ת סי' רלג אות ז.   [39] סי' רלג סעיף א.   [40] רמ"א שם, מ"ב סק"ד,
שעה"צ סק"ח, לוח א"י.   [41] מ"ב סק"ב.   [42] מ"ב סק"א, שעה"צ סי' רלד
סק"א. ואף דמשמע בסי' רלג שאינו נוקט כמו הרא"ש לכתחילה אלא רק אם
יוצא לדרך וכו', בסי' רלד אינו נראה כן, ולכן סתמנו בפנים שזה לכתחילה
גמור.   [43] מ"ב סי' רלג ס"ק יד.   [44] שם, ועיין תפילה כהלכתה פ"ג סעיף
מה בשם הגריש"א שבא"י היינו 13 דקות אחרי השקיעה וי"א 10 דקות, דינים
והנהגות חזו"א פ"ח אות ה.   [45] מ"ב סי' רל"ג ס"ק יד, ועיין תשובות
והנהגות ח"א סי' פה בשם הגה"ץ רבי שמואל יוסף רבינוב שזה נאמר רק
באקראי אבל בקביעות מותר אחר השקיעה אם א"א בלא"ה. ובקונטרס
מבית לוי ניסן תשנ"ו (קובץ ט) עמוד נז כתב שעדיף להתפלל בציבור ולא
קודם השקיעה ביחידות.   [46] סי' רל"ה סעיף ג מ"ב ס"ק כו.   [47] סי' רל"ג

סעיף א, ומ״ב סק״ט וי״א, וסי׳ רל״ה סעיף א, וסי׳ רס״ז סעיף ב׳, שו״ת חלקת
יעקב חיו״ד סי׳ רלד.   [48]   מ״ב סימן רלג ס״ק יא, וסימן רסז סק״ג.   [49]
סימן רלה סעיף א, שעה״צ ס״ק טז, ועיין ביה״ל ד״ה ואם הציבור מקדימים
וכו׳ דעת הגר״א.   [50]   סימן רלה סעיף ג ומ״ב ס״ק כז.   [51]   עיין מ״ב סי׳
רלה ס״ק כז שהמתאחר בקריאת שמע אחרי חצות מקרי עובר על דברי
חכמים, ועיין סי׳ קח ס״ק טו דה״ה שמו״ע, אבני ישפה פי״א סעי׳ יא.   [52]
סי׳ רפו סעיף א.   [53]   רמ״א שם ומ״ב סק״ה.   [54]   סעיף א, ביה״ל ד״ה
יותר, מ״ב סי׳ תרכ סק״ב, מ״ב סי׳ רלג ס״ק יד לגבי מנחה ופשוט דה״ה מוסף.
ולגבי לגמור לפני שבע שעות כך שמענו מאת הגר״צ ובר. ולענין תפלת מוסף
אחר שקיעה מותר לאיש בשעת הדחק כמו במנחה, אבל אסור לאשה כי
בלא״ה יש ספק אם חייבת, כן שמענו מאת הגרמ״א לינדר.   [55]   עיין סי׳
רפו סעיף א שזמנה כל היום, ומסתבר שדינו כמנחה. ולגבי נשים עיין מ״ב
סי׳ קו סק״ד שיש מחלוקת אם נשים חייבות במוסף ולכן נראה שלא תתפלל
אחרי השקיעה. וכן שמענו מאת הרמ״א לינדר.   [56]   סי׳ רפו סעיף ד, ביה״ל
ד״ה עד.   [57]   שם ורמ״א.   [58]   כן נראה מסקנת המ״ב סי׳ רפו ס״ק יג,
ובלא״ה דבר זה מצוי יותר בנשים ונחלקו הפוסקים אם חייבות במוסף, עי׳
מ״ב סי׳ קו סק״ד. וכן פסק בשבט הלוי חלק י׳ סי׳ יז שאלה ה.

פרק ג - תפילת תשלומין (סי׳ קח)

[59]   סעיף א, ז.   [60]   ביה״ל ד״ה טעה, מ״ב סק״ב, סעיף ח.   [61]   מ״ב סי׳
קח סק״ב.   [62]   לגבי אשה שלא התפללה שחרית עיין אשי ישראל פ״ל
סק״ו בשם הגרי״י נויבירט, ואם לא התפללה מנחה עיין מ״ב סי׳ רסג ס״ק מג
שמתפללת מעריב שתים. ובספר הליכות בת ישראל פרק ב הערה נ מבואר
בשם הגרשז״א שאפילו אם לא רגילה להתפלל מעריב יכולה להתפלל
מעריב כדי לאפשר תפילת תשלומין, דהיינו שתתפלל שמו״ע של מעריב
פעמיים, אבל להתפלל מעריב פעם אחת אינו מועיל, ומשמע שאין חיוב בזה.
[63]   סעיף ד, שש״כ פמ״ג הערה קי.   [64]   הליכות בת ישראל במלואים
(עמוד שמב) לפרק ב סעיף כ בשם הגרשז״א.   [65]   הגרחפ״ש הובא ברגשי
לב עמוד 123 סעיף 17.   [66]   סעיף ו, מ״ב ס״ק טז.   [67]   סעיף ד, ה, מ״ב
ס״ק יט. ולגבי שבת ויו״ט עיין ס״ק לג.   [68]   מ״ב סי׳ קה סק״א, וסי׳ קח ס״ק
יב, יג.   [69]   שם וס״ק יא.   [70]   סק״ד, ולגבי מעריב עיין אשי ישראל פ״ל
סעיף יב בשם שו״ת ויען אברהם סי׳ יב.   [71]   סק״י, יא.   [72]   ס״ק טו. ולגבי
שבת ויו״ט עיין ס״ק לג.   [73]   שם.   [74]   סעיף א ומ״ב סק״ו.   [75]   שם,
ומ״ב ס״ק ז, ח.   [76]   ביה״ל ד״ה ואם.   [77]   סעיף ט ומ״ב ס״ק כה, סעיף י.
[78]   שם, ומ״ב ס״ק כח.   [79]   סעיף י.   [80]   כן מבואר בסעיף י ובמ״ב ס״ק
כט שאם היפך אינו יוצא אלא בדיעבד, שו״ת דברי חיים ח״ב יו״ד סו״ס סח.
[81]   מ״ב ס״ק כט.   [82]   סי׳ רסג סעיף טו.   [83]   מ״ב סי׳ קח ס״ק לה.   [84]
ס״ק לג, לד.   [85]   הליכות שלמה ח״א פ״ח הערה 82.

פרק ד - מקומות הראוים לתפילה

[86] סי׳ צ סעיף יח, חיי״א כלל יז סעיף א, ברכות ח/א.   [87] מ״ב ס״ק כח.
[88] שם, ועיין גם בערוה״ש סי׳ צ סעיף טו לגבי רוב עם בביכ״נ שמדברים
בשעת התפילה.   [89] מ״ב שם ס״ק נה. אמנם, עי׳ תפלה כהלכתה פ״ב ס״ק
לו בשם הגרשז״א שבזמנינו כמעט כל ביהכנ״ס דינו כביהמ״ד, אבל עיין
בחיי״א שם שמעלת ביהמ״ד היינו כשלומדים שם כל היום.   [90] מנח״י ח״ז
סי׳ ה, הליכות שלמה ח״א פ״ה סעיף כב-כג, וע״ע אג״מ או״ח ח״ב סי׳ כג
וח״ד סי׳ לג.   [91] ברכות ו/א, סי׳ צ סעיף ט ומ״ב ס״ק לג.   [92] הליכות
שלמה ח״א פ״ה סעיף יח, אבני ישפה פ״ו סעיף ח הערה 13 בשם הגריש״א.
[93] הליכות בת ישראל פ״ב סעיף כו, הגר״ש ברעוודה הובא ברגשי לב
עמוד 181 הערה 12.   [94] מ״ב סי׳ צח סק״ג.   [95] סי׳ צ סעיף יט, ברכות
ו/ב.   [96] הליכות שלמה ח״א פ״ה סק״ב.   [97] שם.   [98] סי׳ צח סעיף ד,
שפת אמת וצל״ח ברכות שם.   [99] תפלה כהלכתה פ״ב סעיף ד, מ״ב סי׳ צ
סק״ס.   [100] מ״ב ס״ק נט.   [101] שערים מצויינים בהלכה סי׳ יב קו״א
סעיף י.   [102] כה״ח סי׳ צ ס״ק קיח.   [103] סי׳ צ סעיף כא.   [104] סי׳ צח
סעיף ד, לבוש שם (וז״ל דוגמת הקרבן שחציצה פוסלת בינו לבין הכלי וביונו
לריצפה) ובלבוש סי׳ צ סעיף כא.   [105] סי׳ צ סעיף כא, מ״ב ס״ק סד, סו.
[106] שו״ע שם וברמ״א, סעיף כב, ועי׳ מ״ב ס״ק סט.   [107] מ״ב ס״ק סג.
[108] סעיף כג, מחה״ש ס״ק לז, ומ״ש בסוף שמותר לאחוז הסידור בפניו כן
נראה.   [109] מ״ב ס״ק עא.   [110] שם.   [111] סי׳ צ סעיף כ, אשי ישראל
פ״ט ס״ק סו, נקיות וכבוד בתפילה תשובה קצא.   [112] סי׳ צ סעיף ה, מ״ב
סק״י, יב, צי״א חי״ח סי׳ יח, א״א בוטשאטש ד״ה ונראה.   [113] מ״ב ס״ק יא.

פרק ה - מקומות שאסור להתפלל

[115] סי׳ עה , עו.   [116] סי׳ עה סעיף ד, סעיף א, מ״ב סק״ח, ולגבי אמירת
דברים שבקדושה עיין מ״ב סי׳ עו סק״ב.   [117] סעיף ד, מ״ב ס״ק כג, סק״ו,
חזו״א סי׳ טז סק״ח, הליכות בת ישראל פ״ד הערה ח.   [118] מ״ב סק״ג,
ביה״ל ד״ה טפח.   [119] מ״ב ס״ק כט, כה, א.   [120] סעיף ב, סק״ה, ועיין
אג״מ או״ח ח״א סי׳ מב שמיקל בשעת הדחק ע״פ דברי הערה״ש.   [121]
לגבי קר״ש ותפילה נגד ערוה עיין מ״ב ס״ק כו. לגבי קר״ש נגד טפח מגולה
עיין סק״ד (ואם היה רק ראיה ולא התכוון להסתכל א״צ לחזור לקרות שמע)
ושאר תפילות וברכות לומדים מזה מכ״ש. לגבי קר״ש בדיעבד נגד שערות
מגולות עיין מ״ב ס״ק טז שמתיר בדיעבד לגבי קול באשה ונראה דה״ה שער
שדומה לזה, ולגבי שאר תפילות סומכים על שיטת הערוה״ש סי׳ עה סעיף ז
ומשום חומר ברכה לבטלה.   [122] מ״ב ס״ק יז, ולגבי גיל י״א עיין אג״מ
או״ח ח״א סי׳ כו, וע״ע ואת הברכה פט״ז סעיף ו (עמוד 149) בשם הגרח״ק
שזה מגיל ז׳.   [123] סי׳ עו, עז, עט, ולגבי אמירת דברים שבקדושה עיין מ״ב
סי׳ עו סק״ב.   [124] סי׳ עו סעיף א.   [125] סי׳ עט סעיף א. ולגבי גיל ג׳

חדשים עיין בירור הלכה סי' פא.   [126] סי' עט סעיף ט מ"ב סק"ל-לא,
מהרש"ם ח"ב סו"ס לח, מנחת יצחק ח"ח סי' ט.   [127] סי' עו סעיף א ומ"ב
סק"ג.   [128] אשי ישראל פנ"ב סעיף יח.   [129] נקיות וכבוד בתפלה פ"ו
סעיף נג.   [130] סי' פז סעיף א, וזאת הברכה פט"ז סעיף ה, והיינו דוקא אם
עשוי מפלסטיק וכדו', וזה אורחא דמילתא.   [131] נקיות וכבוד בתפלה פ"ח
סעיף יד בשם הגר"ש ואוזר והגרנ"ק אסרו, ובזאת הברכה שם סעיף ו בשם
הגריש"א לאסור, ולאג"מ מותר.   [132] מ"ב סי' עט ס"ק כג.   [133] עיין סי'
עו סעיף ח וסי' פא סעיף ב ומ"ב שם.   [134] שע"ת סי' ד סק"ח.   [135]
אג"מ ח"א סי' לט.   [136] אג"מ ח"ה סי' יב סק"א.   [137] אג"מ ח"א סי' לא.
[138] אג"מ ח"ג סי' כה.   [139] סוף סי' צד, ומ"ב סק"ל.

פרק ו - הכנת הלבוש לתפילה

[140] שבת י/א, סי' צא סעיף ה ומ"ב סק"א, וסי' צח סעיף ד.   [141] סי' צא
סעיף ה ומ"ב ס"ק יב, וסי' עד ס"ק כד.   [142] עיין סי' צא סעיף ו שזה דרך
החכמים ותלמידיהם, ועיין כה"ח שם ס"ק כו דה"ה כל אדם, וכתב הגרח"ק
הובא באשי ישראל פ"י סעיף ג שיש בזה חיוב גמור.   [143] עיין הליכות
שלמה ח"א פ"ב ס"ק כג שאסור, ועיין ארחות רבינו ח"א שבת ס"ק קנ וח"ג
עמוד רז (ז) בשם החזו"א שהתיר, וכ"כ בנקיות וכבוד בתפלה פי"א ס"ק 4
בשם הגרח"ק.   [144] עיין במ"ב ס"ק יב, וכ"כ בסידור בית יעקב עמוד כב
בהנהגת הבוקר סדר לבישה ס"ק כא, ערוה"ש סי' צא סעיף ו שכתבו שיש
בזה חיוב, אבל היום שהרבה הולכים לפני אנשים חשובים בלי כובע, יש
מקום להקל.   [145] הליכות שלמה ח"א פ"ב סעיף טו, הגרי"י נויבירט הובא
באשי ישראל פ"י ס"ק טו, אבני ישפה פ"א הערה 8.   [146] תפלה כהלכתה
פ"ז ס"ק עח בשם הגריש"א, הגרחפ"ש הובא ברגשי לב עמוד 111 הערה 38.
[147] ערוה"ש סי' צא סעיף ו, הליכות שלמה ח"א פ"ב סעיף יח.   [148] עיין
מ"ב ס"ק יב שאוסר, ובהליכות שלמה שם מתיר, ומפרש דברי המ"ב לעניין
כפפות של פועלים.   [149] בהליכות שלמה שם כתב שיש להקל בימות
הגשמים כשהוא מהודק יפה לכובע, וכ"כ הגרשז"א הובא באשי ישראל
סק"כ, ושם בשם ר"ח קניבסקי שנכון להוציא הניילון.   [150] ערוה"ש סעיף
ה.   [151] מ"ב ס"ק יב.   [152] לקט הקמח החדש סי' צא סק"ח, אבני ישפה
פ"א הערה 9.   [153] מ"ב שם, אשי ישראל שם סעיף ו.   [154] ע"פ גמרא
שבת קיד/א "תנא דבי רבי ישמעאל לימדך תורה דרך ארץ בגדים שבישל
בהן קדירה לרבו אל ימזוג בהן כוס לרבו". וכן מבואר בסי' צח סעיף ד,
הליכות שלמה ח"א פ"ב סעיף טו, כה"ח שם ס"ק כט, לקט הקמח החדש סי'
צח סק"ו, ואבני ישפה שם. ולעניין סינר, עיין תפלה כהלכתה פ"ז הערה עט.
[155] מ"ב ס"ק יא.   [156] פשוט, שכן היה מקבל פני אדם גדול. וע"ע אשי
ישראל פ"י ס"ק יג, ותפלה כהלכתה פ"ז ס"ק עח שנכון ללבוש מעיל,
ולכאורה זה נראה משונה.   [157] מ"ב סי' צא סק"ב, ועי' אג"מ יו"ד ח"ג סי'
סח סוסק"ד שכתב "ובשעת הדחק מותר להתפלל כי אינו מעכב".   [158]

אבני ישפה פ״א סעיף ו.   [159] כן נראה מק״ו שאם תפלה בזמנה דוחה
תפלה בציבור ק״ו שדוחה לבוש מכובד.

פרק ז - הכנת הגוף לתפילה

[160] סי׳ צב סעיף ד, ה, מ״ב ס״ק כה.   [161] ברכות טו/א, פרישה סי׳ רלג
סק״ו, חיי״א ריש כלל ז.   [162] סי׳ רלג סעיף ב, ומ״ב ס״ק טו.   [163] שם
ס״ק טז, תשובות והנהגות ח״ג סי׳ ה.   [164] מ״ב סי׳ רלג ס״ק יח.   [165]
סי׳ צב סעיף ה, מ״ב סי׳ רלג ס״ק יח, יט.   [166] חיי״א כלל ז׳ סעיף ד,
תשובות והנהגות שם.   [167] חיי״א כלל ז׳ סעיף א, קשו״ע סי׳ יב סעיף ה.
[168] מ״ב סי׳ צב ס״ק כו, ולגבי בין האצבעות עיין סימן ד מ״ב ס״ק נז.
[169] סימן ב סעיף ו ומ״ב ס״ק יג, וסי׳ צב סעיף א ומ״ב סק״א.   [170] מ״ב
סי׳ צב סק״ה.   [171] שם.   [172] שם.   [173] שם.   [173] מבית לוי ניסן תשנ״ז (קובץ
יא) עמוד סו (ב).   [174] מ״ב סי׳ צב סק״ו, ז, הגרח״ק הובא באשי ישראל פ״י
ס״ק מז.   [175] סעיף ב, מ״ב סק״ט, וי״ב.   [176] שם סק״ט, ביה״ל שם ד״ה
קורא כדרכו, ודברי הגרח״ק לגביו באשי ישראל פ״י ס״ס סט.   [177] מ״ב
ס״ק יא.   [178] שם, ונראה שלא צריך לפסוע הג׳ פסיעות.   [179] שם. סי׳
קיד ס״ק כא.   [180] עיין מקורות 652.   [181] מ״ב סי׳ סו ס״ק כג.   [182]
ביה״ל ריש סי׳ צב.

פרק ח - תפלה בציבור

[183] סי׳ צ סעיף ט, מ״ב ס״ק נב, אג״מ או״ח ח״ב סי׳ כז וח״ג סי׳ ז. ולענ יין
נשים עיין מקורות 93.   [184] ברכות ח/א, יסוד ושורש העבודה שער ב פ״ז
בשם זוה״ק.   [185] אג״מ או״ח ח״ג סי׳ ז.   [186] סי׳ צ סעיף טז, מ״ב ס״ק
נב, שיעור מיל מבואר בסי׳ תנט סעיף ב ומ״ב ס״ק טו, ומיל עצמו כיותר
ממיל – מ״ב סי׳ צב ס״ק יט, אג״מ ח״ב סי׳ כז, ועיין אשי ישראל פ״ח ס״ק סט-
ע.   [187] הליכות שלמה ח״א פ״ה סעיף ד, שו״ת שבה״ל ח״ו סי׳ כא סק״ג,
ועיין שו״ת שבה״ל ח״ח סי׳ סח מעשה נורא במשפחה שנסעה לנופש במקום
שאין יהודים וטעו בחשבון בימים ושמרו שבת ביום ראשון.   [188] מ״ב סי׳
קי ס״ק יב.   [189] שו״ת רבבות אפרים ח״א סי׳ סו.   [190] שבת קכו/א,
תפלה כהלכתה פ״ח סעיף כג בשם הגרשז״א.   [191] תפלה כהלכתה פ״ח
סעיף כד, כה. וצ״ע במקום שיתבייש מחמת האיחור.   [192] רמ״א סי׳ צ
סעיף יח, ועיין אג״מ ח״ב סי׳ כז שמי שתורתו אומנתו היינו כרשב״י וחבריו
ולא שייך בזמננו, ועיין מ״ב סוס״ק כט.   [193] סי׳ נה סעיף א.   [194] מ״ב
סי׳ נה ס״ק מז, וסי׳ קכו סק״ב, שו״ת מנח״י ח״ג סי׳ סה, ועיין תפלה כהלכתה
פ״ח ס״ק קג בשם שו״ת דברי חיים שה״ה ההולך בלי כיסוי ראש ברה״ר
בשאט נפש (והיום רובם תינוקות שנשבו).   [195] מ״ב סי׳ נה ס״ק מו, אג״מ
ח״א סי׳ כג, ועיין אשי ישראל פט״ו ס״ק נב באריכות.   [196] מ״ב שם, וה״ה
כל שאר איסורים שעובר בשאט נפש.   [197] הליכות שלמה ח״א פ״ה סעיף
י, ועיין כה״ח ס״ק נח שנאמן דוקא אם נראה מיושב בדעתו ויר״ש.   [198]

סעיף ד, מ״ב ס״ק כד, הליכות שלמה ח״א פ״ה סעיף ט, ועיין אג״מ ח״ב סי׳ [199] יח שהקיל בשעה״ד לצרף ילד בן י״ב האוחז ס״ת, ועיי״ש עוד פרטים. [201] מ״ב קצשו״ע סי׳ טו סעיף ג. [200] סי׳ נה סעיף יג ומ״ב ס״ק מח. ס״ק נב, נח. [202] מ״ב ס״ק נב, ועיין שו״ת שבה״ל ח״ט סי׳ כ שאינו מצטרף בכל אופן דעז״נ נחשב לרשות אחרת לגמרי. [203] סעיף יד מ״ב ס״ק נב. [204] מ״ב ס״ק מח. [205] שו״ת מנח״י ח״ב סי׳ מד. [206] מ״ב סי׳ נב סק״א, ארחות יושר עמוד קא סעיף ב. [207] ברכות מז/ב, שו״ע סי׳ צ סעיף יד ועט״ז שם, חסד לאלפים סי׳ צ סק״ח. [208] סי׳ נב סעיף א ומ״ב סק״א, וסי׳ צ ס״ק כח. [209] מ״ב סי׳ נב סק״ב, ה, ו. [210] מ״ב סק״ז. [212] שע״ת סק״א, שלמת חיים (בני ברק תשנ״ה) סי׳ קכה. [213] סי׳ צ סעיף י, מ״ב סי׳ סו ס״ק לה, אג״מ או״ח ח״ג סי׳ ד. ועיין אבני ישפה פ״ו הערה 24 בשם הגריש״א שאינו נחשב תפלה בציבור אא״כ הציבור לא גמרו אבות. [214] סי׳ קט סעיף א ומ״ב סק״ב. [215] סי׳ קט סעיף ב, מ״ב ס״ק יג-יד, ועיין אג״מ ח״ג סי׳ ט. [216] אג״מ שם. ולגבי אם יאמר קדושה בקול עיין בארחות רבינו ח״א עמוד סא אות רד שהההחזו״א התיר בדוחק. [217] הגרח״ק הובא באשי ישראל פל״ג ס״ק יט. [218] מ״ב ס״ק יא. [219] פשוט. [220] הליכות שלמה ח״א פ״ח סעיף ס״ק סד, ועיין ציץ אליעזר חי״ג סי׳ נא (שמתיר לענות אמן גם אחרי ברכת באהבה). [221] פשוט. [222] דעת הגריש״א, הגר״ש ואזנר, הגרחפ״ש שהיא תדלג כדי להספיק תפלה בציבור. ודעת הגרשז״א, הרבב״א, והגר״מ שטרנבוך שלא תדלג כדי להספיק תפלה בציבור. וכ״ז באבני ישפה פט״ז סעיף ו, ורגשי לב פ״ז. [223] עיין מקורות 865. [224] סי׳ קט סעיף א, מ״ב ס״ק יד. [226] סי׳ צ סעיף ט. [227] תפלה כהלכתה פ״ח ס״ק טז בשם הגרשז״א והגריש״א. [228] פר״ח סי׳ צ סק״ט. [229] אבני ישפה פ״ו סעיף ז בשם הגריש״א. [230] עיין מקורות 91.

פרק ט - דיני שליח ציבור

[231] א״ר סי׳ נג סק״ה בשם אבודרהם, מ״ב סוף הסימן. [232] סי׳ נג סעיף ד, מ״ב ס״ק יב. [233] סעיף ו, מ״ב סי׳ קכו סק״ב. [234] שם, אשי ישראל פי״ד סק״ט, תפלה כהלכתה פכ״ו הערה מ*. [235] סי׳ נג סעיף יג, מ״ב סי׳ יח סק״ד. [236] מ״ב סי׳ יח סק״ד-ה, וסי׳ תקפא סק״ו. [237] סעיף טז, תשובות והנהגות ח״א סי׳ קיב. [238] ארחות רבינו ח״א עמוד מא אות קיד בשם החח״ח, ודלא כשו״ת אג״מ או״ח ח״ב סי׳ כט. [239] אג״מ או״ח ח״א סי׳ סה ואה״ע ח״ד סי׳ קח בס״ד, ועיין הליכות שלמה ח״א פ״ה סעיף כ. [240] מ״ב סוף הסימן. [241] פשוט, ועיין מ״ב סי׳ קכד ס״ק יג. [242] אג״מ או״ח ח״ב סי׳ כב. [243] סי׳ נג סעיף יא, מ״ב ס״ק לו. [244] שיח תפלה שער ז׳ סי׳ א סק״ו. [245] שיח תפלה שם סק״ח, שו״ע סי׳ סב סעיף ה, סי׳ סא סעיף ג ומ״ב סק״ח, מ״ב סי׳ קלב סק״ג. [246] עיין אשי ישראל פי״ז ס״ק פג באריכות, ושם בשם הגרח״ק שלסיים בלחש הוא מנהג יפה, מ״ב

סי' סו ס"ק לה, ועיין הליכות שלמה ח"א פ"ז הערה 62 שרש"ז עצמו נקט שנכון לסיים הברכה בקול. [247] סי' קכד סעיף ב ומ"ב סק"ד, אשי ישראל פכ"ד סעיף ט וסק"ל. [248] דרך החיים דיני שמו"ע סעיף סו הובא באשי ישראל פכ"ד ס"ק קנו. [249] הגרח"ק הובא באשי ישראל ס"ק קנה. [250] סי' קכב סעיף ה, אג"מ או"ח ח"ד סי' ע (ח). [251] הגרח"ק בשם החזו"א הובא באשי ישראל פכ"ט ס"ק סא, הליכות שלמה ח"א פ"ט סעיף א. [252] מ"ב סי' קיא סק"י, תפלה כהלכתה פי"ג ס"ק סג בשם הגריש"א. [253] סי' קכד סעיף ד. ולגבי להמתין עד רוב הציבור גמרו תפלתם עיין הליכות שלמה ח"א פ"ט סק"ב, הגרח"ק הובא באשי ישראל פכ"ד סעיף יא וס"ק מג, תפלה כהלכתה פי"ג ס"ק עא בשם שו"ת אז נדברו ח"ב סי' עט (ג). [254] שם מ"ב ס"ק יג, וסי' קד סק"א. [255] פשוט, ולא מצאתי מפורש. [256] מ"ב סי' קיא סק"י. [257] סי' קיא סעיף ב, ומ"ב שם. [258] מ"ב סי' קכד ס"ק לז, כב. [259] הליכות שלמה ח"א פ"ז הערה 62, אג"מ או"ח ח"ג סי' ד, ועיין שו"ת שבט הלוי ח"ט סי' רעו סק"ב. [260] ביה"ל סי' קכה סעיף א סד"ה אלא, אג"מ או"ח ח"ג סי' ד, ועיין שו"ת שבט הלוי הנ"ל שהש"ץ אומר קדושה ביחד עם הציבור בקול. [261] לקט הלכות שליח ציבור להגרי"א דינר פ"ד הל' י. [262] מ"ב סי' קכד ס"ק מא. [263] שם וסי' קכז סק"ג. [264] סי' קכט סעיף א, מ"ב סק"ח, סי' קכז סעיף ב, מ"ב ס"ק יב, ו. [265] מ"ב סי' קכז סק"ח, ועיין אשי ישראל פכ"ד ס"ק קמא בשם נמוקי או"ח סי' קכז דיפנה פניו בלא להשתחוות לאותו צד. [266] מ"ב ורמ"א סו"ס קכג. [267] סי' קכג סעיף ה, מ"ב ס"ק יח. [268] כה"ח סי' קכג ס"ק כח, קצוה"ש סי' כב סעיף יא, רמ"א סי' קכג סעיף ה. [269] מ"ב ס"ק יח, ומקור דבריו בפרישה סי' קכב סק"א ומוכח מיניה שדין זה תלוי בפסיעות.

פרק י - הפסקות בתפילה

[270] סי' סו סעיף ג, מ"ב ס"ק יח וסי' נא סק"ח. [271] חיי"א כלל כב סעיף א-ב. [272] פשוט. [273] חיי"א שם סעיף ב. [274] שו"ת שלמת חיים (בני ברק תשנ"ה) סי' סב, הליכות שלמה ח"א פ"ו סעיף יב. [275] מ"ב סי' סו סק"י. [276] חיי"א כלל ה סעיף יג. [277] שם. [278] מ"ב סי' נא סק"ח .ועיין גם במקורות הבאות. [279] שם, הליכות שלמה ח"א פ"ו סעיף יא וס"ק יד, ועיין אג"מ ח"ד סי' יד שמתיר לענות אמן של תתקבל ושל על ישראל, אבל עיין מ"ב סי' סו ס"ק יז שמשמע לא כן. [280] מ"ב סי' נא סק"ח, שונה הלכות סי' סה סעיף ט, הליכות שלמה ח"א פ"ו סעיף י וס"ק יג, הגרח"ק הובא באשי ישראל פ"כ ס"ק קכז. [281] הליכות שלמה ח"א פ"ו סעיף יא. [282] מ"ב סי' נא סק"ח. [283] מ"ב שם סק"י. [284] סי' נג סעיף ג מ"ב סק"ה. [285] מ"ב סי' נא סק"ב, שונה הלכות סעיף ד, אג"מ או"ח ח"ד סי' יג, ועיין ערוה"ש סעיף ג שכ' שצריך להתיישב למעשה אם מותר להפסיק בחלק הראשון, אבל נראה שמותר לענות בהוב"ש. [286] ביה"ל סי' נא סעיף ב ד"ה ב"ש, וסי' נד סק"ג, אג"מ שם. [287] מ"ב סי' נד

סק"ו, אג"מ או"ח ח"ב סוף סי' טז. [288] סי' סו סעיף ג ורמ"א, מ"ב ס"ק יז,
כ, אג"מ ח"ד סי' כא אות ב. [289] מ"ב סי' סו ס"ק כג. [290] סעיף ה.
[291] סעיף א, מ"ב ס"ק יא, סעיף ה, מ"ב ס"ק כח. [292] מ"ב סי' סה ס"ק
יא, כה"ח סק"ז. [293] מ"ב סי' סו ס"ק כג. [294] מ"ב סי' סו ס"ק כו.

פרק יא - דברים שאסורים לעשות לפני התפילה (סי' פט)

[297] סעיף ב, ג, ו. [298] ברכות יד/א , רש"י ומהרש"א שם, סעיף ב, מ"ב
סק"ט. [299] מ"ב סק"ח. [300] סעיף ב. [301] מ"ב ס"ק טו, טז, שו"ת
שלמת חיים (בני ברק תשנ"ה) סי' קי"ב-קי"ד, שו"ת תשובות והנהגות ח"א סי'
עא, ועי' מחה"ש סק"ט. [302] ס"ק יד, טז, ובתהלה לדוד סק"ב מבואר
שאפ' אם אמר מקצת ברכות סגי. [303] מ"ב ס"ק טז. [304] שו"ת אז
נדברו חי"ד סי' לד, ובשו"ת בצל החכמה ח"ה סי' ע מתיר להשכים לפתח
של הורים או חבר הנוסעים קודם שחרית ולברכם צאתכם לשלום. [305]
הגרי"י נויבירט הובא באשי ישראל פ"ג הערה לב. [306] סעיף ב ומ"ב ס"ק
יד. [307] במ"ב סק"י מבואר שנתינת יד אינו חמור כמו אמירת שלום,
ובלקט הקמח (החדש) ס"ק כב שדינו כמו בוקר טוב. [308] מג"א סי' תקנד
ס"ק כא, כה"ח סי' פט סק"כ. [309] כה"ח שם ס"ק יג. [310] מ"ב סי' צ
סק"מ, סי' פט ס"ק כב, ועיין כה"ח סי' פט ס"ק יב שמה טוב שלא לדבר דיבור
חול משייקץ עד שמתפלל. [311] מ"ב ס"ק יז ול"ז, וסי' מז ס"ק לא. [312]
סעיף ג, הליכות בת ישראל פ"ב סעיף ד סק"ב, מ"ב ס"ק לו. [313] ברכות
יד/א ורש"י שם. [314] רמ"א סעיף ג. [315] מ"ב ס"ק לו, תפלה כהלכתה
פ"ו ס"ק לח, רצ"ע אם מותר לקנות גם עוד דברים באותה הזדמנות. [316]
תפלה כהלכתה שם. [317] שם ס"ק לט, הגרחפ"ש הובא ברגשי לב עמוד
108 הערה 28. [318] כן שמענו מאת הגר"ח ובר. [319] הגרחפ"ש הובא
ברגשי לב עמוד 106 סעיף c10. [320] תפלה כהלכתה פ"ו ס"ק לו בשם
הגרש"זא. [321] שם. [322] שם. [323] שם פ"ו סעיף כג. [324] שם
סעיף כ, שו"ת שבט הלוי ח"ט סי' א (ב), אבל בהליכות שלמה ח"א פ"ב סעיף
ח כתב אפשר דמותר. [325] מ"ב ס"ק לו, הליכות שלמה ח"א פ"ב סעיף ז.
ועיין א"ר דכתב דלא עדיף משאר מלאכות, ועיין רמ"א סעיף ג. [326]
ברכות י/ב, מ"ב ס"ק כא. [327] מ"ב סי' פט ס"ק כז, כח, הגרשז"א הובא
בלב אברהם ח"ב עמוד כ. [328] מ"ב ס"ק כב, ובזה"ז לא שייך גאוה בחלב
וסוכר שכל העולם שותים כך, עיין דעת תורה סי' פט סעיף ג ד"ה אבל מים
מותר, וארחות רבינו ח"א עמ' נז אות קפא בשם הסטייפלר והגרשז"א,
ובתפלה כהלכתה פ"ו ס"ק כו בשם הגריש"א. [329] נלמד מדין חולה
שצריך להתפלל קצת אם צריך לאכול ולא די לו בשתייה, עיין מ"ב ס"ק כב.
[330] הגרחפ"ש והגר"מ שטרנבוך מובאים ברגשי לב עמוד 98, ואינם דומים
לתה רגיל משום שרוב אנשים אינם רגילים בהם. [331] אשי ישראל פי"ג
סעיף כז והערה עח ע"פ מ"ב ס"ק כב, ולגבי תפלה קודם האכילה עיין שש"כ
פ"מ סעיף מה, תשובות והנהגות ח"א סי' עג. [332] סעיף ד, מ"ב ס"ק כה,

[333] ביה"ל ד"ה וכן, ועיין ששה"כ ח"ב פנ"ב ס"ק מח שמסתפק בדבר. [334] הגרשז"א הובא בלב אברהם ח"ב עמוד כ, ס"ק כד, ערוה"ש סעיף כד. [335] פרמ"ג א"א סי' רפט סק"ד, כף החיים סי' רפו סעיף ל, הליכות בת ישראל פ"ב סעיף ד, הגר"מ הלברשטאם הובא ברגשי לב עמוד 101 הערה 11. ביה"ל סי' רפט ד"ה חובת, אג"מ או"ח ח"ב סי' כו ד"ה ובדבר הקידוש. וכן מבואר בהליכות בת ישראל פט"ו סעיף עג ובשש"כ פנ"ב סעיף יג. ועיי"ש בס"ק מה בשם הגרשז"א שיכולה לאכול אפילו פרוסת עוגה קודם תפילה בלי קדוש, משום חולשה. ועיין אג"מ או"ח ח"ד סי' קא שאשה משעובדת לבעלה לאכול דוקא עמו ולכן חייבת בקידוש כשחל החיוב עליו, ועיין ששה"כ פנ"ב ס"ק מו שהגרשז"א תמה עליו בזה. [336] ביה"ל שם ואג"מ או"ח סי' כו שם מחמירים, ועיין שו"ת חלקת יעקב או"ח סי' צב שמקיל. [337] מ"ב סי' קו סק"ה, מג"א ריש סי' רסט. [338] סי' פט סעיף ו, מ"ב ס"ק לא. [339] מ"ב שם. [340] ביה"ל סי' קו סעיף ב סד"ה מי, שו"ע סי' פט סעיף ו, לבוש שם. [341] מ"ב ס"ק לד. [342] תפלה כהלכתה פ"ו ס"ק יג. [343] כן משמע ממ"ב סי' פט ס"ק יט, וכ"כ אשי ישראל סעיף כג. [344] מ"ב סק"כ. [345] שם. [346] שם, וסי' צ סעיף יז ומ"ב שם ס"ק נג. [347] אשי ישראל פי"ג סעיף לא. [348] שם. [349] שם הערה צ בשם הגרשז"א. [350] שם. [351] שם.

פרק יב - דיני השכמת הבוקר

[352] קש"ע סי' א סעיף ב, מדרש תנחומא משפטים סי' טז. [353] תפלה כהלכתה פ"ט סעיף א, מ"ב סי' א סק"ח. [354] תפלה כהלכתה שם סעיף ג. [355] רבבות אפרים ח"א סי' לז סעיף ב, וע"ע הליכות שלמה ח"א פ"ב הערה 17. [356] כה"ח סי' מו סק"א. [357] מ"ב סי' א ס"ק ח. [358] סי' ד סעיף כג, מ"ב סק"ס, סא. [359] מ"ב סי' ד סק"א, ח. [360] סעיף י, מ"ב סק"י. [361] מ"ב ס"ק כב. [362] מ"ב סק"י, הליכות בת ישראל פ"א הערה כב. [363] מ"ב סי' א סק"ב, סי' קס ס"ק כג, ועיין אשי ישראל פ"ב סעיף ז וס"ק מא שיש מחמירים לכסות המים, סי' ד סעיף ג, ה, ז, מ"ב ס"ק יד, ב. [364] הגרשז"א הובא באשי ישראל פ"ב ס"ק עב. [365] סידור ווילנא עמוד יז בשם קיצור של"ה, ביה"ל ריש סי' א. [366] מ"ב סי' ד סק"ד, וסי' ו סק"ט, י, ורמ"א שם סעיף ב. [367] מ"ב סי' עד ס"ק כב. [368] סי' ד סעיף יד ברמ"א ומ"ב ס"ק לג, וסי' מז סעיף יג ומ"ב ס"ק לא. [369] רמ"א ריש סי' ד, מ"ב סי' ז סק"ו בס"ד. [370] רמ"א ריש סי' ד, מ"ב סק"ג. [371] מ"ב סי' מו סק"ג, כט, וסי' ו ס"ק יב. [372] מ"ב סי' מו ס"ק כד, שיח תפלה שער ב סי' ח אות ה. [373] רמ"א סי' מו סעיף ט, וע"ע מע"ר אות ח שיש לאומרם קודם קרבנות. [374] טור וב"ח סי' מז. [375] שם, ומ"ב סק"א, ב, י. [376] ערוה"ש סי' מז סק"ז, תשובות והנהגות ח"ב סי' לז, צי"א חט"ו סי' ב. [377] סי' מז סעיף ט ומ"ב ס"ק כא. [378] סעיף ב, ד, שע"ת סק"ב [לברך], מ"ב סק"ז. [379] סעיף ג, מ"ב סק"ד. [380] רמ"א סעיף ד. [381] מ"ב סי' מז

ס״ק כז, כח.   [382] בית ברוך על חיי אדם כלל ט בהגה״ה על ס״ק יא,
קצוה״ש סי׳ ה סעיף ח, לקט הקמח החדש סי׳ מז סק״ב.   [383] סי׳ מז סעיף
יד, ובהי״ל שם, הליכות בת ישראל פ״ב סעיף ו.   [384] כך שמענו מאת
הגרצ״ו כי לדעת הגר״א אין איסור.   [385] מ״ב סק״א.   [386] שע״ת סק״א.

פרק יג - טלית ותפילין

[388] באה״ט סי׳ יז סק״ד, תפלה כהלכתה פ״ז הערה קיט.   [389] סי׳ תקנה
סעיף א, רמ״א סי׳ יח סעיף א, צ״ע ביחיד המתפלל מוסף מאוחר ביום אם
לובש טלית.   [390] מ״ב סי׳ יד סוס״ק יא, ביה״ל סי׳ ח סעיף ט ד״ה קודם.
[391] מ״ב שם.   [392] מור וקציעה סי׳ כה ד״ה וכן נלע״ד יותר.   [393]
מ״ב סי׳ סו ס״ק טז, מ״ב סי׳ נג סק״ה, סי׳ נד ס״ק יב, יג, ועי׳ שו״ת שבט הלוי
ח״ג סי׳ טו סק״ז שתמה על מ״ש במ״ב סי׳ סו סוס״ק טז שמותר לברך על
טלית אף בין הפרקים אם מתבייש.   [394] סי׳ ח סעיף ב, מ״ב סק״ג, ד.
[395] שערי אפרים שער ג, סעיף יח.   [396] סי׳ יד מ״ב ס״ק יא, ביה״ל סעיף
ג סוף ד״ה שאלה בשם שערי אפרים ובאה״ט.   [397] מ״ב סי׳ יח סק״ה, וסי׳
תקפא סק״ו.   [398] עיין מקורות 396.   [399] סי׳ יח סעיף ג, תפלה
כהלכתה פ״ג סעיף ד והערה ט*.   [400] הליכות שלמה ח״א פ״ג סעיף יד.
[402] סי׳ לז סעיף א, מ״ב סק״א, ב, ג, ד.   [403] סי׳ כה סעיף יג, סי׳ לא
סעיף א, סי׳ תקנה סעיף א.   [404] סי׳ לא סעיף ב, מ״ב סק״ח, לוח א״י.
[405] אג״מ או״ח ח״ד סי׳ קה (ה), מנחת יצחק ח״ט סי׳ נד (א).   [406] ס׳ ל
סעיף א, ג.   [407] סי׳ כה סעיף א.   [408] שם, מ״ב סק״ג.   [409] רמ״א
שם.   [410] פשוט.   [411] מ״ב סי׳ סו סק״מ.   [412] שם, ועיין סי׳ נח סק״ה.
[413] סי׳ כה סעיף ט, י.   [414] ביה״ל שם ד״ה אם בשם ארה״ח, אג״מ ח״ב
סי׳ קי.   [415] סי׳ כה סעיף יג, ומ״ב ס״ק נו.   [416] מ״ב שם.

פרק יד - ברכות השחר (סי׳ מו)

[417] מג״א בהקדמתו ע״פ נתיב חיים שם, מ״ב בהקדמתו, יסוד ושורש
העבודה שער ב פ״י.   [418] כן נראה פשוט.   [419] א״ר סוס״ק טו, אלף
המגן (על מטה אפרים) סי׳ תקפד ס״ק יב-יג.   [420] מ״ב סק״א, וסי׳ ה סק״א.
[421] מ״ב סי׳ ע סק״ב, ערוה״ש סק״א.   [422] סי׳ מו סעיף ב, רמ״א סוס״י
נב ומ״ב סק״ט.   [423] סי׳ מז סעיף יג ומ״ב ס״ק לא.   [424] מ״ב סי׳ נב
סק״י.   [425] בספר בסתר רעם פ״ב סעיף ח כתב בשם הגריש״א שמוטב
לברך כל ברכות השבח בעמידה אם אפשר, ועיין אשי ישראל פ״ה ס״ק מח,
תפלה כהלכתה פ״ט סעיף מט, ועיין בספר שאלת רב (שו״ת מהגרח״ק עמוד
קמז מש״כ בזה).   [426] מ״ב סי׳ מו ס״ק כד.   [427] רמ״א סעיף ח, ומ״ב
ס״ק כה. ועיין רבבות אפרים ח״ג סי׳ מז אות ג שמי שטס באווירון יכול לברך
רוקע הארץ על המים.   [428] הליכות בת ישראל פ״ב סעיף ה, וכן משמעות
שו״ע סי׳ מו סעיף ד.   [429] עיין באשי ישראל פ״ה סעיף ז וס״י כא* כמה
שיטות בזה.   [430] סעיף א, מ״ב סק״ז.   [431] מ״ב סי׳ כה ס״ק יג.   [432]

סי' מו סוף סעיף א.   [433] מ"ב סק"כ.   [434] מ"ב שם וס"ק טז.   [435] מ"ב סק"כ.   [436] שם וסי' רט סק"ו.   [437] מ"ב סי' ה סק"א.   [438] חסד לאלפים סי' מז סעיף ח.   [440] טור סי' מו וגר"א סעיף ט, תשובות והנהגות ח"ב סי' לח.   [441] רמ"א בסוף הסימן ומ"ב ס"ק לא.   [442] ט"ז סק"ט, מעשה רב אות יא, דינים והנהגות להחזו"א פ"א אות י.   [443] ט"ז ומעשה רב שם.   [444] תענית כז/ב, ועי' יסוד ושורש העבודה שער ב פי"א שמפליג בחשיבות אמירתן.   [445] רמ"א ר"ס מ"ח, סי' א סעיף ט, ארחות יושר עמוד צה.   [446] ביה"ל סו"ס מז, הליכות בת ישראל פ"ב סעיף ז והערות שם.   [447] מ"ב סי' א ס"ק יט.   [448] מ"ב סי' מח סק"א, ארחות יושר עמוד קב (י). ועיין ערוה"ש סי' א סעיף כו שמחלק בין כהן, ללוי וישראל, ובדעת תורה סי' מח מחלק בין שחרית למנחה.   [449] מ"ב שם.   [450] ביה"ל סי' א סעיף ה ד"ה ופרשת, קצות השלחן סי' יד סעיף א, אבני ישפה פ"ט סעיף יב בשם הגריש"א.   [451] א"א בוטשאטש ריש סי' מח.   [452] אבני ישפה שם בשם הגריש"א, ועי' מ"ב סי' קלב ס"ק יד בשם של"ה.   [453] יסוד ושורש העבודה שער ב פי"א, הובא ג"כ בכה"ח סי' קלב ס"ק יח.   [454] סי' א סעיף ט, אבני ישפה פ"ט הערה 13*.   [455] רמ"א סי' קלב סעיף ב, מ"ב ס"ק יד.   [456] רמ"א שם ומ"ב ס"ק יז.   [457] סי' נ ומ"ב סק"ב.   [458] קצות השלחן פי"ד סעיף א.

פרק טו - דיני הניעור כל הלילה

[459] רמ"א סי' ד סעיף יג, מ"ב ס"ק לא.   [460] הגרשז"א במבקשי תורה סיון תשנ"ט סי' קסו (ד).   [461] מ"ב סי' ד סק"ג, ל, דיני הניעור כל הלילה (תשנ"ט) פ"ד הערה 18 בשם הגרח"ק.   [462] מ"ב סי' מו ס"ק כד, שיח תפלה שער ב סי' ח אות ה.   [463] מ"ב סי' מז ס"ק כח, ולענין חצי שעה עיין מקורות 467.   [464] שם.   [465] ס"ק יד.   [466] מ"ב סי' מו ס"ק כד, סוף סעיף א.   [467] לגבי ענט"י ואש"י עיין ביה"ל סי' ד סעיף יג ד"ה כל. לגבי ברכת אל"י והמעביר שינה עיין מ"ב סי' מו ס"ק כד. לגבי ברכות התורה עיין סי' מז ס"ק כח. ולענין זמן ס' נשמין עיין ביה"ל סי' ד סעיף טז שהביא כמה שיטות, ועיין קצשו"ע סי' ב סעיף ח שכתב חצי שעה וכן המנהג, ועיין אשי ישראל פ"ו ס"ק סו עוד מקורות.   [468] ארחות רבינו ח"ג עמ' רג (ז) בשם החזו"א, ועיין אשי ישראל הנ"ל בשם הגרח"ק שביאר דהיינו אפילו במטה.   [469] הליכות שלמה ח"א פ"ו סעיף א וסק"ב-ג, ועיין אשי ישראל הנ"ל.

פרק טז - פסוקי דזמרה

[471] טור סי' נא, סידור בית יעקב אולם ברוך שאמר (עמוד מה/ב) סק"א, לבוש סי' א סעיף ט, וסי' נד סעיף ג.   [472] מ"ב סי' ע סק"ב, קובץ תשובות ח"א סי' יד, תפלה כהלכתה פ"י סק"ד בשם הגרחפ"ש פוסקים שחייבות, אבל הגר"ז סעיף א, ערוה"ש סעיף א, ומחז"א סי' טו מסיקים שפטורות.   [473] מ"ב סי' נב סק"א.   [474] סי' נא סעיף ח, ומ"ב סק"כ. ועיין גר"ז סי' נג סעיף ג

שהוא חצי שעה (!). [475] סי' א סעיף ד, ערה"ש סי' נא סק"ט, אבני ישפה
פ"ט סעיף כז. [476] יסוד ושורש העבודה שער ג פ"ג, ערה"ש סי' נ סק"ד,
מעשה רב אות כו, ועי' אשי ישראל פט"ז ס"ק סד לענין דברים שאומרים
לפני ברוך שאמר. [477] סי' נא סעיף ז ברמ"א, מ"ב ס"ק יט, קש"ע סי' יד
סעיף ד. [478] באה"ט סי' צה סק"ג, ליקוטי מהרי"ח (המפואר, עמוד קב).
[479] סי' צו סעיף א, ב, מ"ב סק"א, ד, ועיין הליכות שלמה ח"א פ"ז סק"ד.
[480] סי' נא סעיף ד ומ"ב סק"ט. [481] שו"ת תשובות והנהגות ח"ב סי' מ.
[482] מ"ב סי' סו סק"י, מ"ב סי' נא סק"ד. [484] עיין מקורות 283. [485]
עיין מקורות 284. [486] מ"ב סי' נא סק"י. [487] מ"ב סי' נא סק"א,
אבודרהם (ברוך שאמר ופסוקי דזמרה). [488] רמ"א סי' נא סעיף ט, וסי'
תרסד סעיף א. [489] לקט הקמח החדש סי' נא ס"ק לט. [490] רבבות
אפרים ח"ח סי' סג, שיח תפלה שער ד סי' ב סעיף ז. [491] ברכות ד/ב,
מהרש"א שם, סי' נא סעיף ז, ועיין יביע אומר ח"ו סי' ה אות ו בעניין ג'
פעמים. [492] שו"ע שם. [493] מ"ב ס"ק טז, תפלה כהלכתה פ"י סעיף טז.
[494] טעמי המנהגים עמוד תקמח סעיף קעז. [495] סי' צב סעיף י, מ"ב
ס"ק לו. [496] רמב"ם הל' תפלה פ"ז הי"ג, מ"ב סי' נא ס"ק יז, כה"ח סק"מ,
מא, ובערוה"ש סי' נב סעיף א בשם הזוהר שנסמך לברכת קר"ש משום
חשיבותא, ולכן מקומו אחרי הכתובים ולא לפניהם, עיי"ש. [497] שיח
תפלה שם סעיף יד. [498] סי' נב סעיף א, תפלה כהלכתה פ"י סק"ד.
[499] כה"ח סק"א. [500] הגרש"א הובא באשי ישראל פט"ז ס"ק נב,
הגריש"א הובא באבני ישפה פ"ט סעיף לד. [501] מ"ב סק"ו, סי' נג סעיף ב
ומ"ב סק"ג. [502] סי' נב סעיף א, מ"ב סק"ד, ולגבי אז ישיר עיין א"ר סק"ב
שאינו נחשב מן הסדר, ובחיי"א כלל יט סעיף ה שהוא מן הסדר. [503]
כה"ח סק"ג. [504] מ"ב סק"ה, ולגבי רננו צדיקים לנוסח ספרד עיין קצות
השלחן סי' פג בדי השלחן סק"ב. [505] אג"מ או"ח ח"ב סי' טז. אמנם,
שמענו מאת הגר"י כגנוף שלדעת הרמב"ם פ"ז הי"ג מותר לומר אז ישיר
אחרי ישתבח, וצ"ע לדינא. [506] סימן נב סעיף א, חיי"א כלל יט, ה.
[507] יש פוסקים לברך ברכות השחר קודם פסוד"ז אפילו אם צריך לדלג -
הגריש"א, הגר"י קמינצקי, והגרשז"א, וכן שמענו מאת הגר"צ ובר, ודעת
הגרחפ"ש והגרח"ק שיכול לאומרם אח"כ ולא ידלג על פסוד"ז. עיין תפלה
כהלכתה פ"י ס"ק עג, אשי ישראל פט"ז ס"ק עב, הליכות שלמה ח"א פ"ו
סעיף ז. [508] סי' נג סעיף ב ביה"ל ד"ה אמר, ועי' שבה"ל ח"י סי' יז סק"ז
שכ' שא"י לברך ב"ש אם גמר כל ההללוקות ואם יש לו זמן יאמר שוב
הללוקה האחרון עם ב"ש. [509] הגרשז"א הובא באשי ישראל פט"ז סעיף
לה, הגרח"ק הובא שם ס"ק קד שיכול לומר ישתבח בברכות קר"ש בין
הפרקים. [510] אבני ישפה פ"ה סעיף ו בשם הגריש"א והגר"ש ואזנר,
אמנם שמענו שהגריש"א לא אמר כן. ועיין הליכות שלמה ח"א פ"ו סק"כ.
ועיין תשובות והנהגות ח"א סי' פט. ובשם הגרחפ"ש שמענו שיש לדלג אם

גמר ההללוקות. [511] ביה"ל סי' רפא, מ"ב סק"ב, שיח תפלה תשובה טו.
[512] מ"ב סי' נג סק"ט. [513] שם. [514] שיח תפלה שער א סי' י סעיף ג,
ועיין מ"ב סי' נד סק"ב. [515] סי' נד סעיף ג מ"ב סק"ד, ערוה"ש סי' נג
סק"ד.

פרק יז - שמע וברכותיה

[517] מ"ב סי' נז סק"ב. [518] כן מדווייק מהט"ז סי' קמו סק"א בס"ד.
[519] סי' קיג סעיף ג וביה"ל שם, וסעיף ז, קצשו"ע סי' יח סעיף יא. [520]
סי' נה סעיף א. [521] משנה ברכות יא/א. [522] סי' נח סעיף ו, מ"ב ס"ק
כו, וביה"ל שם. [523] לגבי ב' ברכות הראשונות פשוט שהן פטורות משום
שהן מצוות שהזמן גרמא ואין סיבה נוספת לחייבן. לגבי ברכת אמת ויציב
עיין מ"ב סי' ע סק"ב שהביא ב' דיעות, ועיין סי' קו סק"ד שסתם שהן חייבות.
וכ"כ בהליכות בת ישראל פ"ב סעיף ח, וקובץ תשובות חא"א סי' יד. [524]
הגרשז"א הובא בהליכות ביתה פ"ה סעיף ה וסק"י, הגריש"א הובא ברגשי
לב עמוד 159 הערה 29, ולגבי סוף זמן ברכות קר"ש עיין סי' נח סעיף ו, ומ"ב
סי' סז סק"ג. ואינה יכולה לברך ברכת קר"ש עד חצות כמו איש (עיין 522)
שהיתר זה לא נאמר אלא באונס לאיש שחייב בהם. [525] כן נראה פשוט.
ואח"כ מצאתיו בשיח תפלה שער יח סי' ב אות ט. [526] מחשש ברכה
לבטלה, אפשר לסמוך על השיטות שמותר לומר ברכת קר"ש עד חצות, וכן
שמענו מאת הגר"ץ ובר. [527] באה"ט סי' נט סק"א, כה"ח סק"ב וכתבו שם
למשמש, ולא לנשק אבל עיין קיצשו"ע סי' י סעיף יז שהיכן שממשמש גם
נושק. [528] מ"ב סי' נט ס"ק כה. [529] שם. [530] סי' נח סעיף א, ו,
מ"ב סק"ה, יא, ג, שיח תפלה שער ה סי' ב אות ב. [531] מ"ב סק"ד. [532]
אג"מ ח"א סי' כד. [533] מ"ב סי' מו ס"ק לא. [534] רע"א סי' מו על מג"א
ס"ק טז, ולעניין ברירה עיין מנחת שלמה חא"א סי' פ סד"ה ולכן נראה ברור.
[535] הליכות שלמה חא"א פ"ז סעיף יב. [536] מ"ב סי' מו ס"ק לב. [537]
סי' ע סעיף א. [538] א"א מבוטשאטש סי' ע הובא בהליכות בת ישראל פ"ב
סעיף י, שמענו מאת הגר"ץ ובר. [539] מ"ב סי' ע סק"ה, הליכות בת
ישראל שם הערה כג, הגרחפ"ש הובא ברגשי לב עמוד 136 ס"ק 35, ושם
בסעיף יד. [540] רמ"א סי' סא סעיף ג. [541] מ"ב שם סק"ו, ועיין מדרש
תנחומא פרשת קדושים אות ו שמביא הפסוק 'שמרני כאישון בת עין'.
[542] שע"ת סי' סא סק"ב והיינו כשהוא עומד בתוך קר"ש, ואם הוא עומד
אחרי הבוחר בעמו ישראל וכו' עיין אשי ישראל פ"כ ס"ק סה בשם ספר
החיים שישתוק ויכוון לש"ץ. [543] שם הערה סב, ופשוט. [544] סי' סא
סעיף ה. [545] מ"ב ס"ק יז, קונטרוס איש איטר דין יט. [546] שו"ת אז
נדברו חי"ב סי' נג. [547] סי' כד סעיף ב ומ"ב סק"ד, סי' סא סעיף כה
משמע רק ב' ציציותיו, ובשו"ת רדב"ז ח"ג ס' תקעא שצריך כל הציצית לפניו
בשעת קר"ש כדי לקיים וראיתם אותו, ובערוה"ש סי' ס' סעיף ט מביא ב'
דיעות, ועיין שם בסי' כד סעיף ד. [548] סי' סג סעיף א, ב. [549] סי' ס

סעיף ד, ה, מ״ב סק״י, יא, וסי׳ סא סעיף א ומ״ב סק״ג. ולא יכוון לשם מצוה
אחר שעבר זמנה מחשש בל תוסיף.　　[550]　סי׳ סג סעיף ד ומ״ב ס״ק יב.
[551]　דברים ו:ד וראשונים שם.　　[552]　כוונת שמות בסי׳ ה, ענין השגחה
פרטית בסידור הגר״א בפירוש אבני אליהו, ענין עדות באבודרהם הל׳ קריאת
שמע ד״ה והטעם, ענין עתיד לבא בערוה״ש סי׳ סא סעיף ד, ועי׳ יסוד ושורש
העבודה שער ד פ״ה.　　[553]　אג״מ או״ח ח״ה סי׳ ה סק״ב, הליכות שלמה
ח״א פ״ז סעיף ה.　　[554]　עיין א״ר סי׳ ה סק״ב שיכוין תחלה, ובהליכות
שלמה ח״א פ״א סעיף ד שיכול לכוין אח״כ, ומשמעות המ״ב סי׳ ס ס״ק יא
ושו״ע סי׳ סא סעיף ו שיכוין בשעת האמירה.　　[555]　סי׳ סא סעיף ו וד״מ
סק״ה.　　[556]　יסוד ושורש העבודה שער ד פרק ה, ארחות רבינו ח״א עמוד
נג אות קע.　　[557]　מ״ב סי׳ ס סק״י ושעה״צ סי׳ רלט סק״ב, ועיין שו״ת שבט
הלוי ח״י סו״ס טז שאם נזכר באמצע הפסוק יכוין שם וא״צ לחזור.　　[558]
מ״ב סי׳ סא ס״ק כב.　　[559]　מ״ב סי׳ סד סק״ז.　　[560]　עולת תמיד, עיין
תפלה.　　[561]　מ״ב סי׳ סא סק״ל, סי׳ תריט סעיף ב סק״ח.　　[562]　מ״ב סי׳ סג
ס״ק יב, ערוה״ש סי׳ סא סעיף ו, ועיין ביה״ל סי׳ סא סעיף יג ד״ה אחר.
ומש״כ במ״ב הנ״ל צ״ל דמיירי שעדיין לא התחיל ואהבת, ודו״ק.　　[563]　סי׳
סא סעיף א, ב, יז, כ, כא, מ״ב סק״ד, ועיין יסוד ושורש העבודה שער ד פ״ז
רשימה שלמה של דקדוקים בקר״ש.　　[564]　סי׳ סג סעיף ו, מ״ב ס״ק יז, יח.
[565]　מ״ב סי׳ קד סק״א, ונראה דה״ה פרשה ראשונה של קר״ש, עיין סי׳ סג
סעיף ו.　　[566]　תשובות והנהגות ח״א סי׳ סא, הגרח״ק הובא באשי ישראל
פ״כ ס״ק פג.　　[567]　עיין בשו״ת שלמת חיים (בני ברק תשנ״ה) סי׳ סא
שחייב לעמוד אפילו בפרשה ראשונה, שזה בכלל קבלת עול מלכות שמים,
ובשו״ת אז נדברו ח״ב סי׳ ד שאין לקום בפרשה ראשונה, ובציץ אליעזר חי״ד
סי׳ י שאין לעמוד בשעה שעסוק במצוה דאורייתא, ומשמע בזמן שקורא א׳
מהג׳ פרשיות אבל בין הפרקים לכאו׳ מותר לעמוד, וכן מבואר בשו״ת שבט
הלוי ח״ו סי׳ קמו שחייב לעמוד בין הפרשיות, וע״פ השיטות אלו כתבנו
פשרה בין השיטות.　　[569]　סי׳ סד סעיף ב.　　[570]　סי׳ סד סעיף ג.　　[571]
סי׳ סד סעיף ב ומ״ב סק״ו.　　[572]　סי׳ סא סעיף כה ומ״ב ס״ק לט, קצשו״ע
סי׳ י סעיף יז.　　[573]　סי׳ כד סעיף ד, קצשו״ע סי׳ יז סעיף ז.　　[574]　מ״ב שם
סק״ד.　　[575]　עיין מקורות 280, 292.　　[576]　סי׳ סה סעיף ב, ג, מ״ב סק״י,
ערוה״ש סק״ז.

פרק יח - שמונה עשרה

[577]　מ״ב סי׳ צה סק״ג, קצשו״ע סי׳ יח סעיף ב.　　[578]　מ״ב שם, קצשו״ע
שם, תפלה כהלכתה פי״ב סעיף ג בשם הגרחפ״ש.　　[579]　מ״ב סי׳ קכג ס״ק
יג, ועיין מ״ב סי׳ ב סק״ה.　　[580]　קצשו״ע סי׳ יח סעיף ב, ועיין מ״ב סי׳ סו
ס״ק לח דמשמע שלא יפסיע אחר גאל ישראל, ובתהלה לדוד סי׳ קיא סעיף
א מבואר שהג׳ פסיעות אחרי גאל ישראל לא נחשבים הפסק. מ״ב סי׳ קיא
סק״א.　　[581]　לפי הביה״ל סי׳ קכג סעיף ג ד״ה כשפוסע ע״פ דברי המג״א

[582] הובא במ"ב ס"ק יג, וכאן שמתקרב לתפלה צריך לעקור ימינו ראשון. [583] מ"ב ס"ק יד, ערוה"ש סי' קכג סעיף ה. [584] שלחן שלמה (לרש"ז אב"ד דמיר) סי' קכג סעיף ב. [585] סי' סו סעיף ז, מ"ב ס"ק לה, ועיין אשי ישראל פי"ז ס"ק פג שהביא כמה שיטות בזה לכאן ולכאן. [586] סי' סו סעיף ט, ברכות ד/ב ורבינו יונה (דף ב/ב בדפי הרי"ף ד"ה איזהו), מ"ב סי' קיא סק"ב. [587] שם. [588] רמ"א סי' קיא סעיף א, מ"ב סק"ח-ט. [589] כן שמענו מאת הגר"ח ובר, ועיין תפלה כהלכתה פי"ב סק"נ שחילק בין יום חול לשבת. [590] סי' צד סעיף א, מ"ב סק"ג. [591] סעיף ג. [592] מ"ב שם, ערה"ש ס"ק יג. [594] סי' צד סעיף ח, מ"ב ס"ק כב, כג, כד, שו"ת שבה"ל ח"י סי' יט (א). [595] מ"ב סי' צה סק"ב. [596] סי' צח סעיף א. חובות הלבבות שער חשבון הנפש פרק ג. [597] סי' צד סעיף א ומ"ב סק"ג, סי' צח סעיף א ברמ"א, סעיף ג, ה, מ"ב סק"ה, סי' צג סעיף ב, ג. [598] סי' קא סעיף א, מ"ב סק"ג, ביה"ל ד"ה ואם, תשובות והנהגות ח"ג סי' לו. [599] רמ"א שם, מ"ב סק"ד, לענין חזרה במחשבה עיין אשי ישראל פי"א ס"ק יח בשם החזו"א, ולענין כונה במודים עיי"ש ס"ק טו ועיין מ"ב סק"ב, ועיין בהליכות שלמה ח"א פ"ח סעיף ט שהביא ב' העיצות. [600] הליכות שלמה שם סעיף ח. [601] שם. [602] סי' קא סעיף ב, ומ"ב סק"ו. [603] מ"ב שם. [604] מ"ב סק"ה, ביה"ל ד"ה בלבו. [605] סעיף ב, מ"ב סק"ט. [606] דינים והנהגות מהחזו"א פ"ד ס"ק כד, וע"ע כה"ח סי' רלו ס"ק יז. [607] אלף המגן סי' תקפב ס"ק מג לגבי תפלה בר"ה שיש מתירים להגביה קולו בשמו"ע שכן עונין, עיי"ש, שו"ת שבט הלוי ח"ג סי' טו (א). [608] מ"ב סי' צה סק"ה. [609] סי' קיג סעיף א. [610] מ"ב ס"ק יב. [611] סעיף ד, ה, מ"ב סק"י. [612] סעיף ו. [613] קצשו"ע סי' יח סעיף יא. [614] סעיף ו. [615] סעיף ה. [616] סעיף א, ב, סי' תקפב סעיף ד ומ"ב שם, אלף המגן ס"ק כז, ועיין במעשה רב אות רג שכתב שמתפללין מעומד ולא בכריעה. [617] סי' קיב סעיף א, סי' קיט סעיף א. [618] סי' קיט מ"ב סק"ז, י. ובסק"ג מבואר לכו"ע שאסור להוסיף בתחילת הברכה ומה נחשב אמצע הברכה. [619] סק"א. [620] מ"ב סי' קכב סק"ח. [621] שם, סידור בית יעקב (תחנונים שונים אחר התפילה סק"ב). [622] הליכות שלמה ח"א פ"ח ס"ק 60. [623] עיין אריכות בזה באשי ישראל פכ"ג הערה קפח-קפט. [624] שם, הליכות שלמה שם סעיף יז. [625] הליכות שלמה שם ס"ק 60. [626] שם. [627] סי' קיז סעיף א, ועיין בבית יוסף בשם אבודרהם שיום ששים יבוא בכ"ב מנובמברי אם היה אותו פיברי"ר מכ"ח יום אבל אם היה פיברי"ר מכ"ט יום תהיה השאלה בכ"ג נובמברי, עיי"ש עוד. ובהגהות והערות לטור מכון ירושלים אות ב כתב "התאריכים הכתובים באבודרהם הם לפי מנין הנוצרים בזמנו. אולם בשנת שמ"ג שינו חכמי הנוצרים ברומא את סדר חשבון השנים שלהם". ועיי"ש עוד שחשבון זה רק עד שנת אלפיים ומאה למספרם, שאז יתקדם שוב ביום אחד. [628] מ"ב סי' קיט סק"ד.

[629] מ"ב סי' קכב סק"ג, ז. [630] שם סק"ח. [631] קצשו"ע סי' יח סעיף טו, רש"י מיכה פרק ו פסוק ט. [632] שיח תפלה שער ו סי' ה אות ה. [633] סי' קכג סעיף א, מ"ב סק"ג. [634] סעיף א, ג, מ"ב ס"ק יג. [635] מ"ב שם, ביה"ל ד"ה כשפוסע. [637] סי' קב סעיף ה. [638] סי' קכג סעיף א, מ"ב סק"ה. [639] סי' קכג סעיף ב, הליכות שלמה ח"א פי"א סעיף יב, ועיין מ"ב ס"ק יא בשם ב"ח ומג"א איך ישער הזמן, ושמענו מאת הגר"צ ובר שזה שיטה תמוה ולא קיי"ל הכי. [640] מ"ב סק"י. [641] מבקשי תורה סיון תשנ"ה סי' קסג במכתבי הגרשז"א. [642] מ"ב סק"ח. [643] מ"ב סק"ט. [644] מ"ב סי' ב סק"ה. [645] כך כתב הגרח"ק לשואל שהאיר. [646] מ"ב סי' נא סק"ט, הגרח"ק הובא באשי ישראל פכ"ג סעיף ע וס"ק רמה. אבל אסור לומר תהילים במוסף דראש השנה ביום חול משום הפסק בתקיעות (עיין ספרנו להלכות ימים נוראים שאלה 85).

פרק יט - הפסק בשמונה עשרה

[647] סי' קד סעיף א, ב, מ"ב סק"א, סי' צז סעיף א. [648] סי' קד סעיף ב, ג, ד, מ"ב סק"י. [649] לא מצאתי מפורש, אבל כן משמע מסתימת הדברים שאינו מסיים שמו"ע, עיין סעיף ב. [650] סעיף ה, מ"ב ס"ק טז. [651] תפלה כהלכתה פי"ב סעיף פו בשם הגריש"א. [652] עיין מקורות 660 וה"ה כאן. [653] תפלה כהלכתה שם. [654] מ"ב סי' קד סק"א. [655] לקט הקמח החדש סי' קד סק"ב. [656] שם בשם החזו"א. [657] חנוך לנער פי"א סק"י, ועיין אשי ישראל פל"ב ס"ק מה בשם הגרי"י נויבירט דמסתבר שרק בין ברכה לברכה שרי. [658] תפלה כהלכתה פי"ב סעיף פט בשם אבני ישפה פ"ז סעיף י-יא. [659] מ"ב סי' צו סק"ז, שו"ת באר משה ח"ג סי' יג. [660] מ"ב סי' קד סק"ב, ולענין לחזור למקומו דעת הגר"י נויבירט הובא באשי ישראל פל"ב סק"ב שצריך לחזור, וכן שמענו מאת הגר"צ ובר שהביא אותה ראיה. [661] מ"ב שם. [662] פשוט. [663] מ"ב סי' צו סק"ז [ואינו מבואר שם היתר הליכה]. [664] סי' צז סעיף ד ומ"ב ס"ק יג, יד, טז. [665] סי' צז סעיף א, מ"ב סק"א, ובתפארת שמואל על הרא"ש ברכות פ"ט ס"ק לט דה"ה כשאין אדם רואהו, משום כבוד שמים. ועיין אשי ישראל פל"ב סעיף ט שכתב ליתן ידו בשניהם, ולא דק. [667] סי' קד סעיף ז, ערוה"ש סעיף יג. [668] הליכות שלמה ח"א פ"ח סעיף לח. [669] כה"ח סי' קד סק"י לו, וכן משמע באג"מ ח"ג סי' ה ד"ה ובאחד שעומד. [670] מ"ב סי' קד סק"י כז. [671] ערוה"ש סעיף יג. [672] סי' קט סעיף א. [673] שם. [674] אגרות משה או"ח ח"ד סי' כא סוסק"ב, הגרשז"א הובא באשי ישראל פל"ב ס"ק נה. [675] רמ"א סו"ס קח, מ"ב סי' קד ס"ק כה. [676] הגרשז"א הובא במבקשי תורה סיון תשנ"ה סי' קסו אות סו. [677] רמ"א סי' קד סעיף ז. [678] מ"ב סי' צז סק"ג. [679] סי' קכב סעיף א, מ"ב סק"ב, ד. [680] סי' קכב סעיף א, מ"ב סק"ה, ו, הגרח"ק הובא באשי ישראל פל"ב ס"ק עג*. [681] מ"ב סי' קד ס"ק כט. [682] הגר"י נויבירט הובא

באשי ישראל פל"ב סק"ה.   [683] מ"ב סי' קכב סק"ד. ולענין תהילים כן דעת הגרשז"א הובא במבקשי תורה סיון תשנ"ה סי' קסו (נד). ולענין דיבור בתורה, עיין בכתר ראש (בסידור הגר"א) אות לג להתיר, ומ"ש באשי ישראל פל"ב ס"ק עג בשם החזו"א לאסור, שמענו מאת הגר"ח ובר בשם הסטייפלר שזו חומרא.

פרק כ - טעויות בשמונה עשרה

[684] פשוט.   [685] ביה"ל סי' קיא סעיף ב.   [686] סי' קיט סעיף ג, מ"ב ס"ק טו, וסי' קיד ס"ק לד.   [687] תהל"ד סי' קכד סעיף ו.   [688] מ"ב סי' קיט ס"ק יד, ביה"ל סי' קיז סעיף ה ד"ה אם לא.   [689] סי' קיט סעיף ג, ביה"ל ד"ה אם דילג, מ"ב סי' קיד ס"ק לד, סי' תקצב סק"ז.   [690] בספר תפלה כהלכתה פי"ב סעיף צז ובספר אשי ישראל פל"א סעיף ב נקטו כמו החיי"א כלל כד כד ס"ק כא שאין צריך לחזור על הברכה שמסתפק שמא אמרו, אלא דוקא על מה שודאי לא אמר. אבל דעת הגרי"י קניבסקי (קהלות יעקב סי' יג), וכן הסכים החזו"א (ארחות רבינו ח"ג עמוד רז אות י) הובא במקורות שם ושם, שצריך לחזור אפילו על מה שמסתפק אם אמרו, וכן הגרי"ש"א הביא ראיה לזה.   [691] סי' קז סעיף א, תפלה כהלכתה פ"א ס"ק עה.   [692] מ"ב וביה"ל סי' סו"ס קכו, אג"מ או"ח ח"ד סי' יח.   [693] ביה"ל שם.   [694] ביה"ל סי' קיד ס"ק אין, מ"ב ס"ק כט, סעיף ה ס"ק כז, ס"ק לב, סעיף ו, מ"ב סק"ל-לא, סעיף ה-ו, ועיין אג"מ או"ח ח"ד סי' צג שס"ל שלא יאמר למדני חוקיך אלא יסיים הברכה ויאמר שם משיב הרוח.   [695] סעיף ג, כה"ח ס"ק כו, סעיף ד, חיי"א כלל כד סעיף ו (ועיין מ"ב ס"ק לב, סעיף ד מ"ב ס"ק כא). ואם נזכר תכ"ד נחלקו בזה הגרשז"א והגרי"ש"א אם יכול לתקן מיד – עיין אשי ישראל פכ"ג ס"ק קח.   [696] סי' קיד סעיף ח, מ"ב ס"ק לו, לז.   [697] מ"ב שם ס"ק לח.   [698] סי' קיז סעיף ד, ה, מ"ב ס"ק טו, יח, יט.   [699] סעיף ג, מ"ב ס"ק יד, ביה"ל ד"ה אם, חיי"א כלל כד סעיף יד.   [700] סי' קיז סעיף א, הגהות רע"א סעיף ג, תהל"ד סק"ב, הליכות שלמה ח"א פ"ח סעיף יח.   [702] סי' תכב סעיף א, מ"ב סק"ה, ועי' אג"מ או"ח ח"ד סי' צג שס"ל שלא יאמר למדני חוקיך אלא יסיים הברכה ויאמר יער"י לפני מודים.   [703] סי' תצ סעיף ב.   [704] מ"ב סי' קח ס"ק לח.   [705] סי' תרפב סעיף א, מ"ב סק"ד.   [706] סי' תקסה סעיף ב, מ"ב סק"ו-ז.   [707] סי' רצד סעיף א, ד, כה"ח ס"ק יז.

פרק כא - חזרת הש"ץ

[708] סי' קכד סעיף א, ג, מ"ב ס"ק יב, טור.   [709] סעיף ד, מ"ב סק"ב, כו.   [710] מ"ב ס"ק יט, ולגבי תפלת נדבה בשבת וביו"ט עיין מ"ב סי' קח ס"ק לג, ושמענו מהגר"ח ובר שבא"י בשחרית לא יתנה כי אין הכהנים רשאים לישא כפיהם בתפלת נדבה.   [711] סעיף ז, מ"ב ס"ק כז, עיין תרגום אונקלוס בראשית ד:יג.   [712] מ"ב ס"ק יז.   [713] סעיף ד, אג"מ או"ח ח"ד סי' יט,

ושמענו מאת הגרחפ"ש שאסור ללמוד בשעה שהש"ץ חוזר על שמו"ע אפילו
אם זהיר לענות אמן, משום חילול ה'. [714] סעיף ה, מ"ב ס"ק כב, שעה"צ
ס"ק כד, מעשה רב אות מג. [715] סעיף ח ורמ"א, מ"ב סק"ל. [716] מ"ב
ס"ק לד. [717] מ"ב ס"ק לג. [718] סעיף ו מ"ב ס"ק כה. [719] סעיף יב
מ"ב ס"ק מז. [720] רמ"א סעיף ד, מ"ב סק"כ, יחוה דעת ח"ה סי' יא בשם
לקט יושר עמוד כז, סי' קכה סעיף ב, אשי ישראל פכ"ד סעיף לח, תפלה
כהלכתה פי"ג ס"ק עח. [721] שלחן שלמה (לרש"ז אב"ד דמיר) סי' קכד
סעיף ד. [722] אבני ישפה פ"ט סעיף נה. [723] מ"ב סי' קכה סק"ה.
[724] מ"ב סק"ד. [725] סעיף ב, מ"ב ס"ק ו. [726] רמ"א שם, מ"ב סק"ח.
[727] רמ"א ומ"ב סק"ז, תפלה כהלכתה פי"ג ס"ק קיב בשם בא"ח פרשת
תרומה ד-ו, ודלא כערוה"ש סק"ג. [728] כ"כ לי הגרח"ק, ועי' מנהג ישראל
תורה סי' קכה סק"ב. [729] מ"ב סק"ב, ביה"ל ד"ה אין. [734] הליכות
שלמה ח"א פ"ט סעיף ו. [735] אשי ישראל פכ"ד סעיף כח. [736] שם
סעיף כז, ועיי"ש ס"ק קכו שי"א שחייב לענות. [737] נראה שזה דומה
להולך ברחוב או נמצא בחדר אחר ביהכנ"ס. [738] מט"א סי' תקפב סעיף
ח. [739] לקט הלכות שליח ציבור להגרי"א דינר פ"ד סעיף טז בשם סידור
יעב"ץ. [740] סי' קיט סעיף ד, מ"ב ס"ק טז. [741] סוטה מ/א, ב"י סי' קכז
ד"ה מצאתי. [742] מ"ב סי' קכד ס"ק כה. [743] אשי ישראל פכ"ד סעיף
לח, שא"א להשתחוות אלא בעמידה, יחוה דעת ח"ה סי' יא בשם לקט יושר
עמוד כז. [744] סי' קכו סעיף א, מ"ב סק"ה, ביה"ל ד"ה הכל, גר"ז סק"א.
[745] הגרשז"א הובא באשי ישראל פכ"ד ס"ק קכג. [750] מ"ב סי' קט
סק"ה, הליכות שלמה ח"א פ"ט סעיף ו. ואם לומד בחדר אחר אינו חייב
לענות כמש"כ בתשובה הבאה ולכן לא יענה משום ביטול תורה. [751]
אשי ישראל פכ"ד ס"ק קכז. [752] סי' קכח סעיף יג, סי' קכו סעיף ב, מ"ב
ס"ק יא, ועיין ערוה"ש סק"ד שיש מוספין בזכות אברהם, בזכות יצחק, בזכות
יעקב, מ"ב סי' קל סק"ו, ועיי"ש אדיר במרום בשעה שאומר הש"ץ
וטוב בעיניך, רצ"ע אם כן המנהג.

פרק כב - תחנון (סי' קלא)

[753] מ"ב סק"ט בשם טור, ב"י סוף הסימן, ערוה"ש סעיף ב, ועיין פלא יועץ
ערך נפילת אפים שמנה ז' מעלות למי שמכוין בו, ועי' רבינו בחיי במדבר
טז:כב עוד ענינים. [754] הליכות בת ישראל פ"ב סעיף יב, הליכות ביתה
פ"ז סעיף א. [755] יסוד ושורש העבודה שער ה פ"ז. [756] אג"מ ח"ג סי'
פט וח"ד סי' לד, סי' תקסה סעיף ה. [757] מג"א סק"ה, ומחה"ש שם.
[758] אשי ישראל פכ"ה ס"ק כא לגבי אמירת תחנון קודם והוא רחום,
ונראה דה"ה כאן. [759] רמ"א סעיף ב, לוח א"י (צום גדליה), ועיין הליכות
שלמה ח"א פי"א סעיף יא. [760] רמ"א שם, מ"ב ס"ק יג, טו. [761] מ"ב
סק"ג. [762] רמ"א סעיף א, פרמ"ג משז"ז סק"ב. [763] כן נהגו. [764]
מעשה רב אות מט, ועי' תפלה כהלכתה פט"ו ס"ק יד בשם הגרי"שא

והגרחפ״ש שכן הוא מנהגנו.   [765] סעיף ב, מ״ב סק״י [ושם מביא עוד
דוגמא, דהיינו שסיים תפלתו וצריך לעמוד במקומו כדי הילוך ד׳ אמות,
והציבור מתחילים נפ״א מיד, שאומרו בעמידה], לקט הקמח החדש סי׳ קלא
סק״כ, ועיין ד״א של תפלה סי׳ ב ס״ק יב שאולי לשיטת האוה״מ סמיכה
נחשבת כישיבה.   [766] מ״ב סק״ט.   [767] טור סי׳ קלד.   [768] כל בו סי׳
יח, מ״ב סי׳ קלד סק״ב.   [769] הגרח״ק הובא באשי ישראל פכ״ה סעיף ה
וס״ק כב.   [770] סעיף א, מ״ב סק״ג, רבבות אפרים ח״ו סי׳ סא (ב). וענין
פורץ גדר הובא גם בסי׳ תקנא סעיף יא לגבי אכילת בשר בט׳ הימים, יו״ד סי׳
לט סעיף א לגבי אכילה בלא בדיקת הריאות, וגם לגבי המתנת ה׳ ימים קודם
ז׳ נקיים (יו״ד סי׳ קצו סעיף יג).   [771] סעיף א, מ״ב סק״ד.   [772] שע״ת
ר״ס קלא.   [773] הגרשז״א הובא באשי ישראל פכ״ה סעיף ה, הגריש״א
הובא בתפלה כהלכתה ס״ק כו.   [774] הגרח״ק הובא באשי ישראל פכ״ה
סעיף יג ושו״ת קנה בושם ח״ב סי׳ ח, וע״ע הליכות שלמה ח״א פי״א סעיף א.
[775] סעיף ו, ז, מ״ב ס״ק לג, לו, שע״ת ס״ק ז [יט].   [777] מ״ב ס״ק כא, כו.
[778] מ״ב ס״ק כו.   [779] מ״ב ס״ק כא, ערוה״ש סעיף טז, שו״ת שבט הלוי
ח״ז סי׳ יח, ועיין עוד בזה בספר שיח תפלה שער יא סימן ד.   [780] שו״ת
שבט הלוי ח״ה סוס״י יב, ח״ח סי׳ כד (ב).   [781] סעיף ד ובברכי יוסף סק״ה.
[782] מ״ב סי׳ קלא סק״ק כד.   [783] הגרח״ק הובא באשי ישראל פכ״ה ס״ק
קב.   [784] מ״ב ס״ק כב, אשי ישראל ס״ק צח בשם שנות חיים (להגר״ח
נאה).   [785] מ״ב ס״ק כה.   [786] שו״ת מנחת יצחק ח״א סי׳ יא, הליכות
שלמה ח״א פי״א סעיף ט.   [787] פסק״ת הערה 144, מנהג ישראל תורה
ח״א עמוד רא.   [788] תפלה כהלכתה פט״ו הערה לז* בשם הגרמ״פ
והגריש״א, ועיין הליכות שלמה ח״א פי״ג סק״ז שאם נמצא במקום שלא
אמרו תחנון ביום זה, כגון יום מסוים שחל בו יא״צ של רבם, אינו צריך
לאמרו אח״כ ביחידות, ומשמע דוקא בכגון זה, אבל מקום שלא אומרים
תחנון ברגילות מטעם זה, צריך לאמרו אח״כ.   [789] שו״ת שבט הלוי ח״ח
סי׳ כד.

פרק כג - סיום התפילה (סי׳ קלב)

[790] ערוה״ש סק״א, ב.   [791] שם סק״ג.   [792] מ״ב סי׳ קלא סק״ק לה,
לוח א״י, לגבי אסרו חג עיין חג ארחות רבינו ח״א עמ׳ סט בשם החזו״א, ועיין
ש״ך סי׳ רסה ס״ק כד שיש שמנהגים שונים אם הבעלי ברית פוטרים מאמירת
למנצח, ועיין קצות השלחן סי׳ כה סק״ב (בדי השלחן) שאפשר שהחתן או
בעלי ברית אין אומרים אא״א, ולכאורה ה״ה למנצח.   [793] סי׳ קלב סעיף
א, מ״ב סק״א-ב.   [794] מג״א סי׳ נט סק״ב, פרמ״ג שם, ועיין ערוה״ש סוף
הסימן שטוב לומר אשרי ובל״צ בישיבה, כה״ח סי׳ נט סעיף כ, ובשו״ת שבט
הלוי ח״ו סי׳ יג מביא שהוא עצמו אומר בעמידה אבל לדינא דעביד כמר
עביד ודעביד כמר עביד. ובדינים והנהגות להחזו״א פ״ד אות לח שאמר
בעמידה.   [795] מ״ב סי׳ קלב סק״ג.   [796] שם, זה השלחן הובא באשי

ישראל פכ״ו ס״ק יט.　[797] מ״ב סק״ד.　[798] כל בו סי׳ טז, רמ״א סעיף ב,
מ״ב סק״ז.　[799] רמ״א שם, מ״ב סק״ט.　[800] מ״ב שם, שלחן שלמה
(רש״ז אב״ד דמיר) סי׳ קלב סעיף ב, קצוה״ש סי׳ כד סעיף יא.　[801]
הגרשז״א הובא בקובץ מבקשי תורה קסו אות סח, הגרח״ק
הובא באשי ישראל פכ״ו ס״ק מג.　[802] מ״ב סי׳ סה סק״ט, ערוה״ש סעיף ו.
[803] מסכת סופרים ריש פרק יח, שש״כ פמ״ב ס״ק יא.　[805] שע״ת סק״ו
[ד] בשם נו״ב.　[806] סי׳ קלג ומ״ב סק״א, ב.　[807] מ״ב בהקדמה לסי׳ סט,
והיינו דוקא במקום שאין לחוש למחלוקת.　[808] הגר״א גרינבלאט הובא
ברגשי לב עמוד 143 סעיף 23, ועיין קובץ תשובות ח״א סי׳ יד.　[809] רגשי
לב שם סעיף 22.　[811] סידור אוצר התפילות עמוד רכב/א, סידור הגר״א
בשם החיד״א.　[812] פשוט.　[813] עיין מ״ב סי׳ נה ס״ק יד שכתב והוא
שכבר שמע קדושה והקדישים עד עלינו, אבל באשי ישראל פכ״ו סעיף כג
וס״ק נט נ הביא שמקור לדברי המ״ב בדה״ח, ושם כתוב עד אחרי עלינו, וכ״כ
בחיי אדם כלל יט סי׳ ח. סי׳ קלב סעיף ב, ארחות יושר עמוד קא סעיף ג.
[814] רמ״א סו״ס קלב, קצשו״ע סי׳ כה סעיף ז.

פרק כד - דיני קדיש

[815] ערוה״ש סי׳ נה סעיף א, ברכות ג/א.　[816] ערוה״ש שם, לבוש סי׳ נו
וכן בתוס׳ ברכות ג/א ד״ה ועונין.　[817] פרמ״ג מ״ז סי׳ נה סק״א, רמ״א סי׳
קלב סעיף ב, מס׳ סופרים פי״ט הל׳ ט, מ״ב סי׳ נד סק״ט.　[818] מ״ב סי׳ קלב
סק״י, גשה״ח פ״ל סי׳ ח סעיף ד.　[819] מהרי״ל (מנהגים) סוף הל׳ תפלה.
[820] רמ״א יו״ד סי׳ שעו סעיף ד, אלף למטה דיני קדיש שער ד סק״ב.
[821] פני ברוך פל״ד סעיף לג והערה סא.　[822] גשר החיים פ״ל סי׳ ח
סעיף ח, וע״ע אג״מ יו״ד ח״א סי׳ רנד.　[823] פני ברוך שם סעיף לז-לח,
ועיין גשר החיים פ״ל סי׳ י סעיף יב וציץ אליעזר ח״ט סי׳ טז ד״ה (ד) ופתחי
תשובה סי׳ שעו סק״ו.　[824] עיין אג״מ או״ח ח״ד סי׳ לג שכתב ״ובדברים
שנאמרים בקול רם בין מדינא בין מדרך העולם צריך להתפלל בנוסח
הצבור״.　[825] מ״ב סי׳ קלב סק״י, הליכות שלמה ח״א פי״א סעיף טו וס״ק
יט.　[826] רמ״א שם סעיף ב, מ״ב שם ס״ק יא.　[827] מ״ב סי׳ נד סק״ט,
סוטה מט/א.　[828] שו״ע סי׳ נו סעיף ד, גר״א שם, ועיין ערוה״ש שכתב
דאינם כריעות ממש אלא שיש לשחוח מעט. ועיין בספר שיח תפלה עמ׳
רכה שמביא מש״כ בליקוטי מהרי״ח שכבר נהוג עלמא כהשו״ע ואין אחר
המנהג כלום.　[829] מ״ב סי׳ נו סק״ב, בסידור יעב״ץ כ׳ שי״ל בפתח, וכ׳
בליקוטי מהרי״ח עמוד צז דעביד כמר עביד דעביד כמר עביד.　[830] סי׳ נו
סעיף ה, מ״ב סי׳ קבג סק״ג.　[831] רמ״א סי׳ נו סעיף א, מ״ב סק״ח.　[832]
סי׳ נו סעיף א, ומ״ב סק״א, וס״ק י.　[833] חיי״א כלל ה סעיף יג.　[834]
מ״ב סי׳ קד ס״ק כז.　[835] מ״ב סי׳ נו סק״א.　[836] מ״ב סי׳ כה ס״ק נו.
[837] שבת קיט/ב, סי׳ נו סעיף א, ומ״ב סק״א וסק״ה.　[838] מ״ב סק״ב-ד.
[839] מ״ב סי׳ נו ס״ק טו.　[840] מ״ב סק״ט.　[841] הליכות שלמה ח״א

פ״ט סעיף ו. [842] אשי ישראל פכ״ד סעיף כח. [843] שם סעיף כז, ועיי״ש
ס״ק קכו שי״א שחייב לענות.

פרק כה - תפלת מנחה (סי׳ רלב)

[844] ברכות ו/ב, טור. [847] ערוה״ש ס״ק טז לגבי אכילה, אג״מ ח״ד סי׳
צט סק״א ד״ה עכ״פ, שש״כ פנ״ו הערה יב, ועיין פסק״ת הערה 21 שהתיר
יחיד שקובע לו זמנו להתפלל ביחידות. [848] מ״ב סק״ז, יב, כב. [849]
מ״ב סק״ט, ביה״ל סד״ה לבורסקי. [850] מ״ב ס״ק כט, א״א בוטשאטש סי׳
רצט, ועיין מ״ב סי׳ רלה ס״ק יז שגם מדייק כן. [851] מ״ב סי׳ רלב ס״ק כא,
קצוה״ש סי׳ כו ס״ק טו (בבדה״ש). [852] ערוה״ש ס״ק יז, ועיין אשי ישראל
פכ״ז ס״ק פז ביאור בדבריו. [853] מ״ב ס״ק יא, ועיין מקורות 341-340.
[854] מ״ב סי׳ פט ס״ק יט, שו״ת שבט הלוי ח״ח סי׳ יח, שיח הלכה סי׳ פט
ס״ק יז בשם הגרשז״א, אבני ישפה פי״ד ס״ק 38 בשם הגריש״א. [855]
רמ״א סעיף ב, מ״ב ס״ק כד. ולגבי עוד גדרי סעודה גדולה עיין אשי ישראל
פכ״ז ס״ק כח. [856] מ״ב סי׳ רלה ס״ק יח, כח, ועיין ס״ק יז. [857] מ״ב סי׳ רלב
ס״ק כד. [858] רמ״א סעיף ב, מ״ב ס״ק כב, כו, כח, שש״כ פנ״ו ס״ק יב.
[859] סעיף ג, מ״ב ס״ק לד, לה, ולעניין פהב״כ עיין ערוה״ש ס״ק יח שמקיל,
ועיין אשי ישראל סעיף כג ס״ק עו* שמשווה לפת, והראיה ממוסף. [860]
סי׳ רלג סעיף ב. [861] שם, מ״ב ס״ק יח. [862] ס״ק יט. [863] ביה״ל
ריש סי׳ א, רמ״א סי׳ רלד סעיף א, מ״ב סק״ו. [864] שו״ת רבבות אפרים
ח״ח סי׳ פט, סידור יעב״ץ עזרה קטנה סדר תפלת מנחה (ס״ק יז). [865] מ״ב
סי׳ קח ס״ק יד. [866] מ״ב סי׳ קכד ס״ק ו. [867] סי׳ רלב סעיף א, מ״ב סי׳
קכד סק״ז, הגרשז״א הובא בקובץ מבקשי תורה סיון תשנ״ה סי׳ קסו אות עא.
[868] מ״ב שם סק״ח. [869] מ״ב סי׳ קלא ס״ק יז, תפלה כהלכתה פי״ח ס״ק
סד בשם הגריש״א, הליכות שלמה ח״א פי״ג סעיף ד. [870] סי׳ קלא סעיף
ו, ז, מ״ב ס״ק לה, לג, לו, לוח א״י. [871] עיין מקורות 774.

פרק כו - תפלת ערבית (סי׳ רלה-ו)

[874] סי׳ רלה סעיף ב, מ״ב ס״ק יז. [875] מ״ב שם וס״ק יח. [876] עיין
מקורות 341, 342. ולגבי אכילה לפני מעריב עיין מ״ב סי׳ רלה ס״ק טז, ועיין
אשי ישראל פכ״ז ס״ק עג בשם הגר״י נויברט. [877] שבות יצחק ח״ב עמוד
דש בשם והגריש״א, ועיין שש״כ פמ״ז ס״ק קא. [878] שבו״י שם עמוד רפז
בשם הגרשז״א. [879] מ״ב סי׳ רלה ס״ק יט. [880] מ״ב סי׳ רלג ס״ק טו.
[881] שם ס״ק יח. [882] שם ס״ק טז. [883] ביה״ל ריש סי׳ א. [884]
טור סי׳ רלו. [885] מ״ב סי׳ רלו סק״א. [886] תפלה כהלכתה פי״ט סעיף
יא. [887] שו״ת אבני ישפה ח״ג סי׳ כו בשם הגריש״א ע״פ הליכות שלמה
ח״א פ״ו סק״כ. [888] כן מדוייק מהט״ז סי׳ קמו סק״א בס״ד. [889] אבני
ישפה פי״א ס״ק 5, תפלה כהלכתה פי״ט סק״ל. [890] סי׳ רלו סעיף ג, מ״ב
ס״ק יב, קובץ מבקשי תורה סיון תשנ״ה סי׳ קסה בשם הגרשז״א, הגרשז״א

הובא באשי ישראל פכ״ח ס״ק צב, עיי״ש עוד.   [891] מ״ב ס״ק יא, מנח״י
ח״ח סי׳ טז, אבני ישפה פי״א סעיף י, ועיין אשי ישראל פי״ב ס״ק נז.   [892]
שו״ת קנין תורה ח״ב סי׳ קמא.   [893] שלמת חיים (בני ברק תשנ״ה) סי׳
ריח-ריט, שערים מצויינים בהלכה סי׳ ע סק״ג, ודין האמצעי פשוט.   [896]
סי׳ סג סעיף א, מ״ב סק״ז.   [897] רבבות אפרים ח״א סי׳ קעד.   [898] מ״ב
סי׳ רלו סק״י.   [899] מ״ב סי׳ רלו סק״ז, שעה״צ סק״ד, כה״ח ס״ק יז.   [901]
עיין מקורות 253.   [902] מ״ב סי׳ נה ס״ק לב, חיי״א כלל כט סעיף א,
קצשו״ע סי׳ טו סעיף ז.

Dedicated in Memory

of

HaRav Shmuel Scheinberg

ר׳ שמואל בן ר׳ יעקב יצחק זצללה״ה

By his children

Dedicated in memory of

our beloved father

Moshe Grossbard z"l
ר׳ משה בן ר׳ אהרן ז״ל

and our dear grandparents

Aharon & Esther Grossbard z"l
ר׳ אהרן בן ר׳ אליהו דוב ז״ל
מרת אסתר פייגא בת ר׳ משה ע״ה

Dovid & Rella Gelberman z"l
ר׳ דוד בן ר׳ משה ז״ל
מרת רבקה ריינא בת ר׳ יצחק אייזיק ע״ה

Their children & grandchildren

Dedicated in loving memory of

our dear parents

Dovid & Rella Gelberman z"l
ר׳ דוד בן ר׳ משה ז״ל
מרת רבקה ריינא בת ר׳ יצחק אייזיק ע״ה

Sam & Rebecca Bakunow z"l
ר׳ נחמיה בן ר׳ מנחם מענדל ז״ל
מרת רבקה בת ר׳ משה בצלאל ע״ה

and our dear brother-in-law

Moshe Grossbard z"l
ר׳ משה בן ר׳ אהרן ז״ל

George and Estelle Gelberman

May the use of this book
bring merit to the soul of

ר׳ שמחה ב״ר מאיר הלוי ז״ל

Sidney Silinsky

Dedicated by

his children Shmuel and Alyce

and his wife Bonnie Silinsky

ת.נ.צ.ב.ה.

לע"נ

ר' עזריאל זאב (וועלוועל)
בן ר' צבי הירש ז"ל

נפטר י"ג ניסן תשס"ד

ת.נ.צ.ב.ה.

Dedicated in Memory of

ר׳ אליהו חיים בן
ר׳ דוד חייו ז״ל

ת.נ.צ.ב.ה.

לעילוי נשמת

האי גברא יקירא, מוקיר רבנן,
קובע עיתים לתורה, גומל צדקה וחסד,

הר״ר זישא אלכסנדר
בן ר׳ פינחס זצ״ל
פלוס

נלב״ע כ״ג בשבט תשנ״ח

ת.נ.צ.ב.ה.

לזכר נשמות

יצחק דוד בן מרדכי הלוי ז״ל
ג׳יקובס
נפטר ערב שבת קודש י״ט מנחם אב תשס״ד

ואשתו מרת דבורה לאה בת בנימין ע״ה
נפטרה מוצאי שבת קודש ד׳ אייר תשנ״ז

ת.נ.צ.ב.ה.

May the learning of this ספר be a זכות
for my beloved parents

ר׳ דוד בן ראובן ז״ל
(David Ross)

נפטר כ״ב סיון תשנ״ב

מרת מלכה בת ישראל ע״ה
(Queenie Ross)

נפטרה ג׳ דחול המועד פסח תשס״ג

Dedicated by Laurence Ross and family

ת.נ.צ.ב.ה.

לע״נ

ר׳ שניאור זלמן בן נפתלי משה ז״ל
נביס

שנפטר ערב שבת קודש
ט״ז אייר תשס״ד

ת.נ.צ.ב.ה.

לע"נ

ר' דוד בן אהרן דנדרוביץ ז"ל

נפטר ב' חשון תשנ"ה

מרת דרשנא בת ר' נחמן גיטלמן ע"ה

נפטרה ר"ח אייר תשנ"ג

ת.נ.צ.ב.ה.

May the learning of this ספר be a זכות
for our beloved sister

מרת חיה חנה בת שמואל שניאור ע"ה

Along with our parents

מרת מרים בת שרגא ע"ה
ר' שמואל שניאור בן יצחק יעקב ז"ל
מרת חיה בת פסח ע"ה

Dedicated by the Sherwood family

ת.נ.צ.ב.ה.

לע"נ

ר' שלמה חיים ב"ר משה צבי ז"ל

מרת גיטל בת ר' חיים יצחק ע"ה

אהרן יעקב ב"ר חיים שלמה הכהן ז"ל

ת.נ.צ.ב.ה.

לע"נ

ר' שלמה ב"ר משה ז"ל

מרת רייזל דבורה בת ר' יעקב מרדכי ע"ה

ר' יצחק ב"ר זאב ז"ל

מרת לאה בת ר'אברהם יהודה ע"ה

Dedicated by
Rabbi Max & Mrs. Marilyn Karmen

ת.נ.צ.ב.ה.

לע"נ

ר' בנימין
ב"ר נח ליב ז"ל

נלב"ע י"ב סיון תשס"ב

ת.נ.צ.ב.ה.

In Loving memory of

ר' נחמן ב"ר אברהם משה שלגמן

מרת חנה בת ר' יעקב שלגמן

ר' משה ב"ר מרדכי ראבין

ת.נ.צ.ב.ה.

לע"נ

ר' אברהם יצחק
ב"ר אליהו מענדל הכהן ז"ל

ואשתו מרת
פערל בת ר' שמעון לייב ע"ה

ת.נ.צ.ב.ה.

לע"נ

מרת פרידא
בת ר' שמעון הכהן ע"ה

ת.נ.צ.ב.ה.

לע"נ

מרת ביילא ע"ה
בת ר' לייב נ"י

ת.נ.צ.ב.ה.